Global Issues in Civil Procedure

Cases and Materials

Thomas O. Main
University of the Pacific
McGeorge School of Law

AMERICAN CASEBOOK SERIES®

Mat #40347845

American Casebook Series and West Group are trademarks registered in the U.S. Patent and Trademark Office.

© 2006 Thomson/West
       610 Opperman Drive
       P.O. Box 64526
       St. Paul, MN 55164–0526
       1–800–328–9352

ISBN–13: 978–0–314–15978–6
ISBN–10: 0–314–15978–9

 TEXT IS PRINTED ON 10% POST CONSUMER RECYCLED PAPER

This book is dedicated to Tim,
who has taught me not to mistake boundaries for walls;
and to Greg,
who has taught me that there is no view from nowhere.

*

Preface

The cases and materials in this book were selected to introduce first year civil procedure students to a range of comparative, transnational, and international perspectives. I have included ten chapters introducing issues regarding access to justice, pleadings, discovery, the jury, personal jurisdiction, service, subject matter jurisdiction, conflict of laws, and enforcement of foreign judgments. This book can be used to supplement any civil procedure casebook, and the chapters can be used in any combination or order.

This book is designed to be very accessible for first year law students. The magnificent complexity of comparative, transnational and international perspectives is reserved for other courses. Instead, this book provides law students with a vocabulary of terms and concepts that globalization has introduced. An annotated bibliography provides students and professors with a roadmap for more detailed study.

This project has benefited greatly from the input and ideas of others. I wish to thank publicly Professors Debbie Bassett, Rick Freer, and Margaret Woo for reviewing an earlier draft of the manuscript and offering very useful suggestions—many of which I have been able to incorporate into the finished product. Correspondence with Professor Kevin Clermont has also been instructive and inspiring. I would also like to thank Professors Rick Marcus, John Oakley, Linda Silberman and Roger Trangsrud; this book was enriched by insights that each of them shared this past summer at the Globalizing the Law School Curriculum Workshop, Pacific McGeorge at Tahoe. Professor Steve Subrin was also an active participant in the workshop, and is a teacher, mentor, and friend par excellence.

Louis Higgins and Roxy Birkel have demonstrated that Thomson West is a first-rate, professional operation. Thank you for your support of the Global Issues series and, in particular, for your efforts in getting this volume to press.

At Pacific McGeorge, Kim Clarke, James Wirrell and other librarians were very helpful in gathering materials for this book. Students David Keyzer and Elhahm Mackani provided valuable research assistance. Deans Elizabeth Rindskopf Parker, Christine Manolakas and John Sprankling provided their typical yet remarkably generous financial and other support. And Professor Frank Gevurtz has envisioned and championed a series of books that could become an important part of the transformation of legal education.

To each of these colleagues and friends, thank you for providing me with the opportunity to work with you.

And to students studying civil procedure with a global perspective, I hope that you find these materials rewarding and fun—yes, fun!

THOMAS MAIN

October 2005

Acknowledgments

Andrew S. Bell, Forum Shopping and Venue in Transnational Litigation (2003).

Oscar G. Chase, American "Exceptionalism" and Comparative Procedure, 50 Am. J. Comp. Law 277 (2002). A version of this article appears as a chapter in the book, Oscar G. Chase, Law, Culture, and Ritual: Disputing in Cross-Cultural Context (NYU Press 2005).

Kevin M. Clermont, Preface, in Kuo-Chang Huang, Introducing Discovery into Civil Law (Carolina Academic Press 2003).

W. Kent Davis, The International View of Attorney Fees in Civil Suits, 16 Ariz. J. Int'l L. & Compl. L. 361, 371-414 (1999).

Owen M. Fiss & Judith Resnik, Adjudication and its Alternatives (2003).

Llewellyn Joseph Gibbons, Creating a Market for Justice; A Market Incentive Solution to Regulating the Playing Field: Judicial Deference, Judicial Review, Due Process, and Fair Play in Online Consumer Arbitration, 23 Nw. J. Int'l L. & Bus. 1 (2002).

Geoffrey C. Hazard, Jr., From Whom No Secrets are Hid, 76 Tex. L. Rev. 1665 (1998).

Herbert Jacob et al., Courts, Law & Politics in Comparative Perspective (Yale 1996).

David McClean, Morris: The Conflict of Laws (5th ed. 2000)

Principles and Rules of Transnational Civil Procedure copyright 2005 by the American Law Institute (ALI) and, for the "Principles" also the International Institute for the Unification of Private Law (UNIDROIT). Reprinted with permission. All rights reserved. The complete work is available from Cambridge University Press (www.uk.cambridge.org).

Rest. 3rd, Restatement of the Foreign Relations Law of the United States copyright 1987 by the American Law Institute. Reprinted with permission. All rights reserved.

Linda J. Silberman, Judicial Jurisdiction in the Conflict of Laws Course: Adding a Comparative Dimension, 28 Vand. J. Transnat'l L. 389 (1995).

Linda J. Silberman & Allan R. Stein, Civil Procedure: Theory and Practice (Aspen 2001).

Stephen N. Subrin, Discovery in Global Perspective: Are We Nuts?, 52 DePaul L. Rev. 299 (2002).

Annotated Bibliography
of Recommended Resources

Andrew Bell, Forum Shopping and Venue in Transnational Litigation (2003).

> Written for American and European lawyers, this book's analysis of forum shopping may be of interest to first year law students.

International Judicial Assistance in Civil Matters (Dennis Campbell ed., 1999).

> This book offers a survey of how selected issues in transnational litigation are being handled in various jurisdictions worldwide.

Mauro Cappelletti, International Encyclopedia of Comparative Law, Vol. XVI. Civil Procedure (Mauro Cappelletti, ed., 1987).

> Chapters of this very well-respected encyclopedia focus on specific topics of comparative law, including trends and ideas in civil procedure. The book is dated, but it is a classic for good reasons.

Sofie Geeroms, Foreign Law in Civil Litigation: A Comparative and Functional Analysis (2004).

> This book analyzes foreign law in civil litigation by looking at Belgium, England, France, Germany, the Netherlands, and the United States. The book is divided into two parts, considering foreign law at the levels of both trial and review.

Claire Germain, Germain's Transnational Law Research: A Guide for Attorneys §§ 1.01-1.23 (1991).

> This regularly updated looseleaf guide is intended as a starting point for attorneys researching transnational legal issues. The first chapter covers procedural and practical issues. Among other strengths, the book provides an excellent annotated list of authoritative sources.

Shelby R. Grubbs, International Civil Procedure (2003).

> This book provides a country-by-country analysis of a series of topics, including pre- and post-trial proceedings, jurisdiction, venue, and alternative dispute resolution. Most European countries, several South American countries, and some Asian countries are covered.

Richard H. Kreindler, Transnational Litigation: A Basic Primer (1998).

> This book is a compact, distilled version of *Transnational Litigation: A Practitioner's Guide*.

Transnational Litigation: A Practitioner's Guide (Richard H. Kriendler and Judith Holdsworth, eds., 2004).

> This regularly-updated three volume looseleaf set covers nearly all aspects of transnational litigation and provides commentary on the systems of major countries. Additionally, relevant international conventions, statutes and regulations that affect transnational litigation are included. This Guide is the dream-come-true for practitioners, and a phenomenal resource for interested students.

International Encyclopaedia of Laws: Civil Procedure (P. Lemmens, ed., 2005).

> This regularly updated multi-volume looseleaf set is published as part of the *International Encyclopaedia of Laws* series, which covers a variety of legal topics. It provides detailed information on various components of the legal systems of thirty different countries. This set contains a great deal of information, and is very well-organized and accessible.

International Litigation: Defending and Suing Foreign Parties in U.S. Federal Courts (David J. Levy, ed., 2003).

> Examining international civil litigation from an American lawyer's perspective, topics in this book include service of process and personal jurisdiction over foreign parties, and a discussion of procedural concepts using international cases.

Joseph M. Lookofsky, Transnational Litigation and Commercial Arbitration : An Analysis of American, European, and International Law (2d ed. 2004).

> This book offers a comparative study of rules and procedures that govern the resolution of transnational commercial disputes. The book's coverage of commercial arbitration makes it an especially useful book.

Lawrence W. Newman and Michael Burrows, The Practice of International Litigation (2d ed. 2004).

> This regularly updated one volume looseleaf volume offers an overview of international litigation. It is organized topically and offers a more condensed discussion of various transnational and comparative issues.

Louise Ellen Teitz, Transnational Litigation (1996).

> This well organized and easy to read guide for American attorneys focuses on international civil procedure from an American perspective. Although intended as a basic guide for U.S. lawyers engaging in transnational litigation, it can also serve as a very useful and accessible resource for law students.

*

Summary of Contents

*

Table of Contents

Table of Cases

The principal cases are in bold type. Cases cited or discussed in the text are roman type. References are to pages. Cases cited in principal cases and within other quoted materials are not included.

*

Global Issues in Civil Procedure

Cases and Materials

*

Chapter 1

INTRODUCTION

An important purpose of any system of civil procedure is to administer the substantive law fairly and efficiently. Although that statement may be generally accepted, the consensus really ends there. Reasonable minds will disagree about the scope and meaning of the aspirations of "fairness" and "efficiency." Moreover, even among those fortunate enough to be united in purpose, discussion of the methods for implementing those aims often reveals profound differences.

Dissent looms because the stakes can be very high when choosing one procedural rule over another. Although one might believe (and will frequently read) that procedure is technical or secondary, in fact procedure is an instrument of power and social control. Procedures alter the conduct of groups and individuals, and thus can prefer some over others. And procedures can, in a very practical sense, negate, resuscitate, or generate substantive rights. The study of procedure, then, is an exploration of the values that a system serves or could serve. "[N]o legal technique is an end in itself, none is ideologically neutral."*

Mastery of American civil procedure is hard enough. Why, then, add additional reading introducing global issues? There are at least a couple of answers to that question. First, the contemporary practice of law requires some fluency with these concepts. In this era of increasing globalization, provincialism can be not only an embarrassment, but a professional liability. Although litigation in a global context may seem at times as complicated as a game of three-dimensional chess, pretending that it is as simple as a game of checkers is not adequate preparation for the real thing.

* Mauro Cappelletti, *Social and Political Aspects of Civil Procedure—Reforms and Trends in Western and Eastern Europe*, 69 Mich. L. Rev. 847, 882 (1970–1971).

Second, globalization can actually make the study and mastery of the civil procedure course easier. One key to law school success is *learning* the material rather than memorizing it. Rules and doctrines that are memorized can be forgotten—especially during an exam when you may be stressed, anxious, and exhausted. But if you can instead learn those rules and doctrines within some meaningful context—say, for example, by comparing and contrasting other systems' approaches to the same problem—the steps of analysis and application become unforgettable, even intuitive.

This book uses three different categories of materials to "globalize" the course: transnational, comparative and international. Not everyone assigns these familiar terms the same meanings, so it is important to appreciate the context of the reference whenever the terms are invoked. In this book, "transnational" refers to domestic litigation that has some foreign component—for example, where the defendant resides in another country. "Comparative" refers to the exploration of another legal system to understand how that country articulates priorities, strikes compromises, and achieves ends. And finally, "international" refers to systems, treaties, and reform efforts that transcend national boundaries. Although there is overlap among these three categories,* the remaining materials in this chapter introduce each in turn.

A. TRANSNATIONAL PERSPECTIVES

David McClean
Domestic Litigation in Transition

Morris: The Conflict of Laws 1 (5th ed. 2000)

On many an office or seminar-room wall, there hangs a political map of the world. Each State, except the very smallest, has its own colour. Sixty years ago, the colour scheme was rather simpler: pink for the British Empire, perhaps green for the French possessions, and some other colour for the many republics which made up the Soviet Union. The boundaries between the different colours once meant a great deal. Many individuals lived and died without ever visiting a foreign country. Patterns of trade and commerce tended to follow the imperial colour schemes, so that British companies would have their branches in the colonies, where legal

---

* For example, one might imagine reviewing how the Italian court system ensures that a French defendant is properly notified of the filing of a court action. That inquiry would be *comparative* because we would be looking at the Italian court system's approach to a problem that we face in our own procedural system. That inquiry would be *transnational* because it would involve the intersection of French and Italian systems and values. And because there happens to be a treaty between those countries on this matter, the inquiry would also involve matters *international*.

rules and commercial practice followed English models. All this has now changed.

Mass tourism has made foreign travel commonplace. Students cross the world in search of higher education, or to offer voluntary service, or simply for adventure. Employees of British companies find themselves working in Tokyo or the Gulf, and a trip to Brussels or Frankfurt has little novelty value. Many national boundaries, such as those in "Schengen land" can be crossed without formality. Love knows not national boundaries: tourist, student, or worker may find romance and marry someone whose home is on the other side of the world. Independence may increase the number of colours on the map, but the old empires are replaced by regional common markets, such as those in Europe or the Caribbean. The regional organisations soon move beyond a concern with economic issues and acquire legislative powers. Each individual country nonetheless retains its own body of law, its own system of courts, its own legal personnel. Individual and corporate activity may be increasingly international, but there is no corpus of international law and no system of international courts to resolve any legal issues and disputes that arise. They have to be addressed through the courts of a particular national legal system and the legal rules which those courts choose to apply....

Andrew S. Bell
Transnational Litigation

Forum Shopping and Venue in Transnational Litigation 3–5 (2003)

The advent of the subject of transnational litigation has been coincident both with the emergence of a truly global economy and the achievement in recent decades of great technological advances, particularly in the fields of transportation and telecommunications and, more generally, through the internet's facilitation of international commerce including the electronic transfer of funds and the ability to transact business in cyberspace. These developments have been remarked upon by both courts and commentators alike. Part of the explanation for this economic trend lies in the fact that rapid and inexpensive transportation has led to greater international trade and an increase in labour mobility. The relative freedom of international trade, and efforts under the auspices of the GATT agreement to secure this goal to an even greater extent, mean that primary and secondary products are regularly penetrating new markets, especially since the end of the Cold War. The same may also be said in relation to various service industries.

One feature of economic globalization has been the great diversification of corporate holdings, both in terms of commodity portfolios and geographical spheres of operation, and a company's plant, equipment, and other assets will frequently be located in a strategic range of countries. Such diversification characterizes the corporate behaviour of vast multinational corporations which are able to co-ordinate their businesses by virtue of sophisticated communications networks. More generally, the flow of international commerce has been facilitated by the development of systems of electronic funds transfer and, more recently, e-commerce. Furthermore, co-operative joint ventures often see corporations from different countries combining to invest in a third. As these developments have occurred, the world economy has not been a paragon of stability and the effect of various international crises has produced great fluctuations in world currency, share, and commodity markets. . . .

The emergence of an ever more integrated global economy has obvious ramifications for transnational litigation. One commentator has observed that "in a world where daily transactions routinely involve multiple countries, litigants are increasingly likely to find themselves embroiled in simultaneous contests in multiple theatres." Quite simply, more international trade means more transnational disputes, contractual, quasi-contractual, and arising from the negligent provision of goods and services. One consequence of a global economy—the posting of employees abroad—may also give rise to disputes as to the application of the employment law protections of the state from which the employee has been posted. And another consequence is the diversification of assets against which judgments may be enforced. As Sir Michael Kerr observed extrajudicially, *"quot contractus, tot contentions, tot lites"*. This has had the consequence that "the business of litigation, like commerce itself, has become increasingly international." It is no coincidence that the last twenty years have seen the burgeoning of "international law firms", offering not only the personnel and facilities to co-ordinate complex transnational litigation but also knowledge of and familiarity with the procedural and other advantages to be secured through litigating in particular forums.

This collective bargaining of transnational activity is seen most clearly in, but is by no means confined to, international commerce. Complexities of transnational litigation are also presented as a consequence of the growth of international tourism and greater mobility generally, meaning that one also encounters "fights about where to fight" across the legal firmament, including, often sadly, in the context of family law both in the area of divorce and in relation to the custody of children whose separated parents wish to live in different countries. . . .

B.   COMPARATIVE PERSPECTIVES

Comparative law is often described as providing both a window into other cultures as well as a mirror for one's own. Increased tolerance, respect, and understanding are among the "soft" values that comparativism promotes; that others can do things differently yet still succeed is an important reminder. But there are also benefits that might be characterized as "hard" values. To be an effective advocate, students must be prepared to deal effectively with foreign systems and foreign lawyers. Moreover, foreign legal systems can be sources for data and ideas about the causes of and solutions to universal problems.

Important caveats accompany most efforts at comparativism, and they apply to our inquiries as well. Understand that any procedural system is a complex and dynamic amalgam with interconnected parts influenced by culture, language, and other forces. Consideration of another country's procedural rule on any given subject is unavoidably removed from that important context. To appreciate such a rule fully would require learning not only the other parts of the procedural schema, but the entire legal system, the native language, the local culture and more. In the following excerpt Professor Clermont discusses two objectives of the study of comparative civil procedure.

Kevin M. Clermont
Why Comparative Civil Procedure?

Preface, Kuo–Chang Huang, Introducing Discovery into Civil Law ix, xi-xix (2003)

Transplants

The comparativist could look abroad for superior procedural devices in order to transplant them into the local system. This transplanting could be through voluntarily borrowing by the system or through involuntary imposition on the system.

The fact is, however, that actual transplanting of procedure, as opposed to the mere seeking of inspiration abroad for locally generated reform, is not common. Transplants that impinge on the system's organizing principles or constitutional norms are obviously impractical. But even less intrusive transplants of foreign devices are problematic. The reason is that procedure is a field especially marked by the interrelatedness of its parts and its inseparability from local institutional structure. Also, although it is a technical subject, procedure is surprisingly culture-bound, reflecting the fundamental values, sensibilities, and beliefs of the society.

All this is not to say that transplants are impossible. ... But any such transplant must be limited in scope and sensitive to context....

Insights

The procedural comparativist can ... seek illumination by the cross-border study of theory, doctrine, or practice. The aim is to better understand one's own law: "The purpose of comparative study is to help understand what is distinctive (and problematic) about domestic law."[36] ...

[A]s to examining the foreign law, one must do so carefully while being attentive to culture. But one does not always need systematic knowledge of the foreign system. "Even unsystematic knowledge can be very useful in a practical way for, say, law reform." "Moreover, it is quite legitimate for comparatists to base their comparisons on literature produced by foreign law specialists, at least to a substantial degree." To do comparative study, as opposed to scholarship on foreign law itself, one need be neither a linguist nor an anthropologist....

[Comparative study can yield] across-the-board insights into domestic law. Because any willing scholar can pursue this task, every legal scholar should do so, as an adjunct to his or her primary focus. Indeed, the universality of this purpose of simply seeking insight raises the question of what is distinctive about this endeavor. Maybe studying comparative law, so viewed, is no different from being broadly read. This view might explain why Professor Bermann refers to [this particular] purpose of comparative law as the pursuit of "the culturally edifying," while suggesting that a main purpose of comparative law is to reach the point at which all of law study is comparative.[54]

———

Comparative study begins with awareness of the two dominant legal traditions of the world. The following excerpts introduce those traditions.

Herbert Jacob et al.
The Civil Law and Common Law Traditions

Courts, Law & Politics in Comparative Perspective 3–6 (1996)

Western law has conventionally been divided into two distinct categories: a civil code tradition and a common-law tradition. The

36. John H. Langbein, *The Influence of Comparative Procedure in the United States*, 43 Am. J. Comp. L. 545, 548–49 (1995).

54. George A. Bermann, *The Discipline of Comparative Law in the United States*, in L'avenir du droit compare 306, 314 (Société de Législation Comparée 2000).

civil code finds its ancient roots in Roman law but is also the product of the French revolution. Where French armies conquered they imposed the Napoleonic civil code. Thus the legal systems of almost the entire continent of Europe can be traced to this common ancestor. In the intervening years, each country has added or subtracted details, but the common parentage remains apparent. A distinctive feature of the civil code was its design as a seamless body of legal prescriptions, based on simple principles that could best be understood by lay people. Scholars were its principal drafters, and they considered law as a science rather than as a political art. In keeping with the contempt with which French revolutionaries held judges of the old regime and the revolutionaries' commitment to popular sovereignty, the drafters of the civil code granted little authority to the judiciary. Judges were to apply the law, but their decisions were not given authority as precedents. At the same time, lawyers remained overshadowed by magistrates and judges in the conduct of trials. Courts were *state* institutions rather than a battleground for attorneys sponsored by private interests.

The second category of Western legal systems is those based on what is described as the common law. Its origins lie in England with the gradual development of legal authority as interpreted by the monarchy's judges. In the English version, however, parliamentary authority became supreme; no written constitution provided opportunities to declare Acts of Parliament unconstitutional. However, Parliament did not begin to write comprehensive legal codes until the twentieth century, and many gaps existed in the law. Courts filled that vacuum by decisions in disputes brought to them. By citing their earlier decisions as precedent, courts built up a large body of case law without challenging the authority of Parliament. English settlers brought this common law to the American colonies. However, the adoption of a written constitution in the United States quickly allowed judges to exercise judicial review in a manner unknown to nineteenth-century England. In addition, both in England and in the United States the principal drafters of law have been judges, lawyers, and politicians rather than academic scholars. Law is not considered a science, but rather a pragmatic endeavor. Moreover, lawyers play a central role in litigation. Courts (and judges) sit passively until activated by private interests as represented by lawyers.

These two types of law, however, no longer are as distinct as they were during the nineteenth and early twentieth centuries. In the 1970s judges began to cite their own decisions as precedent in many civil code countries and even dispute the authority of legislatures. Over time the seamless structure of the civil code showed ruptures as new laws addressed novel social and economic problems. At the same time, common law countries—particularly the United States—codified segments of their law, though not with the same single-minded attentiveness to basic principles as the civil code. Common law judges have become somewhat more active although not yet equaling their civil code peers; civil code lawyers have become more aggressive although not yet matching their common law counterparts.

While common law and civil code legal systems demarcate significant variations in national legal practices, one must also take into account national differences in the willingness of people to employ the law to resolve their disputes and in the perceived acceptability of litigation as an alternative to other modes of processing. Some American researchers find that when people in the United States seek to resolve disputes they act "in the shadow of the law." Mnookin and Kornhauser suggest that remedies that might be obtained by litigation lurk in the background during many negotiations and that court action is often viewed as a viable strategic alternative.[8] It is not true, however, that Americans think about law in all their disputes, and abundant evidence exists in other countries that multiple normative orders exist which some- times push litigation to the periphery of dispute processing. Some scholars argue that social norms and habitual behaviors lead some people away from thinking about legal rights when they confront a dispute; the Japanese are sometimes identified as reflecting such preferences. However, current scholarship has challenged this in- terpretation and points instead to legal institutions that restrict access to courts and to legal remedies in addition to attitudes toward the law.

The combination of circumstances that lead people to invoke the law, therefore, vary not only with public attitudes toward law but also with institutional arrangements. A willingness to mobilize the law to challenge the actions of government agencies depends not only on the perceived legitimacy of such a challenge but also on such particulars as the availability of legal aid, the willingness of courts to accept jurisdiction, the presence of alternative forums for hearing such complaints, the costs and risk associated with making complaints, and the benefits that may be gained by proceeding one way or another. Resort to law for more personal remedies—such as compensation for injuries resulting from auto accidents or damages arising from contractual disputes—also varies with such circum- stances, which are the product of government policy as well as social customs.

---

8. Robert H. Mnookin and Lewis Kornhauser, "Bargaining in the Shadow of the Law: The Case of Divorce," Yale Law Journal 88 (1979), pp. 950-997.

Geoffrey C. Hazard, Jr.
Fundamental Differences
Between Procedural Systems

From Whom No Secrets Are Hid, 76 Tex. L. Rev. 1665, 1672–74 (1998)

The fundamental differences in civil procedural systems are, along one division, differences between the common-law and civil-law systems. . . .

The common-law systems all derive from England and include the United States, Canada, Australia, New Zealand, South Africa and India, as well as other smaller regimes such as Israel, Singapore, and Bermuda. The civil-law systems originated on the European continent and include systems derived more or less from Roman law (the law of the Roman Empire codified in the Justinian Code) and canon law (the law of the Roman Catholic Church, itself substantially derived from Roman law). The civil-law systems include those of France, Germany, Italy, and Spain and virtually all other European countries and, in a borrowing or migration of legal systems, those of Latin America and Japan.

There are many significant differences between common-law and civil-law systems. First, the judge in civil-law systems rather than the advocates in common-law systems, has responsibility for development of the evidence and exposition of the legal concepts that should govern decision. However, there is great variance among civil-law systems in the manner and degree to which this responsibility is exercised, and no doubt variance among the judges in any given system. In general, however, in the civil-law systems the final selection of witnesses to be examined and the examination itself are done by the judge and only indirectly by the advocates, who nominate the witnesses and who may suggest questions that should be asked. Second, civil-law litigation proceeds through a series of short hearing sessions—sometimes less than an hour each—focused on development of evidence. The products of this are then consigned to the case file until an eventual final stage of analysis and decision. In contrast, common-law litigation has one or more preliminary or pretrial stages, and then a trial at which all the evidence is received consecutively, including all "live" testimony. Third, a civil-law final hearing usually takes less time than a common-law trial of a similar case. This is partly due to a difference in the role of judge and advocates, but it also results from the different character of a common-law trial and a civil-law final hearing. Fourth, a civil-law judgment in the court of first instance (i.e., trial court) is generally subject to a more searching re-examination in the court of second instance (i.e., appellate court) than a common-law judgment. Also, re-examination in the civil-law systems extends to facts as well as law. Fifth, a judge in a civil-law system serves his entire professional career as a judge, whereas the judges in common-law systems are almost entirely selected from the ranks of the bar. Thus, civil-law judges lack the experience of having been a lawyer, which may affect their views.

These are important differences, but not worlds of difference. The American common-law system, however, has differences from most other common-law systems that are of equally great if not greater significance. The American system is unique in many respects. First, jury trial is a broadly available right in the American federal courts and, more or less to the same extent, in the state court systems. No other country routinely uses juries in civil cases. Second, the American version of the adversary system generally affords the advocates far greater latitude in the form and style of the case's presentation than in other common-law systems. This is in part because of our use of juries. Third, in the American system, each party, including a winning party, pays his own lawyer and cannot recover that cost from a losing opponent. This rule has been changed by statute for specific types of cases but almost invariably in the direction of allowing recovery of litigation costs only by a successful plaintiff. In most all other countries the winning party, whether plaintiff or defendant, recovers at least a substantial portion of his litigation costs. Fourth, American rules of discovery give wide latitude for exploration of potentially relevant evidence.... Fifth, American judges are selected in a variety of ways in which political affiliation plays an important part. In most of the other common-law countries, judges are selected on the basis of professional standards.

––––––

Standards of proof are a sixth important difference between the procedural systems of the civil law and common law traditions. Where the common law countries tend to impose, in civil cases, a standard requiring a preponderance of the evidence (i.e., more likely than not), many civil law countries, including Japan, require proof to a higher degree of probability. The higher standard in those countries tends to be something resembling "clear and convincing evidence" or even "proof beyond a reasonable doubt."

C. INTERNATIONAL PERSPECTIVES

Comparative perspective and transnational conflict lend themselves to international solutions that transcend national boundaries. These solutions can take several forms, including international court systems, multinational treaties, and multilateral reform efforts. Although the materials in this book emphasize the latter two, all three are introduced in these introductory pages.

Owen M. Fiss & Judith Resnik
International Tribunals

Adjudication and its Alternatives 46–49 (2003)

The power of courts is tied to the power of the government of which they are a part. Governments in turn have long measured their authority by reference to the physical boundaries over which they have control. As technology and transportation reduce the import of geographical borders, new questions are posed for courts. The pressures for international, transnational, and multi-national responses, based in both public courts and private contracts, stem from all arenas (from family life and commercial transactions to organized crime and war) and raise many conceptual problems about the role of national courts and the place of international dispute resolution mechanisms. One set of questions relates to the reach of national courts, seeking to adjudicate events involving persons or activities beyond their borders. Another set of issues addresses the role of international courts and the reach of their jurisdiction, sometimes limited only to nations that consent to a specific instance and otherwise conceived to be more broad-ranging. Another concern relates to the interaction between national, subnational, and international adjudication. As judicial bodies of varying kinds have proliferated during the later part of the twentieth century, the import of such problems for both domestic and international tribunals has similarly grown.

In some instances, when individuals violate a nation's law but are not physically within that country's boundaries, national courts claim jurisdiction by seizing the person of the defendant—either by requesting that, pursuant to a treaty, another country extradite that person or by forcibly bringing that person to a jurisdiction for trial. In other instances, the injuries occur beyond that country's boundaries. For example, beginning in 1789 with the First Judiciary Act, Congress has given federal courts jurisdiction over tort claims filed by aliens alleging a "violation of the law of nations;" cases have been filed under this statute challenging torture and property seizure that occurred in countries other than the United States. See 28 U.S.C. § 1350.

International tribunals may also respond and, some argue, are especially important to deploy in cases when jurisdiction beyond the nation-state is sought to be exercised. For example, in 1948, the United Nations [UN] Charter established the International Court of Justice (the ICJ). All state members of the UN are subject to the ICJ's jurisdiction, although in some instances, member states decline to participate. For example, in the 1980s the United States declined to do so when Nicaragua sought redress for this country's alleged involvement in its civil war; the ICJ, however, ruled on the merits that the United States had violated international customary law by intervening. In the 1970s, the Court had but a few cases on its docket; by the 1990s, its docket grew to about ten cases a year and, as of 2000 it had twenty-three cases before it.

In addition to the ICJ, the UN also has many conventions addressed to specific issues (such as racism, discrimination against women, and the rights of children), and these conventions often create expert bodies or committees that receive information from countries and review their work in a quasi-administrative capacity. Some have optional protocols permitting individuals to bring complaints, although the remedies provided may be advisory rather than binding. Further the UN has set up special tribunals to deal with individual claims arising out of events such as the Gulf War and the 1981 Iranian revolution.

More recently, proposals have sought to establish courts with jurisdiction to provide transnational responses to all "crimes against humanity," such as genocide. After World War II, ad hoc tribunals (the Nuremberg and Tokyo Tribunals) were constituted. In the 1990s under the auspices of the United Nations, special courts have been convened to deal with prosecutions arising in Rwanda and the Former Territories of Yugoslavia. Their mandates rely on the crimes detailed in the Geneva Protocols of 1949 and the 1977 Additional Protocols. In 1999, many countries joined in the Rome Treaty for an International Criminal Court (ICC) to establish a permanent prosecutorial and adjudicatory body that would have the power to adjudicate crimes against humanity, as specified by that Treaty. That proposal has engendered substantial controversy about which persons would be called to account for what forms of behavior. Since the Rome Treaty has been ratified by more than a requisite sixty countries (although not the United States), the ICC entered into force on July 1, 2002. The International Criminal Court is expected to supplement many existing institutions and to be used in lieu of the ad hoc responses to specific conflicts.

The World Trade Organization (WTO) is yet another source of courts; its 1995 initiating agreement includes a "dispute settlement understanding" that created a Dispute Panel and Appellate Body. Private traders and investors have the power, pursuant to their respective domestic laws, to request that their governments take action against unreasonable foreign trade measures. Access to GATT [General Agreement on Tariffs and Trade] and WTO processes do not always require exhausting local remedies, and the speed of resolution and volume of cases has grown considerably. As of 1999, there were about 100 cases in the WTO system.

In addition to proceedings under specific UN Conventions and the WTO processes, regional federations have also created courts with a jurisdictional span broader than a single nation-state. The European Union, comprised of 15 states, and the Council of Europe (41 states) have two such courts: the European Courts of Justice (both trial and appellate), ... and a specialized court, the European Court of Human Rights.... The latter court deals with claims by individuals seeking review of decisions from their own domestic courts alleged to be in contravention of the European Convention on Human Rights.

As is true domestically, international agreements often include alternative dispute resolution provisions. Sometimes private international organizations or commercial entities contract to use such processes; nation-states may also incorporate these dispute resolution mechanisms in their treaties. For example, the International Olympic Committee prompted the creation of the Court of Arbitration for Sport, with 150 arbitrators sitting for four-year terms, dealing with both individual parties' disputes and sports federation discipline, and providing advisory opinions. The North American Free Trade Agreement (NAFTA) and many bilateral investment treaties also permit individuals to pursue claims through the United Nations Commission for International Trade Law (UNCITRAL) and the International Center for the Settlement of Investment Disputes (ICSID). All of these systems have to face questions about enforceability of their judgments in case of noncompliance, which in turn often relate to whether "local law" recognizes the authority of such contracts and defers to such decision-makers.

All multi-national courts and dispute resolution processes have the challenge of developing forms of processing that resolve differences among competing national paradigms....

Geoffrey C. Hazard, Jr.
International "Harmonization" of Procedural Law

From Whom No Secrets Are Hid, 76 Tex. L. Rev. 1665, 1666–69 (1998)

The human community of the world lives at closer quarters today than in ancient days: international trade is at an all time high and steadily increasing; international investment and monetary flows increase apace; businesses from the developed countries establish themselves all over the globe directly or through subsidiaries; business people travel abroad as a matter of routine; and increasing numbers of ordinary citizens live temporarily or permanently outside of their native countries. As a consequence, there are positive and productive interactions among citizens of different nations in the form of increased commerce and wide possibilities for personal experience and development. There are also inevitable negative interactions, however, including increased social friction, legal controversy, and litigation.

In dealing with these negative consequences, it is recognized that the costs and misery resulting from legal conflict can be mitigated by reducing differences in legal systems, whereby the same or similar "rules of the game" apply no matter where the participants may find themselves. The effort to reduce differences between national legal systems is commonly referred to as "harmonization." Another term, more often used in other countries, is "approximation," meaning that the rules of various legal systems should be reformed in the direction of approximating each other. Most endeavors at harmonization have addressed substantive law, particularly the law governing commercial and financial transactions. There is a profusion of treaties and conventions governing these subjects, as well as similar arrangements addressing personal rights such as those of employees, children, and married women. A conspicuous example is the North American Free Trade Agreement ("NAFTA")....

Harmonization of the law of procedure is avoided, so it appears, on the supposition that national procedural systems are too different and too deeply embedded in local political history and cultural tradition to permit reduction or reconciliation of differences between legal systems. For example, UNIDROIT ("International Institute for the Unification of Private Law"), an institution engaged for more than 70 years in the work of legal harmonization, traditionally has regarded procedural law as beyond its agenda. There are some international conventions dealing with procedural law—notably The Hague Convention on the Taking of Evidence Abroad and European conventions on recognition of judgments—and effort continues on a more general convention on personal jurisdiction and recognition of judgments. The international conventions on procedural law, however, have thus far addressed the front and back ends of procedural law, but not procedure as such. That is, the conventions and draft conventions govern the bases of personal jurisdiction and the mechanics of service of process to commence a lawsuit on one end of the litigation process and recognition of judgments on the other end. The events in between— the formulation of claims, the development of evidence, and the decision procedure—remain matters governed by local national law.

International arbitration often is a substitute for adjudication in national courts. However, the international conventions on arbitration have the same limited scope as the conventions dealing with international litigation in judicial forums. Thus, the international conventions on arbitration specify aspects of commencement in an arbitration proceeding and specify also the recognition to be accorded an arbitration award, but they say little or nothing about the procedure in an international arbitration proceeding. Rather, the typical stipulation concerning hearing procedure in international arbitration is that the procedural ground rules shall be as determined by the neutral arbitrator.

Nevertheless, The American Law Institute (ALI) is now engaged in a project seeking to take the next step in international harmonization of procedural law. The project is entitled "Transnational Rules of Civil Procedure" and is under the direction of Professor Michele Taruffo, of the University of Pavia, Italy, and myself. Our approach has been to draft proposed procedural rules that a country could adopt for adjudication of private international controversies that find their way into the ordinary courts of justice. Perhaps this venture involves fools walking where angels fear to tread. The project is inspired in part by the model of the Federal Rules of Civil Procedure, undertaken over a half century ago in pursuance of the Rules Enabling Act of 1934. The Federal Rules established a single procedure to be employed in courts sitting in forty-eight different semi-sovereign states, each of which had its own procedural law, its own procedural culture, and its own bar. The Federal Rules thereby accomplished what many thoughtful observers thought impossible—a single system of procedure for four dozen different legal communities. If experience with the Federal Rules proves that it has been possible to establish a single procedure for litigation in Louisiana (civil-law system), Virginia (common-law pleading in 1938) and California (code pleading), the ALI project conjectures that a procedure for litigation in transactions across national boundaries is also worth the attempt.

The ALI is a group of American judges, lawyers and scholars whose past efforts on a variety of fronts have focused primarily on uniformity within American jurisdictions. The ALI and UNIDROIT have joined efforts to synthesize common-law and civil law procedure into a single framework. Excerpts from the Transnational Rules of Civil Procedure appear in this book.

Chapter 2

ACCESS TO JUSTICE

"Justice for all" is both a common pledge and a universal challenge. Justice often requires effective legal representation, and legal representatives must be paid for their professional services. Considered broadly, the system by which lawyers are compensated can reflect a culture's priorities, norms, and biases. Considered more narrowly, compensation can influence a lawyer's obligations and decision-making. Contingency fee arrangements and the so-called "American Rule" are two distinguishing features of the American legal system.

W. Kent Davis
The International View of Attorney Fees in Civil Suits

16 Ariz. J. Int'l & Comp. L. 361, 371–414 (1999)

Contingent Fees and Indigent Access to the Legal System

The United States is unique in its wide use of contingent fees as a method of financing litigation. Under the contingent fee system, a plaintiff's attorney agrees to receive payment for his services out of the funds that the plaintiff wins from the defendant, either through a judgment in court or settlement before judgment. In the event that the case is lost, however, the lawyer receives nothing for his services. The contingent fee is an extremely common form of paying for the services of lawyers in the United States. In fact, it is now the dominant means of financing cases in many important areas of legal practice, including the collection of overdue commercial accounts, stockholder's suits, class actions, tax practice, condemnation proceedings, will contests, and—of course—personal injury litigation. As a sign of just how pervasive contingent fees have become, a report from the Federal Trade Commission has shown that ninety-seven percent of attorneys will only take personal injury cases on a contingent fee basis, refusing to consider hourly rates no matter how generous they are. The contingent fee is now coming to be seen as the basis of an industry "boldly and openly run for profit," and as a weapon of first choice rather than a last resort for those who are desperate and unable to find legal services by any other means. Even large law firms are now reported to work on contingency. And in a trend that is a sure sign of the future of the contingent fee, its use is spreading into new areas of litigation: employment matters, child support, copyrights, and even divorce. . . .

Its supporters maintain that it enables individuals to "press forward with claims that would otherwise remain unprosecuted for lack of funds. They claim, moreover, that feared abuses are not likely to occur, since lawyers have a strong incentive to choose those cases with the greatest chance of success." In theory, this argument makes great sense. An injured person can obtain a lawyer's services without paying for them unless there is a recovery from the one who caused the injury; thus, many people who are unable to afford a lawyer on an hourly rate are allowed access to the legal system. Of course, there are some risks to the attorney. He may spend a great deal of time, effort, and money on a case and get nothing in return if he loses. But for clients—especially poor ones—the offer is practically irresistible. In fact, clients usually prefer contingent fees over an hourly rate even when they could afford it; the obvious reason is that the contingent fee minimizes the very heavy expenses the client may incur if his suit is unsuccessful. It is thus not far off the mark to quote an old saying: "The contingent fee is the poor man's key to the courthouse door."[109] . . .

Despite the lofty notions that contingent fees exist to provide a means of achieving justice for the poor, America has a surprisingly poor view of the right to legal access in civil cases when compared with our international neighbors. While other nations explicitly grant civil litigants the right to representation in civil as well as criminal cases, our courts do not recognize any right of a poor client to the assistance of counsel, paid or unpaid, in civil cases. Although certain judges do have discretionary power to appoint counsel for indigent parties in civil cases, they have been extremely reluctant to do so, knowing that in these cases the appointed attorney would have to take the case pro bono. Some courts, it is also true, have undertaken a slight remedy by authorizing the clerk of the court to keep an official list of attorneys willing to handle pro bono cases. And in yet another exception, some courts have reversed cases on appeal because of the trial court's discretionary refusal to appoint

109. Arthur L. Kraut, *Contingent Fee: Champerty or Champion?*, 21 Clev. St. L. Rev. 15, 29 (1972).

counsel for an indigent civil litigant. But in American courts a civil litigant has no absolute right to representation by an attorney. In commenting on this "archaic" American view, Professor Schlesinger has stated, "By their refusal to recognize the existence of such a right, our courts and legislature make the words Due Process and Equal Protection of the Laws sound rather hollow for the impecunious litigant who loses a meritorious cause of action or defense because of his inability to obtain the assistance of competent counsel."[124] It is curious that a system that now pushes contingent fees so strongly as a means of helping the poor litigants of the nation has not adopted a more generous view when it comes to the rights of those same litigants. This unique and apparently contradictory American view of the tools and rights available to the indigent in civil litigation raises an obvious question: Given their charitable view on the right to counsel in civil cases, how do other nations ensure that the keys to the courthouse are available to the poor? . . .

Contingent fees in civil litigation have long been disfavored in both civil law countries and other common-law countries. In fact, the majority view in the world seems to be that they are "intrinsically evil," which has led to a "deeply ingrained attitude of hostility toward the contingent fee." This view has made contingent fees illegal, unethical, or both in virtually all countries outside the U.S. . . . [The] view among our international neighbors is simply that parties to a suit are not very good at looking out for themselves; that no direct means of policing lawyer's conduct is likely to be even halfway effective at discouraging unethical practices; and therefore the best line of ethical defense is to insulate lawyers from a direct stake in the outcome of a case. . . .

A few caveats are in order when discussing the international view of contingent fees. First, there are a few foreign nations that allow some form of contingent fee, including Japan, Indonesia, and Thailand. . . . Furthermore, there are signs that some versions of contingent fees may be creeping into nations that have traditionally held a very poor view of them. For instance, though the straightforward contingent fee contract is still illegal in France, since 1991 an agreement which adds a supplemental payment based on the result reached in a case to a fixed fee for the legal services performed has been permitted. And while contingent fees are still illegal in England, there is an informal quasi-contingent fee system in place under which an unsuccessful solicitor for a plaintiff does not seek a fee from his client, even though the plaintiff must still pay the winner's costs. Moreover, as of 1994 there were some signs of

124. Rudolf B. Schlesinger et al.,   als 361 (5th ed. 1988).
Comparative Law: Cases, Text, Materi-

change in the overall view of contingent fees in England. A preliminary study by the Lord Chancellor showed a willingness to study the introduction of contingent fees in England, Scotland, and Wales. It cannot be denied, however, that the overwhelming view of contingent fees among our international neighbors remains unfavorable.

Given the lack of contingent fees overseas, it is important to inquire into the measures that other nations take to ensure access to the legal system for lower income civil litigants. From the beginning of this discussion, however, a few words should be said of the fact that civil litigation in foreign nations is usually not as expensive as in the United States. For many reasons involving the trial process itself—such as the lack of discovery costs and expert opinion witnesses by the parties—the costs of civil litigation have generally been low in other countries. Another factor that has tended to keep litigation costs down overseas is the common existence of statutory tariffs for lawyers, which cover the costs an attorney may charge unless the client and attorney agree otherwise. In some nations, it is considered unethical for a lawyer to agree to a fee below these statutory rates. An agreement for a rate above the statutory guidelines, however, is often subject to restrictions, probably to protect the clients from unknowingly submitting to exorbitant costs. Fees in excess of the statutory guidelines, moreover, can be reduced by a court if found to be excessive. For example, a German statute lists in very fine detail every possible type of litigation activity that a lawyer might engage in, and for each activity assigns a monetary amount based on a fraction of what is called a "basic fee." . . . Of course, these tariffs can often be overcome by substituting a contractual fee for the statutory one, but this is usually done to protect the client rather than to give a windfall to the attorney. In short, a host of factors tend to make litigation overseas cheaper than in the United States, a factor that must be considered when discussing indigent access to the legal system.

Despite these factors which tend to decrease costs to individual clients, the cost risks can be quite high in foreign nations, not only because of the lack of contingent fees, but also because of the usual rule that permits the winner in a suit to recover his attorney fees from the loser (fee shifting). In addition to his own modest attorney fees, the loser also has to pay the modest attorney fees for the winner in these nations. Sometimes these two "modest" costs can add up to one big bill. Thus, it is important to consider how these risks, as well as the modest legal costs in general, are taken into account for low and moderate income people to ensure that they have access to the civil litigation system. The foreign measures taken to do this generally break down into three separate areas: (1)

Government-sponsored legal aid; (2) Mandatory pro bono work; and (3) Legal expense insurance.

England is a prime example of legal aid in the common-law world. In 1949 the Legal Aid and Advice Act set up a system of providing legal services without cost to low income individuals. It provides that litigants who have an income above a certain level but below a fixed maximum are eligible for more limited assistance based on their income level. Those with incomes above the maximum are not eligible for legal aid. The actual day-to-day operation of the system is left to the organized bar. The English Law Society has control of a fund composed of government appropriations and payments from parties; money is disbursed from this fund to pay lawyers and court officials for the clients utilizing legal aid. Attorney fees are set by an official of the court (a Taxing Master) in line with the routine costs between the parties and client and lawyer. The fee is thus the same as if the client were not using legal aid (except in cases before the High Court, in which the lawyer's fee is eighty-five percent of the level set by the Taxing Master). The beauty of the English system is that it preserves freedom of selection by the client, allows the bar to largely run the system, and fairly compensates the attorney for his services.

Most civil law nations have also long recognized the use of legal aid, seeing it as superior to the contingent fee with its surrounding ethical concerns. The statutory schemes covering the legal aid systems in these countries make sure that in civil as well as criminal cases an indigent party will have sufficient legal representation. Of course, this notion stems from the differing view in many civil law nations on the right of citizens to legal counsel. Unlike the United States, legal counsel is often seen as a right in civil as well as criminal cases. In fact, the German Federal Constitutional Court has explicitly recognized that an indigent party to a civil action has a constitutional right to be represented by an attorney. Accordingly, under the German system of legal aid, which is fairly typical for the civil-law world, an indigent person merely has to show that his claim or defense "has a sufficient prospect of success and is not frivolously asserted" to apply for legal aid. Under current German law, assistance will be granted to anyone who meets this test and is completely or partly unable to afford an attorney due to his "personal economic circumstances." The assistance is paid out of public funds and sometimes takes the form, for all practical purposes, of a long-term loan which has to be repaid to the government. The person who wishes to apply for legal aid does so to the court. If the court finds that the applicant meets the foregoing requirements, it appoints a lawyer to represent him. If the applicant has indicated a preference for a particular lawyer and that lawyer is willing to take the case, the court must honor that choice.

Defendants as well as plaintiffs may partake of this system. This system of paying for the legal costs of the indigent has been in place for a long time in Germany, and apparently meets with wide approval from the bar and public. And the rates payable to lawyers under the system, while not overly generous, are by no means at charity levels. In fact, court appointments to represent the indigent are often eagerly sought out by the bar, including some of the more experienced members.

In France, a similar system is used, with some minor variations. There, the indigent litigant must first apply to the Legal Aid Bureau instead of directly to the court. The bureau is an independent commission made up of members of government, the judiciary, and the bar. If the application is approved, an avocat will be appointed for the litigant. Until 1972 lawyers appointed to represent the indigent in such cases had to serve without compensation. Under 1972 reforms, compensation is now paid out of public funds for both criminal and civil lawsuits, although the compensation tends to be modest and the cases are generally handled by younger, less experienced lawyers.

Another means of providing access to civil litigation is the use of mandatory pro bono work. Austria and Italy utilize this system, though they appear to have experienced differing results. In Austria, all attorneys are required to handle a number of pro bono cases each year. As indigent parties apply to a court for legal assistance and are approved, lawyers are assigned these cases on an alphabetical basis using the bar roster. If an attorney decides to take pro bono cases on his own, his quota of pro bono cases originating from the bar roster is reduced accordingly. This system is well-accepted by the members of the bar in Austria as part of their professional responsibilities.

In Italy, attorneys are appointed in a fashion similar to that of Germany and the system in place is thought of as a form of legal aid. However, in Italy lawyers appointed to represent the indigent are usually not compensated out of public funds. Thus in reality Italy's system is much like Austria's mandatory pro bono system. In practice, the task of representing such clients is usually left to the younger, less experienced lawyers, leading to an understandably bad reputation when it comes to success of claims. As a result, little use is made of the Italian system by indigent parties; private organizations such as labor unions sometimes try to fill the gap.

In Europe, legal expense insurance was introduced more than sixty years ago and has become another popular alternative to contingent fees as a means of avoiding the risks of litigation costs. In Austria, Switzerland, and Germany, about forty percent of all households carry some form of legal expense insurance. Although at first glance the existence of these policies might lead one to believe that they would bring increased numbers of lawsuits, experience has shown that they have not increased litigation. In fact, one comprehensive study of these policies concluded bluntly that "legal expense insurance does not cause legal costs any more than accident insurance causes accidents." And proponents of legal expense insurance are quick to point out that—when combined with fee shifting—it solves a claimant's problems much better than contingent fees, "not only by paying his own attorney without diminishing the amount of damages actually received by the claimant, but also by paying the costs due the opponent in the event of defeat," thus leaving everyone satisfactorily compensated for attorney fees with little risk. . . .

Fee-Shifting: Who Pays for Attorney Fees After the Trial?

. . . The United States has a general rule that each side in civil litigation has ultimate responsibility for its own attorney fees, and the court will not require the loser to pay any of the cost of the winner's representation. This practice, which has become known as the American Rule, places the United States in a very small minority of the world's nations. The roots of this approach date back to very early in the nation's history. In general, the rule adopted by the colonies did not deviate from the entrenched English fee shifting rule. On both sides of the Atlantic, statutes provided the basis for attorney fee shifting. Throughout colonial times, the statutes that regulated the fees recoverable from the loser in civil litigation also regulated the maximum fees that all lawyers could charge clients. At a very early stage in American history, however, legislative control of attorney fees butted heads with the organized bar's desire for adequate compensation. The resolution of this conflict led to the emergence of the American Rule. After the American Revolution, lawyers were successful in repealing the statutes that regulated both attorney fees in general and the rates payable by losers in civil cases, though revised statutes still allowed the winner to recover small fixed awards as compensation for some of the costs of litigation besides attorney fees. The American Rule thus began as a compromise that allowed lawyers to charge clients higher rates while legislatures could still regulate some of the cost recovery from losers. . . .

But some interesting developments occurred on the way to the full adoption of the American Rule. Recognizing that sometimes the American Rule actually hindered plaintiffs with valid claims from filing suit, courts found ingenious ways around it. Some commentators have even argued that in personal injury cases, the award for pain and suffering evolved as a way for courts to allow the plaintiff to pay his own attorney while still gaining compensation for his loss. Punitive damages are also sometimes seen by courts as a way to allow the plaintiff to recover his own attorney's fees. Legislatures took even more direct steps to get around the American Rule in some cases, mainly as a means of encouraging public policies such as civil rights, consumer protection, and environmental awareness. As a result, many statutes today provide for some form of fee shifting in the United States. Besides providing help to plaintiffs with beneficial claims, legislatures also began to see fee shifting schemes as a way to deter frivolous or bad faith litigation.... Today, federal law includes more than two hundred statutes providing for fee shifting in some form, and individual states have many as well....

In the English legal system, a "loser pay" rule applies. The successful litigant can collect his or her legal fees, or costs, from the loser.... The English Rule has a long history. In the early stages of Roman law, civil procedure evolved as a highly organized, often ritualized form of dispute resolution under the cognizance of high priests and, later, the Roman government. Under this early system, there were no costs to be shifted simply because there were no attorneys; the priests or government handled everything for the parties. By the time of the Byzantine Empire, lawyers had begun to appear and were charging their clients fees. As costs became a reality for clients, the government began to enforce increasingly detailed regulations covering them. Out of this regulatory control evolved a rule that required the losing party to reimburse the winner for costs when the court found that the litigation was frivolous or was instigated in bad faith. Prior to this rule, the winner was allowed double recovery in cases of frivolity or bad faith. As the Byzantine Empire rolled along, reimbursement for the winner in all cases became the norm; the Byzantine Emperor Zenon is credited with first announcing, in 486 A.D., the general rule that the loser must pay the legal costs of the winner. Fifty years after Zenon's announcement, this rule became part of the Code of Justinian, which would heavily influence the laws of the modern European nations. The presumption of the now-codified rule was that the loser had done a wrong by insisting on his legal position, which had been proven in court to be unjustified. In its new form, the rule was adopted into the canon law of the Catholic Church and eventually into the emerging European court systems. This Roman/Byzantine rule also played a strong influence in the emerging court system of England.

The English Rule today reflects the rationale that victory is not complete in civil litigation if it leaves substantial expenses uncovered. Though there are some variations on the English Rule, its basic mechanics are as follows: (1) The objective fact of defeat is sufficient grounds for imposing legal costs on the loser, without regard to bad faith, fault, or frivolity; and (2) The costs to be reimbursed include not only the court fees and related costs but also the attorney fees and other expenses incurred by the winner. The effects of the English Rule are almost always mitigated, divided proportionately, or modified when the winner's victory is only a partial one, for "defeat" is usually understood to mean complete defeat in all major aspects of the case. In most nations using the English Rule, a lawyer and his client may contract for fees higher than those recommended by statutory tariffs, but the loser will not be liable for these excess fees.

A few caveats are in order.... [M]uch like the exceptions to the American Rule in the United States[,] there are many cases when the English Rule does not apply at all. Some of these exceptions focus on the conduct or state of mind of the victor. Others attempt to recognize the good faith efforts of the loser or his economic disadvantage. These exceptions have led to classes of cases where the application of the English Rule has been found unsuitable.... (1) Mandatory no-fault court proceedings, such as no-fault divorce, where there is no presumption of fault; (2) Cases of social and economic imbalance, such as landlord-tenant cases; (3) Sovereign immunity cases. The government is often immune from reimbursing the legal costs of private parties when it is sued. In addition to these exceptions, in some instances a court has discretion to waive the English Rule....

To further understand the mechanics of the English Rule, it is necessary to examine its use in individual countries. In England, at the end of the suit or interlocutory proceeding, an order is made by the court on allocation of costs. Then, a Taxing Master examines the list of costs submitted by the solicitors for the parties and determines the amount to be paid by the loser in a proceeding called "taxation." This procedure existed at the time of the American Revolution, and indeed today the United States has an analogous system of allocating costs. The difference between the two systems is that in England, unlike America, the "costs" include not only court fees and other minor expenses, but also the attorney fees for both the solicitor and barrister. The English system of full indemnity for attorney fees is governed by rules of court and not by statute, unlike the civil law nations which use the English Rule. Thus, the awarding of costs is not automatic as in most civil law countries, but is within the discretion of the court. Courts may, in some circumstances, assess no costs against the loser and may even require the winner to bear the loser's costs if his claim or defense seems oppressive or unnecessary, even though successful. Despite this discretionary power by the courts, however, costs usually "follow the event," as the English often say and fee shifting is the norm. The theory of the rule in England is simple: the winner is entitled to recover his reasonable litigation expenses, including attorney fees, from the loser. In England, the loser pays the attorney fees of the winner even in settlements, regardless of whether formal court action was initiated (although many settlement agreements specify the division of costs). The practice in England is generally followed throughout the English Commonwealth, with jurisdictions such as Australia and Ontario particularly similar.

Despite this seemingly universal rule in England, there are many instances when the English Rule does not apply, usually when speaking of plaintiffs. While most defendants, which tend to be institutional in nature, are almost always liable for costs of successful plaintiffs, individual plaintiffs who lose are often exempted from the English Rule because of the way their litigation was financed. Privately funded plaintiffs are subject to the English Rule win or lose; but those who do not pay for their own attorney fees are exempt from the Rule if they lose. Only about forty percent of English plaintiffs are thus subject to the downside risk of the English Rule, according to the Lord Chancellor's Department. The remaining sixty percent avoid the risk of the English Rule largely by financing their litigation in one of three ways: (1) Legal aid. Litigants who are eligible for legal aid are not subject to the risks of the English Rule except in rare cases; (2) Trade unions. Many English litigants have their cases financed by their trade unions, especially in work-related litigation. The unions absorb all litigation costs, including any assessments of attorney fees under the English Rule; (3) Legal expense insurance. Though only about two percent of English cases involve plaintiffs with legal expense insurance, this method requires the insurer to pay any attorney fees assessed under the English Rule....

With few exceptions, the civil law countries have also embraced the English Rule. Unlike England, however, in most civil law countries the Rule is not a matter for court discretion, but is prescribed in codes as mandatory.[389] Many of these codes specifically

---

389. See Werner Pfenningstorf, *The European Experience with Attorney Fee Shifting*, 47 Law & Contemp. Probs. 37, 45–46 (1984). There is surprising variation in how the English Rule is carried out in the civil law nations of Europe, however. Readers should note these passages from Pfennigstorf as illustration:

[T]he European codes vary in the ways in which they determine costs or control attorney fees for reimbursement purposes.... Most of the countries ... provide for reimbursement of attorney fees, although to different ex-

tents. In Austria and Germany, where attorney fees are fixed by statutory schedule, the amount resulting from the application of the schedule is considered a necessary expense and is routinely allowed. In Switzerland, official fee schedules are common, but courts have traditionally specified the reimbursable expenses at lower amounts.... France and Belgium ... traditionally had two major types of legal professionals to assist parties in litigation.... While it was recognized that traditional notions of justice and the interests of the prevailing party provide that the court is to shift fees to the loser on its own initiative even if the winner has failed to submit a petition for such costs. For example, in Germany the statutory rule is that the loser bears all costs of the winner, including attorney fees and other expenses such as loss of time to travel to and participate in hearings.... The English Rule also finds a civil law application in Austria, where extensive statutory guidelines govern its use. Article 41 of the Austrian Code of Civil Procedure embodies the principle of reimbursement for the winner of civil cases. Similar articles impose punitive costs upon litigants who use dilatory tactics or engage in frivolous litigation.... Mexico has also adopted the English Rule as part of its civil-law system. Accordingly, in Mexico the loser must reimburse the winner for all legal costs (gastos procesales) involved in the case, including the attorney fees. Much like the other civil law nations discussed herein, the reimbursable attorney fees are determined by statutory tariffs related to the amount in controversy and the procedural steps involved in the litigation....

Notes

2–1.   On a per capita basis, the United States government spends $2.25 per year for civil legal aid, with England spending $32, New Zealand and Ontario $12. D. Rhode, Access to Justice 112 (2004). "The best estimates suggest that the nation supplies about one legal aid attorney for every nine thousand poor persons, compared with one lawyer for every three hundred residents." D. Rhode, In the Interests of Justice: Reforming the Legal Profession 120 (2000). Does this data suggest that our system of legal aid is administered more efficiently than other countries or that we may need a more robust infrastructure of legal aid?

2–2.   Are contingent fees an effective substitute for legal aid? How do (or could) contingent fees provide access to justice for poor litigants who are *defendants* (e.g., in actions filed by landlords, lenders, employers, retailers)?

2–3.   A contingency fee means that the lawyer has a financial interest in the outcome of the lawsuit. Does this ensure or does it compromise a lawyer's undivided loyalty to his client?

argued in favor of full reimbursement of attorney costs, whether in the nature of fees or honoraria, as was the rule in other major European countries, it was perceived as equally important to protect the independence of the legal profession against the threat of regimentation, which, it was feared, would be a consequence of full reim-bursement. The result of this conflict of policies has been a continuation of a [rather complicated] dual system for lawyer remuneration.... [In] Spain, ... [as in] England, ... the court is given discretion whether to rule on costs.

Id. at 45, 56–57, 59.

2–4.   One of the most persistent critiques of the American Rule on attorneys' fees is that it allows plaintiffs with weak cases to "extort" settlement offers from defendants who know that it is cheaper to settle a case than to litigate and win. What might explain the United States' singular approach?

2–5.   Because the State of Alaska uses the "English Rule" in its state courts, there is an experiment with fee-shifting in the United States well underway. If you were curious to learn more about its successes and vulnerabilities, (i) what specific questions would you ask an Alaska practitioner?; and (ii) what particular data from the court system would you want to review?

Chapter 3

PLEADING REQUIREMENTS

The materials in this chapter focus on the technical requirements of pleading rules. Pleadings comprise the first stage of a civil
lawsuit in any system. The parties exchange pleadings to inform
each other as well as the court of their respective contentions.
Under the Federal Rules, such notice is the primary function of the
pleadings; hence the characterization of the Federal Rules as establishing a regime of "notice pleading."

Yet notice is not the only important function that can be served
by pleadings. For example, pleadings can also be used to filter
unmeritorious claims, narrow the issues in dispute, and identify
cases that can be resolved on legal determinations without fact-
finding. But to perform these additional functions effectively, pleadings must be written with some precision and must contain specific
facts. And in most parts of the world, pleading rules have been
engineered to demand that level of attention.

Spain's Ley de Enjuiciamiento Civil (LEC) offers a set of
pleading rules that are fairly typical of the civil law countries. The
requirements for a *demanda* or complaint, set forth in Article 399,
include:

- a complete, clear, and accurate narrative of the factual
  background, with clear and accurate mention and reference
  to all documents attached to the complaint, including expert
  reports;
- the legal grounds of the claim, including, not only those
  relating to the merits, but also those referring to the rights
  of action, the capacity of the parties, jurisdiction, and venue;
  and
- the relief sought.

The LEC introduces four pleading requirements, in particular,
that require attention: (i) factual specificity; (ii) legal precision; (iii)

28

pleading evidence; and (iv) static content. Each of these four requirements can be scaled higher or lower in any given system so that pleadings perform more or fewer sorting functions. Although the differences between the LEC provisions and FRCP 8 may appear subtle, the systems are in fact calibrated quite differently.

Factual Specificity. One of the most unusual characteristics of pleading under the Federal Rules is the lack of any requirement of factual specificity. A quick survey of other pleading regimes suggests that most, including the LEC, require a more detailed factual narrative. Australia requires, in summary form, a statement of the material facts on which the party relies. Austria requires a statement of the facts upon which the claim is based. The codes in Argentina, Peru, and other civil law countries in South America tend to require a clear explanation of the facts on which the complaint is based. Similarly, in Japan, a complaint must contain concrete allegations of the facts from which the claim arises. In Singapore, the Rules of Court require that plaintiffs establish their cause of action by pleading the material facts precisely. Turkey requires a list and discussion of the events and material facts on which the plaintiff bases its claim.

Many pleading systems advise *brevity* in pleading, but plaintiffs still are required to plead *facts*. The English Civil Procedure Rules, for example, require a concise statement of the facts on which the claimant relies. The Federal Rules do not require a claimant to set out in detail the facts upon which he bases his claim. To the contrary, the Rules require only a short and plain statement of the claim that will give the defendant fair notice of the plaintiff's claim and the grounds upon which it rests.

Legal Precision. In addition to targeting the facts, pleading rules, such as the LEC, can demand particulars about the plaintiff's legal theory of redress. The expectation is that plaintiffs will have done their legal homework, and will thus identify with precision their cause of action and its constituent elements. In Argentina, for example, plaintiffs are expected to articulate a brief description of the law sustaining the complaint. In Peru, pleaders must offer their legal reasoning. A recent amendment to the code in The Netherlands requires that plaintiffs describe not only their own legal arguments but also the defendant's counter-arguments, if known. Textual nuance and local custom can demand more or less precision regarding identification of the legal right asserted, the source of that right, and the available remedy.

Again pleading under the Federal Rules is the liberal outlier on a continuum of approaches. Although the Federal Rules require that the plaintiff have a cognizable claim, a plaintiff need not articulate the claim with any sophistication or specificity. A pleading states a claim if the pleader offers some narrative for which the law offers relief. The plaintiff need not plead legal theories. Indeed, the drafters of the Federal Rules used the word "claim" when crafting the pleading standard instead of the more familiar, and therefore freighted, term "cause of action."

Pleading Evidence. The Federal Rules draw a sharp distinction between pleadings and evidence. The pleadings are not, themselves, evidence; nor is evidence to be attached to the pleadings. Yet in countries as diverse as The Netherlands, Korea, Mexico, Italy, and Portugal, plaintiffs in many cases are expected to file supporting evidence (or at least a list of their supporting evidence) with their complaint. The LEC requires that documents be attached to the complaint and that references to those documents be incorporated into the complaint. In Israel, documents that are material to the claim must be attached; and if the statement of claim includes any allegations regarding a medical issue, then an expert opinion provided by a physician must accompany the statement of claim. In Peru, the claim must be accompanied by all the documents and means of proof available to the plaintiff. A much less ambitious form of such a requirement requires only that the complaint be verified. In England, for example, the facts set out on the claim form must be verified by the plaintiff under the pains and penalties of perjury.

Demanding evidentiary support for the complaint can invite much more rigorous review of the sufficiency of the pleadings. Not all systems with such a requirement use it aggressively, however. Some systems use the requirement to "fix" the quantum of evidence at issue in the case. *See infra.* Other systems use the requirement largely to effect the disclosure of evidence between the parties. *See* Chapter 3, *infra.*

Static Content. Systems demanding specificity and precision in pleading may be unwilling to review pleadings that are a moving target. Accordingly, under the Spanish LEC, as in Sweden and many other countries, the pleadings fix the basis of the claim and also determine the object and scope of the proceedings. Absent exceptional circumstances, the plaintiff cannot amend the pleadings after the defendant has filed an answer. Even the evidence that can be used to support the claim is circumscribed by the pleadings. By disallowing or discouraging amendments, litigants have the incentive to research and evaluate both the law and the facts with utmost care prior to filing.

Under the Federal Rules and other systems that liberally allow amendments, the pleadings can be a dynamic reflection of the parties' evolving positions. As the interplay of additional evidence and further legal research yields new possibilities, the pleadings are amended accordingly.

Notes

3–1.   The drafters of the Federal Rules created a system where the filtering of weak cases and the narrowing of issues would be undertaken in later stages of litigation. But if rigorous pleading requirements encourage litigants to do their legal and factual homework prior to filing and if challenges to insufficient pleadings can dispose of weak and meritless cases sooner rather than later, why wouldn't every system use pleadings to perform these useful functions? Would this explain the tendency of some federal judges to demand more particularity than is demanded by FRCP 8? *See* Christopher M. Fairman, *The Myth of Notice Pleading*, 45 Ariz. L. Rev. 987 (2003); Richard L. Marcus, *The Puzzling Persistence of Pleading Practice*, 76 Tex. L. Rev. 1749 (1998).

3–2.   What does "notice pleading" mean? Which pleading system provides more and better notice to defendants: the Federal Rules or the LEC? Can a "notice pleading" regime *also* enforce rigorous pleading requirements to filter claims and narrow disputes?

3–3.   The well-documented history of federal procedure in the United States reveals that the introduction of notice pleading in the Federal Rules represented a profound departure from past practice. *See* Stephen N. Subrin, How *Equity Conquered Common Law: The Federal Rules of Civil Procedure in Historical Perspective*, 135 U. Pa. L. Rev. 909 (1987). Yet the procedural codes of other countries remained largely unchanged throughout the early twentieth century—a period of great procedural reform in the United States. The LEC, for example, is still based largely on the Napoleonic Code. Were the codes of Spain and other countries outside the United States not subject to the social, political, and economic forces that spurred procedural reform in the United States?

3–4.   Because of federalism, meaningful "comparative" work can be done even within the American court system. Some states have long maintained pleading standards that require a plaintiff to identify, in their complaint, facts constituting the cause of action. One survey of pleading standards suggests that the pleading standards *applied* in the federal and state courts of those states may be quite similar notwithstanding the textual differences. That survey posits that a legal culture that is common to the federal and state courts in each of those states may have an assimilative effect on the pleading standards. *See* Thomas O. Main, *Procedural Uniformity and the Exaggerated Role of Rules*, 46 Vill. L. Rev. 311 (2001). As cultural differences fade in an era of increasing globalization, should we expect some international convergence on a pleading standard—in practice even if not in form?

3–5. An effort to harmonize procedural law at an international level has already been undertaken jointly by the American Law Institute (ALI) and the International Institute for the Unification of Private Law (UNIDROIT). That effort has produced the Principles and Rules of Transnational Civil Procedure, which nations are invited to adopt or use for the adjudication of international disputes. The pleading standard contained in model Rule 12 provides:

- The plaintiff must state the facts on which the claim is based, describe the evidence to support those statements, and refer to the legal grounds that support the claim, including foreign law, if applicable.

- The reference to legal grounds must be sufficient to permit the court to determine the legal validity of the claim.

- The statement of facts must, so far as reasonably practicable, set forth detail as to time, place, participants, and events. A party who is justifiably uncertain of a fact or legal grounds may make statements about them in the alternative. In connection with an objection that a pleading lacks sufficient detail, the court should give due regard to the possibility that necessary facts and evidence will develop in the course of the proceeding.

How rigorous is this demand for factual specificity and legal precision? (Evidence need not be attached to the complaint. And amendments are to be allowed "upon showing good reason ... within reasonable time limits, when doing so does not unreasonably postpone the proceeding or otherwise result in injustice.")

3–6. The scope of the Transnational Rules is limited to commercial disputes. Would the pleading standard quoted above be suitable only for commercial cases? Does each substantive category require its own standard?

3–7. Imagine that you are a consultant to a country seeking to draft a uniform pleading standard. How, if at all, would the following factors about that country influence the undertaking:

    a. Rigor of the standard already in place.

    b. Cultural expectations about legal representation.

    c. Likelihood of litigation abuse by filing frivolous cases. (How could we gauge or predict this?)

    d. Percentage of cases that typically settle before trial.

    e. Availability of legal aid.

    f. Society's reliance on private litigation for the enforcement of public norms (e.g., protection of the environment, antitrust, consumer protection, employment discrimination).

    g. Coverage of the social safety net (e.g., welfare, the availability and affordability of medical care, job retraining).

What other factors would you want or need to know before offering your advice?

Chapter 4

DISCOVERY

The materials in this chapter focus on the task of gathering evidence for trial—what common law systems label "discovery." This stage is central to the judicial process of any system because it provides litigants with the means to obtain evidence that may be necessary to prove their case. Justice, or at least the ascertainment of truth, would seem to require the consideration of all evidence that may be relevant to the case. Rules that are designed to facilitate discovery of all of that evidence, however, tend to compromise other important values. Indeed, the American system of discovery, while credited for leaving no stone unturned, is also notorious throughout the world for its inefficiency and intrusiveness. This chapter presents comparative materials demonstrating the range of discovery systems, transnational materials revealing conflicts at the intersection of different systems, and international materials documenting efforts at multinational cooperation.

A. NATIONAL PRACTICES

National approaches to discovery can vary widely—even among neighboring countries that are derivative of the same legal tradition. Explanations for these variations would include politics and culture, perceptions about the purposes of litigation and, given the interrelatedness of procedure, other rules and doctrines. Systems can be differentiated by examining their approach as to each of the following protocols: (i) the available mechanisms; (ii) the scope of inquiry; (iii) timing; (iv) the extent of judicial involvement; and (v) the participation of experts.

Discovery Mechanisms. American litigators have at their disposal a number of formal discovery techniques, including document requests, interrogatories, depositions, requests for admissions, and physical examinations. This set is unusually broad. Other common law systems, including Australia, England, Hong Kong, India, the

Philippines and Singapore, offer only a subset of this list. In particular, no common law countries other than the United States and (parts of) Canada liberally allow pre-trial depositions for the purpose of gathering evidence.

The civil law countries tend to maintain a still narrower set of pre-trial discovery mechanisms. In many countries, only documents are exchanged in advance of trial. Pre-trial discovery in Japan is limited primarily to document requests and interrogatories. In Belgium, other than receiving documents, the most that a party can do to elicit detail from their opponent is to use their written submissions to the court to ask questions challenging the other party openly to respond. Many civil and common law countries have other discovery mechanisms (including depositions) available, but these techniques are for the limited use of preserving testimony that might be impossible to obtain at trial.

Among the discovery tools of almost all systems are automatic disclosure requirements. Either with the pleadings or at some later point, parties typically are obliged to disclose documents. Some require the disclosure only of documents that support the disclosing party's position; many others require the disclosure of all relevant documents.

Scope of Inquiry. A system's philosophy toward the gathering of evidence is also reflected in the permissible scope of discovery. At one end of that spectrum, the Federal Rules permit the discovery of any unprivileged matter that is relevant to the claim or defense of any party (provided the request is not unreasonably cumulative or burdensome). Under this regime, litigants tend to make broad requests, seeking unspecified information for the purpose of turning up anything that might be (or become) relevant to the case. These are the sort of "fishing expeditions" that are frequently derided by other systems. In other systems—whether of the common law or the civil law tradition—discovery requests must be more narrowly tailored and must correspond to the allegations and theories in the pleadings. These constraints are especially significant since, in many systems, the pleadings are both fixed and more precise. Generally speaking, then, whether a particular request is sufficiently specific depends upon the circumstances leading to the request and the system's tolerance for discovery.

Timing. The timing and sequence of gathering evidence are fundamentally different in the common law and civil law traditions. In the common law tradition, the discovery stage occurs in preparation for trial where the evidence is then presented in full. In the civil law tradition, certain documents and evidence may be disclosed early in the action, but otherwise the evidence is simultaneously gathered and evaluated by the judge in a series of hearings.

In Italy, for example, the discovery of evidence occurs over the course of a number of separate hearings spanning months or years. The purpose of the earlier hearings is to determine which mechanisms of evidence will be used; the latter hearings involve the "taking" of evidence.

Judicial Involvement. In most common law systems, certain initial disclosures may be required by procedural rule, but discovery otherwise is largely party-controlled. Under the Federal Rules, discovery requests and responses ordinarily are not filed with the court, and only if there is some dispute between the parties is the judge likely even to know whether or what discovery is underway.

In most civil law systems, however, the parties may not compel one another to produce evidence without the participation of the court. Because of the interrelatedness of discovery and trial, civil law systems view evidence-gathering as a judicial function. While the parties may offer the names of witnesses, and will suggest questions to be put to the witnesses, the civil law judge typically decides which witnesses to summon, conducts the questioning, and records the evidence. The gathering and evaluation of the evidence are intertwined, and both tasks are undertaken as an exercise of the judicial function.

Expert Evidence. Under the Federal Rules, the use and selection of experts are largely within the control of the parties. It is not uncommon, then, that so-called "hired guns" engage in a "battle of the experts." Not all common law systems, however, follow this model. In England, the new Civil Practice Rules restrict the use of expert witnesses "to that which is reasonably required to resolve the proceedings."* In particular, no expert witness can be used in any civil proceeding without the court's permission.

The civil law countries tend to be even more restrictive. Parties ordinarily cannot bring their own expert witnesses or present reports from their own experts. Instead, the court, upon acknowledging the need for expert testimony, appoints a neutral expert who submits a report answering the parties' questions and appears for questioning at trial. In Belgium, for example, the judge determines both the need for and the tasks of any expert. At a meeting with the expert, the parties give an overview of their respective positions and the evidence necessary for the expert to offer her opinion. The expert prepares a preliminary report upon which the parties are permitted comment. The expert then prepares a final report that incorporates and responds to the parties' comments. The court is not bound by the conclusions of the expert although, in practice, most courts follow the findings.

* Civil Procedure Rule 35.1.

Stephen N. Subrin
Discovery in Global Perspective: Are We Nuts?

52 DePaul L. Rev. 299, 309–312 (2002)

. . . Our discovery mechanisms are not so irrational when seen in context. Let me sketch out some examples. Consider our historic distrust of concentrated power. Our doctrines of federalism and separation of powers, the right to a jury trial, and the adversary system, including party control, reflect our historic distrust of residing power in one person or limited groups. We do not think that judges would ferret out negative aspects of our opponent's case and positive information to prove our own claims or defenses with the same motivation and intensity that self-interest propels. Perhaps if we had more experience with career judges, elevated as the result of performance based on objective criteria, as opposed to politically-appointed or elected judges, we would have more confidence in turning over discovery to the judiciary. . . .

In the United States, civil litigation plays a more substantial role in the governmental and societal structure than in most other countries. Alexis de Tocqueville noted in the 1830s how many hotly contested political issues end up in the United States courts. These issues are frequently, if not usually, raised by private litigants in civil litigation, as opposed to law enforcement by the state itself. A recent article about the Japanese legal system emphasizes how unusual the United States is in utilizing civil litigation, often through the tort system, to enforce social norms.[53] In this article, the author notes that in Japan, after private individuals sought to enforce environmental and anti-discrimination laws through civil litigation, the government, particularly "the entrenched bureaucracy," sought to curtail private enforcement so that the state could retain its power "as the appropriate enforcer of legal norms." Perhaps a truer comparison of the utilization of discovery in the United States would be between our civil discovery and the methods used in other countries to gain information, through force or otherwise, by the police, prosecutors, and administrative agencies in their attempt to enforce laws. It may well be that other countries permit so little discovery because the bulk of their civil cases are like the routine cases in the United States that engender modest discovery.

Broad discovery seems critical in many situations in which private individuals in the United States use civil litigation to enforce rights. This is particularly true in such cases as civil rights, products liability, securities, and antitrust, in which evidence to make a prima facie case frequently resides in the files and minds of

---

53. Carl F. Goodman, *The Somewhat Less Reluctant Litigant: Japan's Chang-* *ing View Towards Civil Litigation,* 32 Law & Pol'y Int'l Bus. 769 (2001).

the defendants. In these lawsuits, it would often be very difficult, if not impossible, for the plaintiff to plead her facts or evidence with particularity in the complaint, as is required in the pleading rules of other countries. The lack of precise pleading means that the defendant also frequently needs extensive discovery. The United States Supreme Court has repeatedly drawn the connection between notice pleading and liberal discovery. . . . In short, it would be difficult to eliminate extensive discovery in United States civil litigation without also changing the relative places of civil litigation, lawyers, judges, and juries in our culture and the relative roles of pleading, discovery, summary judgment, and other elements of procedure. The rules and the culture are interrelated in complex ways that would be very difficult to disentangle, even if such rearrangements were deemed desirable.

B. TRANSNATIONAL CONFLICT

National differences in discovery practice present circumstances ripe not only for comparative study, but also for transnational conflict. Indeed "no aspect of international litigation has caused as much friction as the issue of discovery."* Most of these conflicts tend to develop when documents or other evidence is located in a foreign country that has a more restrictive approach to discovery.

Imagine, for example, that you are defending a French corporation in an action that is pending in a United States District Court. You receive a document request from the plaintiffs seeking unspecified documents that are only tangentially relevant to the underlying cause of action. Given the French system's attitude toward discovery, your client may be outraged by this "fishing expedition." Yet you would have to produce the document. Indeed, if the documents (no matter their location) were within the control and possession of your client, the refusal to produce them would be sanctionable under FRCP 37.

Many countries were uncomfortable with—even incensed by— the unilateral export of American-style discovery. From their perspective, American courts were acting outside their territorial boundaries and flouting the rights and protections granted by the foreign law. Moreover, American discovery had essentially privatized the gathering of evidence, which in the civil law tradition is an act of the judicial sovereign.

---

* Andreas Lowenfeld, International   ness 137 (1996).
Litigation and the Quest for Reasonable-

Many countries struck back. To protect their citizens and information within their territories, if not also to defend the integrity of their court system, many countries prohibited the disclosure of such information. For example, in 1980 France added to its Penal Code the following offense:

> [I]t is prohibited for any party to request, seek or disclose, in writing, orally or otherwise, economic, commercial, industrial, financial or technical documents or information leading to the constitution of evidence with a view to foreign judicial or administrative proceedings or in connection therewith.

French Penal Code Law No. 80–538. These "blocking statutes" took various forms, including the constructive "seizure" by the (foreign) government of documents otherwise subject to discovery. By invoking these statutes, foreign litigants in American courts could thus argue that it would be a crime for them to cooperate with the discovery requests and/or the documents were not within their custody or control. Through the wonder of globalization, then, a discovery dispute becomes a question of international relations and diplomacy: which country's laws and values should prevail?

Courts balanced the interests and, generally speaking, the blocking statutes worked. The blocking statutes created enough friction to moderate the application abroad of discovery techniques.

C. INTERNATIONAL SOLUTIONS

Foreign resistance to discovery prompted the United States to propose the adoption of a convention on transnational discovery. The Hague Convention on the Taking of Evidence Abroad in Civil or Commercial Matters was intended to establish a system that would be tolerable to the state executing the request yet useful to the requesting state. The United States ratified the Convention by a unanimous vote of the Senate in 1972. Dozens of other countries ("contracting states") have since joined.*

There are three alternative methods for obtaining evidence abroad under the Convention.

(1) A litigant may request the court where the action is pending to transmit a "Letter of Request" to the "Central Authority"** in the country where the evidence is to be ob-

---

* The Hague Conference on Private International Law maintains an excellent website, including a list of the contracting states to conventions such as the Convention on the Taking of Evidence Abroad. *See* http://www.hcch.net (last visited October 1, 2005).

** Article 2 of the Convention requires each Contracting State to designate a Central Authority to receive Letters of Request emanating from other countries and to transmit them to the authority competent to execute them. In the United States, the Department of Justice serves as the Central Authority for incoming requests.

tained. The Central Authority transmits the request to the appropriate foreign court, which conducts an evidentiary proceeding under procedures of the foreign country.

(2) A litigant may request that the evidence be taken before a diplomatic or consular officer in the country where the action is pending. The Convention provides that a contracting state may reserve the right not to allow the taking of evidence before a diplomatic or consular officer.

(3) A litigant may request that a specially appointed commissioner take evidence in the foreign country.

Of the three procedures, the Letter of Request is the most useful. It is the only method which applies to compulsory evidentiary proceedings. The other two methods are subject to limitations in the Convention and many countries have taken a variety of exceptions regarding the use of these procedures. Some of the key provisions of the Convention regarding the procedure for Letters of Request are printed below.

Hague Convention on the Taking of Evidence Abroad in Civil or Commercial Matters

(1972)

The States signatory to the present Convention,

Desiring to facilitate the transmission and execution of Letters of Request and to further the accommodation of the different methods which they use for this purpose,

Desiring to improve mutual judicial co-operation in civil or commercial matters,

Have resolved to conclude a Convention to this effect and have agreed upon the following provisions:

Article 1

In civil or commercial matters a judicial authority of a Contracting State may, in accordance with the provisions of the law of that State, request the competent authority of another Contracting State, by means of a Letter of Request, to obtain evidence, or to perform some other judicial act.

A Letter shall not be used to obtain evidence which is not intended for use in judicial proceedings, commenced or contemplated. . . .

Article 2

A Contracting State shall designate a Central Authority which will undertake to receive Letters of Request coming from a judicial authority of another Contracting State and to transmit them to the authority competent to execute them. Each State shall organize the Central Authority in accordance with its own law.

Letters shall be sent to the Central Authority of the State of execution without being transmitted through any other authority of that State.

Article 3

A Letter of Request shall specify—

a) the authority requesting its execution and the authority requested to execute it, if known to the requesting authority;

b) the names and addresses of the parties to the proceedings and their representatives, if any;

c) the nature of the proceedings for which the evidence is required, giving all necessary information in regard thereto;

d) the evidence to be obtained or other judicial act to be performed.

Where appropriate, the Letter shall specify, inter alia—

e) the names and addresses of the persons to be examined;

f) the questions to be put to the persons to be examined or a statement of the subject-matter about which they are to be examined;

g) the documents or other property, real or personal, to be inspected;

h) any requirement that the evidence is to be given on oath or affirmation, and any special form to be used;

i) any special method or procedure to be followed under Article 9.

A Letter may also mention any information necessary for the application of Article 11.

No legalization or other like formality may be required.

Article 4

A Letter of Request shall be in the language of the authority requested to execute it or be accompanied by a translation into that language.

Nevertheless, a Contracting State shall accept a Letter in either English or French, or a translation into one of these languages, unless it has made the reservation authorized by Article 33.

A Contracting State which has more than one official language and cannot, for reasons of internal law, accept Letters in one of these languages for the whole of its territory, shall, by declaration, specify the language in which the Letter or translation thereof shall be expressed for execution in the specified parts of its territory. In case of failure to comply with this declaration, without justifiable excuse, the costs of translation into the required language shall be borne by the State of origin.

A Contracting State may, by declaration, specify the language or languages other than those referred to in the preceding paragraphs, in which a Letter may be sent to its Central Authority.

Any translation accompanying a Letter shall be certified as correct, either by a diplomatic officer or consular agent or by a sworn translator or by any other person so authorized in either State. . . .

Article 9

The judicial authority which executes a Letter of Request shall apply its own law as to the methods and procedures to be followed.

However, it will follow a request of the requesting authority that a special method or procedure be followed, unless this is incompatible with the internal law of the State of execution or is impossible of performance by reason of its internal practice and procedure or by reason of practical difficulties.

A Letter of Request shall be executed expeditiously. . . .

Article 11

In the execution of a Letter of Request the person concerned may refuse to give evidence in so far as he has a privilege or duty to refuse to give the evidence—

a) under the law of the State of execution; or

b) under the law of the State of origin, and the privilege or duty has been specified in the Letter, or, at the instance of the requested authority, has been otherwise confirmed to that authority by the requesting authority.

A Contracting State may declare that, in addition, it will respect privileges and duties existing under the law of States other than the State of origin and the State of execution, to the extent specified in that declaration.

Article 12

The execution of a Letter of Request may be refused only to the extent that—

a) in the State of execution the execution of the Letter does not fall within the functions of the judiciary; or

b) the State addressed considers that its sovereignty or security would be prejudiced thereby.

Execution may not be refused solely on the ground that under its internal law the State of execution claims exclusive jurisdiction over the subject-matter of the action or that its internal law would not admit a right of action on it. . . .

Article 14

The execution of the Letter of Request shall not give rise to any reimbursement of taxes or costs of any nature.

Nevertheless, the State of execution has the right to require the State of origin to reimburse the fees paid to experts and interpreters and the costs occasioned by the use of a special procedure requested by the State of origin under Article 9, paragraph 2. . . .

Article 23

A Contracting State may at the time of signature, ratification or accession, declare that it will not execute Letters of Request issued for the purpose of obtaining pre-trial discovery of documents as known in Common Law countries.

Article 27

The provisions of the present Convention shall not prevent a Contracting State from—

a) declaring that Letters of Request may be transmitted to its judicial authorities through channels other than those provided for in Article 2;

b) permitting, by internal law or practice, any act provided for in this Convention to be performed upon less restrictive conditions;

c) permitting, by internal law or practice, methods of taking evidence other than those provided for in this Convention.

———

The Evidence Convention outlined a scope and procedure for foreign discovery that, although narrow and administratively cumbersome in comparison with the Federal Rules, identified important common ground. But this common ground confined American litigators familiar with American discovery, who "needed" broader discovery in order to meet their burdens of proof. Those litigators tested the limits and durability of the Convention.

The Court's decision in *Société Nationale Industrielle Aérospatiale*, which follows, addressed the extent to which litigants and courts were obliged to follow the Convention when engaged in transnational discovery. The petitioners to the Court (SNIA) were corporations owned by the Republic of France engaged in the business of designing, manufacturing and marketing aircraft. One of their planes, the "Rallye," was allegedly advertised in American aviation publications as "the World's safest and most economical STOL plane." STOL was an acronym for "short takeoff and landing," and it referred to a fixed-wing aircraft that either takes off or lands with only a short horizontal run of the aircraft. On August 19, 1980, a Rallye crashed in Iowa, injuring the pilot and a passenger.

The plaintiffs (later the respondents in the Supreme Court action) brought separate suits based upon this accident in the United States District Court for the Southern District of Iowa, alleging that petitioners had manufactured and sold a defective plane and were thus liable under theories of negligence and breach of warranty. Plaintiffs sought discovery under the Federal Rules, and SNIA filed a motion for a protective order. SNIA argued that, because they were a French corporation, the Hague Evidence Convention was the only means through which the plaintiffs could conduct discovery. After all, defendants argued, the Hague Evidence Convention had been adopted by the Senate and thus was the law of the land. The plaintiffs argued, however, that compliance with the Convention was not mandatory. The district court agreed with the plaintiffs, and denied the motion for a protective order. The case ultimately found its way to the Supreme Court.

SOCIÉTÉ NATIONALE INDUSTRIELLE AÉROSPATIALE v. UNITED STATES DISTRICT COURT

482 U.S. 522 (1987)

JUSTICE STEVENS delivered the opinion of the Court:

[I]

... In arguing their entitlement to a protective order, petitioners correctly assert that both the discovery rules set forth in the

Federal Rules of Civil Procedure and the Hague Convention are the law of the United States. This observation, however, does not dispose of the question before us; we must analyze the interaction between these two bodies of federal law. Initially, we note that at least four different interpretations of the relationship between the federal discovery rules and the Hague Convention are possible. Two of these interpretations assume that the Hague Convention by its terms dictates the extent to which it supplants normal discovery rules. First, the Hague Convention might be read as requiring its use to the exclusion of any other discovery procedures whenever evidence located abroad is sought for use in an American court. Second, the Hague Convention might be interpreted to require first, but not exclusive, use of its procedures. Two other interpretations assume that international comity, rather than the obligations created by the treaty, should guide judicial resort to the Hague Convention. Third, then, the Convention might be viewed as establishing a supplemental set of discovery procedures, strictly optional under treaty law, to which concerns of comity nevertheless require first resort by American courts in all cases. Fourth, the treaty may be viewed as an undertaking among sovereigns to facilitate discovery to which an American court should resort when it deems that course of action appropriate, after considering the situations of the parties before it as well as the interests of the concerned foreign state. . . .

We reject the first two of the possible interpretations as inconsistent with the language and negotiating history of the Hague Convention. The preamble of the Convention specifies its purpose "to facilitate the transmission and execution of Letters of Request" and to "improve mutual judicial co-operation in civil or commercial matters." 23 U.S.T., at 2557, T.I.A.S. No. 7444. The preamble does not speak in mandatory terms which would purport to describe the procedures for all permissible transnational discovery and exclude all other existing practices.[15] The text of the Evidence Convention itself does not modify the law of any contracting state, require any contracting state to use the Convention procedures, either in requesting evidence or in responding to such requests, or compel any contracting state to change its own evidence-gathering procedures.

---

15. The Hague Conference on Private International Law's omission of mandatory language in the preamble is particularly significant in light of the same body's use of mandatory language in the preamble to the Hague Service Convention, 20 U.S.T. 361, T.I.A.S. No. 6638. Article 1 of the Service Convention provides: "The present Convention shall apply in all cases, in civil or commercial matters, where there is occasion to transmit a judicial or extrajudicial document for service abroad.". . . [T]he Service Convention was drafted before the Evidence Convention, and its language provided a model exclusivity provision that the drafters of the Evidence Convention could easily have followed had they been so inclined. Given this background, the drafters' election to use permissive language instead is strong evidence of their intent.

The Convention contains three chapters. Chapter I, entitled "Letters of Requests," and chapter II, entitled "Taking of Evidence by Diplomatic Officers, Consular Agents and Commissioners," both use permissive rather than mandatory language. Thus, Article 1 provides that a judicial authority in one contracting state "may" forward a letter of request to the competent authority in another contracting state for the purpose of obtaining evidence. Similarly, Articles 15, 16, and 17 provide that diplomatic officers, consular agents, and commissioners "may ... without compulsion," take evidence under certain conditions. The absence of any command that a contracting state must use Convention procedures when they are not needed is conspicuous.

Two of the Articles in chapter III, entitled "General Clauses," buttress our conclusion that the Convention was intended as a permissive supplement, not a pre-emptive replacement, for other means of obtaining evidence located abroad. Article 23 expressly authorizes a contracting state to declare that it will not execute any letter of request in aid of pretrial discovery of documents in a common-law country. Surely, if the Convention had been intended to replace completely the broad discovery powers that the common-law courts in the United States previously exercised over foreign litigants subject to their jurisdiction, it would have been most anomalous for the common-law contracting parties to agree to Article 23, which enables a contracting party to revoke its consent to the treaty's procedures for pretrial discovery.[22] In the absence of explicit textual support, we are unable to accept the hypothesis that the common-law contracting states abjured recourse to all pre-existing discovery procedures at the same time that they accepted the possibility that a contracting party could unilaterally abrogate even the Convention's procedures. Moreover, Article 27 plainly states that the Convention does not prevent a contracting state from using more liberal methods of rendering evidence than those authorized by the Convention. Thus, the text of the Evidence Convention, as well as the history of its proposal and ratification by the United States, unambiguously supports the conclusion that it was intended to establish optional procedures that would facilitate the taking of evidence abroad.

An interpretation of the Hague Convention as the exclusive means for obtaining evidence located abroad would effectively subject every American court hearing a case involving a national of a contracting state to the internal laws of that state. Interrogatories and document requests are staples of international commercial litigation, no less than of other suits, yet a rule of exclusivity would subordinate the court's supervision of even the most routine of

---

22. Thirteen of the seventeen signatory states have made declarations under Article 23 of the Convention that restrict pretrial discovery of documents.

these pretrial proceedings to the actions or, equally, to the inactions of foreign judicial authorities. . . .

We conclude accordingly that the Hague Convention did not deprive the District Court of the jurisdiction it otherwise possessed to order a foreign national party before it to produce evidence physically located within a signatory nation.[25] . . .

[II]

Petitioners contend that even if the Hague Convention's procedures are not mandatory, this Court should adopt a rule requiring that American litigants first resort to those procedures before initiating any discovery pursuant to the normal methods of the Federal Rules of Civil Procedure. The Court of Appeals rejected this argument because it was convinced that an American court's order ultimately requiring discovery that a foreign court had refused under Convention procedures would constitute "the greatest insult" to the sovereignty of that tribunal. We disagree with the Court of Appeals' view. It is well known that the scope of American discovery is often significantly broader than is permitted in other jurisdictions, and we are satisfied that foreign tribunals will recognize that the final decision on the evidence to be used in litigation conducted in American courts must be made by those courts. We therefore do not believe that an American court should refuse to make use of Convention procedures because of a concern that it may ultimately find it necessary to order the production of evidence that a foreign tribunal permitted a party to withhold.

25. The opposite conclusion of exclusivity would create three unacceptable asymmetries. First, within any lawsuit between a national of the United States and a national of another contracting party, the foreign party could obtain discovery under the Federal Rules of Civil Procedure, while the domestic party would be required to resort first to the procedures of the Hague Convention. This imbalance would run counter to the fundamental maxim of discovery that "[m]utual knowledge of all the relevant facts gathered by both parties is essential to proper litigation." *Hickman v. Taylor,* 329 U.S. 495, 507 (1947). Second, a rule of exclusivity would enable a company which is a citizen of another contracting state to compete with a domestic company on uneven terms, since the foreign company would be subject to less extensive discovery procedures in the event that both companies were sued in an American court. Petitioners made a voluntary decision to market their products in the United States. They are entitled to compete on equal terms with other companies operating in this market. But since the District Court unquestionably has personal jurisdiction over petitioners, they are subject to the same legal constraints, including the burdens associated with American judicial procedures, as their American competitors. A general rule according foreign nationals a preferred position in pretrial proceedings in our courts would conflict with the principle of equal opportunity that governs the market they elected to enter. Third, since a rule of first use of the Hague Convention would apply to cases in which a foreign party is a national of a contracting state, but not to cases in which a foreign party is a national of any other foreign state, the rule would confer an unwarranted advantage on some domestic litigants over others similarly situated.

Nevertheless, we cannot accept petitioners' invitation to announce a new rule of law that would require first resort to Convention procedures whenever discovery is sought from a foreign litigant. Assuming, without deciding, that we have the lawmaking power to do so, we are convinced that such a general rule would be unwise. In many situations the Letter of Request procedure authorized by the Convention would be unduly time consuming and expensive, as well as less certain to produce needed evidence than direct use of the Federal Rules. A rule of first resort in all cases would therefore be inconsistent with the overriding interest in the "just, speedy, and inexpensive determination" of litigation in our courts. *See* Fed. R. Civ. P. 1.

Petitioners argue that a rule of first resort is necessary to accord respect to the sovereignty of states in which evidence is located. It is true that the process of obtaining evidence in a civil-law jurisdiction is normally conducted by a judicial officer rather than by private attorneys. Petitioners contend that if performed on French soil, for example, by an unauthorized person, such evidence-gathering might violate the "judicial sovereignty" of the host nation. Because it is only through the Convention that civil-law nations have given their consent to evidence-gathering activities within their borders, petitioners argue, we have a duty to employ those procedures whenever they are available. We find that argument unpersuasive. If such a duty were to be inferred from the adoption of the Convention itself, we believe it would have been described in the text of that document. Moreover, the concept of international comity[27] requires in this context a more particularized analysis of the respective interests of the foreign nation and the requesting nation than petitioners' proposed general rule would generate. We therefore decline to hold as a blanket matter that comity requires resort to Hague Evidence Convention procedures without prior scrutiny in each case of the particular facts, sovereign interests, and likelihood that resort to those procedures will prove effective.[29]

---

27. Comity refers to the spirit of co-operation in which a domestic tribunal approaches the resolution of cases touching the laws and interests of sovereign states. . . .

29. The French "blocking statute". . . does not alter our conclusion. It is well settled that such statutes do not deprive an American court of the power to order a party subject to its jurisdiction to produce evidence even though the act of production may violate that statute. *See Société Internationale Pour Participations Industrielles et Commerc-* *iales, S.A. v. Rogers*, 357 U.S. 197, 204–06 (1958). Nor can the enactment of such a statute by a foreign nation require American courts to engraft a rule of first resort onto the Hague Convention, or otherwise to provide the nationals of such a country with a preferred status in our courts. It is clear that American courts are not required to adhere blindly to the directives of such a statute. Indeed, the language of the statute, if taken literally, would appear to represent an extraordinary exercise of legislative jurisdiction by the Republic of France over a United States dis-

Some discovery procedures are much more "intrusive" than others. In this case, for example, an interrogatory asking petitioners to identify the pilots who flew flight tests in the Rallye before it was certified for flight by the Federal Aviation Administration, or a request to admit that petitioners authorized certain advertising in a particular magazine, is certainly less intrusive than a request to produce all of the "design specifications, line drawings and engineering plans and all engineering change orders and plans and all drawings concerning the leading edge slats for the Rallye type aircraft manufactured by the Defendants." Even if a court might be persuaded that a particular document request was too burdensome or too "intrusive" to be granted in full, with or without an appropriate protective order, it might well refuse to insist upon the use of Convention procedures before requiring responses to simple interrogatories or requests for admissions. The exact line between reasonableness and unreasonableness in each case must be drawn by the trial court, based on its knowledge of the case and of the claims and interests of the parties and the governments whose statutes and policies they invoke.

American courts, in supervising pretrial proceedings, should exercise special vigilance to protect foreign litigants from the danger that unnecessary, or unduly burdensome, discovery may place them in a disadvantageous position. Judicial supervision of discovery should always seek to minimize its costs and inconvenience and to prevent improper uses of discovery requests. When it is necessary to seek evidence abroad, however, the district court must supervise pretrial proceedings particularly closely to prevent discovery abuses. For example, the additional cost of transportation of documents or witnesses to or from foreign locations may increase the danger that discovery may be sought for the improper purpose of motivating settlement, rather than finding relevant and probative evidence. Objections to "abusive" discovery that foreign litigants advance should therefore receive the most careful consideration. In addition, we have long recognized the demands of comity in suits involving foreign states, either as parties or as sovereigns with a coordinate interest in the litigation. American courts should

trict judge, forbidding him or her to order any discovery from a party of French nationality, even simple requests for admissions or interrogatories that the party could respond to on the basis of personal knowledge. It would be particularly incongruous to recognize such a preference for corporations that are wholly owned by the enacting nation. Extraterritorial assertions of jurisdiction are not one-sided. While the District Court's discovery orders arguably have some impact in France, the French blocking statute asserts similar authority over acts to take place in this country. The lesson of comity is that neither the discovery order nor the blocking statute can have the same omnipresent effect that it would have in a world of only one sovereign. The blocking statute thus is relevant to the court's particularized comity analysis only to the extent that its terms and its enforcement identify the nature of the sovereign interests in nondisclosure of specific kinds of material. . . .

therefore take care to demonstrate due respect for any special problem confronted by the foreign litigant on account of its nationality or the location of its operations, and for any sovereign interest expressed by a foreign state. We do not articulate specific rules to guide this delicate task of adjudication.

———

On remand, the French manufacturer agreed to provide the requested information so the "delicate task" requiring "special vigilance" was not undertaken in this case. But since, United States courts have applied a balancing test that is reflected in the Restatement.

RESTATEMENT (THIRD) OF FOREIGN RELATIONS LAW

(1987)

§ 442. Requests For Disclosure; Law Of The United States

(1) (a) A court or agency in the United States, when authorized by statute or rule of court, may order a person subject to its jurisdiction to produce documents, objects, or other information relevant to an action or investigation, even if the information or the person in possession of the information is outside the United States.

(b) Failure to comply with an order to produce information may subject the person to whom the order is directed to sanctions, including finding of contempt, dismissal of a claim or defense, or default judgment, or may lead to a determination that the facts to which the order was addressed are as asserted by the opposing party.

(c) In deciding whether to issue an order directing production of information located abroad, and in framing such an order, a court or agency in the United States should take into account the importance to the investigation or litigation of the documents or other information requested; the degree of specificity of the request; whether the information originated in the United States; the availability of alternative means of securing the information; and the extent to which noncompliance with the request would undermine important interests of the United States, or compliance with the request would undermine important interests of the state where the information is located.

(2) If disclosure of information located outside the United States is prohibited by a law, regulation, or order of a court or other authority of the state in which the information or prospective

witness is located, or of the state of which a prospective witness is a national,

(a) a court or agency in the United States may require the person to whom the order is directed to make a good faith effort to secure permission from the foreign authorities to make the information available;

(b) a court or agency should not ordinarily impose sanctions of contempt, dismissal, or default on a party that has failed to comply with the order for production, except in cases of deliberate concealment or removal of information or of failure to make a good faith effort in accordance with paragraph (a);

(c) a court or agency may, in appropriate cases, make findings of fact adverse to a party that has failed to comply with the order for production, even if that party has made a good faith effort to secure permission from the foreign authorities to make the information available and that effort has been unsuccessful.

With the decision in *Aérospatiale* diluting the significance of the Hague Convention on the Taking of Evidence Abroad, the search for international common ground resumed. The ALI/UNIDROIT Transnational Rules have proposed a set of model discovery rules that reflect a compromise: they are based on a generalized version of a common law system outside the United States. If adopted, they would apply to transnational commercial disputes.

ALI/UNIDROIT
Rules of Transnational Civil Procedure

(2005)

21. Disclosure

21.1 In accordance with the court's scheduling order, a party must identify to the court and other parties the evidence on which the party intends to rely, in addition to that provided in the pleading, including:

21.1.1 Copies of documents or other records, such as contracts and correspondence; and

21.1.2 Summaries of expected testimony of witnesses, including parties, witnesses, and experts, then known to the party. Witnesses must be identified, so far as practicable, by name, address, and telephone number....

22. Exchange of Evidence

22.1 A party who has complied with disclosure duties prescribed in Rule 21, on notice to the other parties, may request the court to order production by any person of any evidentiary matter, not protected by confidentiality or privilege, that is relevant to the case and that may be admissible, including:

> 22.1.1   Documents and other records of information that are specifically identified or identified within specifically defined categories;

> 22.1.2   Identifying information, such as name and address, about specified persons having knowledge of a matter in issue; and

> 22.1.3   A copy of the report of any expert that another party intends to present.

22.2 The court must determine the request and order production accordingly. The court may order production of other evidence as necessary in the interest of justice. Such evidence must be produced within a reasonable time prior to the final hearing. . . .

22.7 The fact that the demanded information is adverse to the interest of the party to which the demand is directed is not a valid objection to its production. . . .

Comment:

R–22A. These Rules adopt, as a model of litigation, a system consisting of preliminary hearings followed by a concentrated form of final hearing. The essential core of the first stage is preliminary disclosure and clarification of the evidence. The principal consideration in favor of a unitary final hearing is that of expeditious justice. To achieve this objective, a concentrated final hearing should be used, so that arguments and the taking of evidence are completed in a single hearing or in a few hearings on consecutive judicial days. A concentrated final hearing requires a preliminary phase (called pretrial in common-law systems) in which evidence is exchanged and the case is prepared for concentrated presentation.

R–22B. Rules 21 and 22 define the roles and the rights of the parties, the duty of voluntary disclosure, the procedure for exchange of evidence, the role of the court, and the devices to ensure that the parties comply with demands for evidence. Proper compliance with these obligations is not only a matter of law for the parties, but also a matter of professional honor and obligation on the part of the lawyers involved in the litigation.

R–22C. The philosophy expressed in Rules 21 and 22 is essentially that of the common-law countries other than the United States. In those countries, the scope of discovery or disclosure is specified and limited, as in Rules 21 and 22. However, within those specifications disclosure is generally a matter of right. . . .

R–22G. Rule 22.1 provides that every party is entitled to obtain from any person the disclosure of any unprivileged relevant evidence in possession of that person. Formal requests for evidence should be made to the court, and the court should direct the opposing party to comply with an order to produce evidence or information. This procedure can be unnecessarily burdensome on the parties and on the courts, especially in straightforward requests. Ideally, full disclosure of relevant evidence should result through dialogue among the parties, whereby the parties voluntarily satisfy each other's demands without intervention of the court. A party therefore may present the request directly to the opposing party, which must comply with an adequate request within a reasonable time. . . .

R–22H. According to Rule 22.1, compulsory exchange of evidence is limited to matters directly relevant to the issues in the case as they have been stated in the pleadings. See Rule 25.2. A party is not entitled to disclosure of information merely that "appears reasonably calculated to lead to the discovery of admissible evidence," which is permitted under Rule 26 of the Fed. R. Civ. P. in the United States. "Relevant" evidence is that which supports or contravenes the allegations of one of the parties. This Rule is aimed at preventing overdiscovery or unjustified "fishing expeditions." . . .

R–22L. In cases involving voluminous documents or remotely situated witnesses, or in similar circumstances of practical necessity, the court may appoint someone as a special officer to supervise exchange of evidence. . . .

23. Deposition and Testimony by Affidavit

23.1 A deposition of a party or other person may be taken by order of the court. Unless the court orders otherwise, a deposition may be presented as evidence in the record. . . .

23.4 With written permission of the court, a party may present a written statement of sworn testimony of any person, containing statements in their own words about relevant facts. . . .

––––––––

Notes

4–1. Does the enactment of a "blocking statute" disrespect the laws and institutions of other nations?

4–2. After *Aérospatiale*, district courts must balance the need for discovery against the policies reflected in a treaty. Although there have been some cases where litigants have been forced to use Hague Convention procedures, in the majority of cases the Hague Convention is held not to apply. *See* Patrick J. Borchers, *The Incredible Shrinking Hague Evidence Convention*, 38 Tex. Int'l L.J. 73, 82 (2003). Justice Blackmun's dissent in *Aérospatiale* noted that "it is the Executive that normally decides when a course of action is important enough to risk affronting a foreign nation or placing a strain on foreign commerce. It is the Executive, as well, that is best equipped to determine how to accommodate foreign interests along with our own." 482 U.S. at 552. Is the question of foreign discovery more appropriately considered by the Executive and by Congress? But isn't the reasonableness of a particular discovery request more appropriately considered by a judge? How should these competing concerns be reconciled?

4–3. Liberal discovery rules in the United States can also be invoked for the *benefit* of foreigners and/or foreign litigation. Section 1782 of Title 28 of the U.S. Code provides that a federal district court "may order" a person "resid[ing]" or "found" in the district to produce documents or provide testimony "for use in a proceeding in a foreign or international tribunal ... upon application of any interested person." Section 1782 is particularly useful because its requirements are much simpler than the Hague Convention procedures. The essential requirements for assistance under Section 1782 are: (1) the person from whom discovery is sought resides in or is found in the forum where the application is made; (2) the discovery is sought for use before a foreign or international tribunal; and (3) the application is made by the tribunal or any interested person. Where those requirements are satisfied, the forum court has broad discretion to decide whether to grant the assistance.

The United States Supreme Court has endorsed the broad and aggressive use of Section 1782. In *Intel Corp. v. Advanced Micro Devices, Inc.*, 542 U.S. 241 (2004), the Court defined "interested person" and "foreign or international tribunal" broadly to include an action initiated by a complainant with the Directorate General Competition of the European Communities. Further, the Court held that the proceeding need only be "within reasonable contemplation" to invoke the federal statute. And finally, the Court found no "foreign discoverability" requirement—i.e., the Court held that the evidence sought in the United States forum need *not* be discoverable in the foreign or international tribunal. Nor would the discovering party need to demonstrate that United States law would allow discovery in domestic litigation analogous to the foreign proceeding. Does Section 1782 encourage foreign countries to emulate the United States' example by providing similar assistance? *See generally* Okezie Chukwumerije, *International Judicial Assistance: Revitalizing Section 1782*, 37 Geo. Wash. Int'l L. Rev. 649 (2005).

4–4. Rules 21–23 of the Transnational Rules strike a compromise between the regimes of broad and narrow discovery. Which of the two extremes is being asked to make the greater sacrifice?

4–5. Is it realistic to suggest that transnational and domestic cases could be litigated under different discovery regimes? Could discovery in domestic litigation in the United States be conducted successfully pursuant to rules similar to the Transnational Rules?

Chapter 5

THE AMERICAN JURY

This chapter explores the nexus between a society's culture and its procedural system. Although all procedural systems share certain general characteristics, the dissimilarities—whether trivial or profound—are sometimes traceable to cultural differences. Procedures can both reflect and project a society's values; to study *why* a particular procedural approach has been adopted is usually more significant (and interesting) than merely recording *that* it has been adopted. Accordingly, understanding the values, beliefs, and idiosyncrasies that animate procedural rules is an important part of comparative study. It is also an essential task if one is to consider or advocate transplanting a particular procedure from one system into another.

In the article that follows Professor Chase explores the ideology that underlies a uniquely American institution: the civil jury.

Oscar G. Chase
American "Exceptionalism" and Comparative Procedure
50 Am. J. Comp. Law 277, 280–83, 287–92 (2002)*

... AMERICAN CULTURE

American "exceptionalism" has been observed and remarked upon at least since Alexis de Tocqueville published his observations of American society over one hundred-fifty years ago. "Tocqueville is the first to refer [to] the United States as exceptional—that is, qualitatively different from all other countries." The qualities that struck Tocqueville, such as individualism, egalitarianism, and a readiness to pursue disputes through litigation have persisted over

* A version of this article appears as a chapter in the book, Oscar G. Chase, Law, Culture, and Ritual: Disputing in Cross-Cultural Context (NYU Press 2005).

time and been observed by other students of society. A leading modern proponent of the "America as unique" thesis is Seymour Martin Lipset, who recently developed his argument in *American Exceptionalism: A Double Edged Sword*. Because Lipset so success-fully captures this standard description of American culture I will center my discussion of it around his work, but the reader should keep in mind that Lipset is only one of many scholars who have identified similar American characteristics. . . .

According to Lipset, America's "ideology can be described in five words: liberty, egalitarianism, individualism, populism, and laissez-faire." As Lipset notes, egalitarianism in the United States "involves equality of opportunity and respect, not of result or condition." Thus, American egalitarianism is consistent with indi-vidualism and laissez-faire. "The emphasis in the American value system, in the American creed, has been on the individual." It is the emphasis on the individual as a person equal in status to all other countrymen that produces populism, rights-orientation and laissez-faire (or anti-statist) attitudes.

Lipset argues that these values explain many distinctive fea-tures of American society, including some that are far from admira-ble, such as high crime rates. More ambiguous effects are those seen in the nature of governmental institutions and practices. He notes the relative weakness of the American central government and its modest involvement in the economy. The Constitution, he observes, "established a divided form of government . . . and re-flected a deliberate decision by the country's founders to create a weak and internally conflicted political system." Almost all other modern states have parliamentary systems under which the majori-ty party exercises power that is virtually plenary. As Mirjan Damas-ka said about American government, "Most astonishing to a foreign eye is the continuing fragmentation and decentralization of author-ity."[23]

Individualism, liberty and laissez-faire values also explain the comparatively low levels of American economic and social regula-tion (except for the strangely co-existing Puritanism that explains sex and drug laws). Meager American governmental support of welfare-state projects, be they cultural activities or universal health care—again typically laissez faire and individualist—is reflected even in constitutions. Many in Europe, but not the American, contain provisions that impose welfare-state obligations on the government. According to Mary Ann Glendon, these constitutional differences "are legal manifestations of divergent, and deeply root-ed, cultural attitudes toward the state and its functions . . . [C]onti-

---

23. Mirjan Damaska, The Faces of Justice and State Authority: A Compara-tive Approach to the Legal Process (1991) at 233.

nental Europeans today, whether of the right or the left, are much more likely than Americans to assume that governments have affirmative duties."[26] At the same time, the Bill of Rights incorporates the American ideal of a citizen as possessing the right to be "let alone" by government. As Jerold Auerbach has it, "Law has absorbed and strengthened the competitive, acquisitive values associated with American individualism and capitalism."[27] If this is true of law in general it is more so the case with dispute procedures in particular.

Since American values strongly influence its governmental arrangements, it would be odd if these same values did not also contribute to an American exceptionalism in disputing. . . .

American individualism and egalitarianism, Lipset also claims, underlies the emphasis on a rights-based legal discourse, and helps explain high rates of litigation compared to other industrialized nations. "In America . . . 'egalitarianism is based on the notion of equal rights of free-standing, rights-asserting individuals.' " The American attachment to courts suggests, perhaps, a weakness in the claim of anti-statism. Courts are governmental institutions and a resort to courts to resolve disputes is unavoidably to invoke governmental authority. While there is a point here, I think that the difference between courts and other governmental institutions is such that the inclination to sue in pursuit of private interest is better understood as of a piece with individualism and laissez-faire. Compared with most governmental institutions, courts are responsive to individualized pursuit of personal claims. Consider that private litigation is for the most part controlled by the litigants, who provide its impetus, its direction and often, its ultimate resolution. (The vast majority of American civil actions are settled before trial.) Courts neither meddle nor rescue unless called upon to do so, and then paradigmatically only for the litigants before them. And, as we shall see in more detail, the values of a distinctly American ideology underlie the forms and structures of disputing in America, and indeed have contributed to an American "exceptionalism" in disputing. . . .

Some Features of American Procedural Exceptionalism

. . . "The jury is one of America's venerated institutions." It has achieved and maintained an importance in American trials that is unparalleled elsewhere in the world. While the jury retains a lively role in criminal cases in most English-speaking nations (but

---

26. Mary Ann Glendon, *Rights in Twentieth Century Constitutions*, in Geoffrey R. Stone, Richard A. Epstein & Cass R. Sunstein (eds.), The Bill of Rights in Modern States (1992) at 521.

27. Jerold Auerbach, Justice Without Law? (1983) at 138.

not in the rest of the world),[64] it is striking that in no other nation has the jury been retained in civil litigation to the degree it has in the United States. The right to a jury trial in civil cases is historic and iconic: it was added to the Federal Constitution by the Seventh Amendment as one of the Bill of Rights ratified in 1791. In 1938, when the Federal Rules of Civil Procedure were promulgated, its drafters thought it desirable to include a provision reminding readers that "The right of trial by jury as declared by the Seventh Amendment to the Constitution or as given by a statute of the United States shall be preserved to the parties inviolate." The Seventh Amendment and the Federal Rules apply only in federal litigation, but the right to a jury in civil cases has been constitutionalized by the states as well. Typical is the provision of the New York Constitution: As adopted in 1777, it provides that the right "shall remain inviolate forever."

Contrariwise, civil juries have never been found in any of the countries that follow Continental procedure. "Truly astonishing in the Continental view was the degree to which decisions of the lay jury—the paradigmatic adjudicator—escaped supervision through regular appellate mechanisms."[69] The United Kingdom, where it originated, has abandoned the civil jury in all but a very few kinds of cases,[70] and most of the countries with legal roots in England world [sic] have followed suit.[71]

It is not hard to see how the historic American attachment to the jury is bottomed on core American values. It is quintessentially an egalitarian, populist, anti-statist institution. It is "strongly egalitarian" because it gives lay people with no special expertise a fact-finding power superior to that of the judge, despite all of his or her training and experience. Although it is true that the judge presiding at the trial may overrule a jury verdict and grant judgment "as a matter of law" against the party favored by the jury, this power is

---

64. Mirjan R. Damaska, Evidence Law Adrift (1997) at 28 (notes that while juries were established in France and elsewhere following the French Revolution, "the Continental love affair with the jury was one of short duration." Juries are used in criminal cases only in Belgium, Switzerland and Denmark. Id. note 5.

69. Faces of Justice, at 219–20. The passage refers to the pre-twentieth century period when "classic civil procedure" was still used in England, including the civil jury.

70. On the decline of the civil jury in the U.K., see Mary Ann Glendon, Michael Wallace Gordon & Christopher Osakwe, Comparative Legal Traditions (2nd ed. 1994) at 613–27. The materials there collected indicate that the atrophy of the civil jury in the U.K. began during the First World War and culminated in 1965 when the Court of Appeal decided that there was no right to a jury trial except where specifically authorized by statute.

71. Kaplan & Clermont, *England and the United States*, in Chapter 6, Ordinary Proceedings in First Instance, Civil Procedure, XVI International Encyclopedia of Comparative Law (1984) at 3, 29 n. 265 (reports that there is some variation among the provinces of Canada and Australia but that in general the jury is seldom used in civil cases in those countries).

circumscribed. It can be exercised only if "there is no legally sufficient evidentiary basis for a reasonable jury to find for that party ..."[73] The jury is also egalitarian in that it is a duty of citizenship imposed on all and that every juror has an equal vote regardless of education or social status. Indeed it is strikingly an institution which plunges people, willy-nilly, into a situation in which communication and cooperation across distinctions of racial, ethnic and wealth are mandatory.

The civil jury is populist, "an avatar of democratic participation in government," because it allows the people to rule directly. A jury can determine, for example that a particular product was designed or manufactured in an unreasonably unsafe manner, thus setting safety standards that might otherwise be governed by statute or regulation. Jurors are well aware of their power to act as a "mini-legislature" in such cases. According to a recent article in the journal of the American Bar Association, "Like no time before, the 12 people seated in the jury box regularly demonstrate an increasing willingness—even a clamoring—to force basic American institutions, such as government, business and even private social organizations, to change the way they operate."[76] The article lists a number of cases in which juries awarded large verdicts in order to "send a message" to the defendant and its industry that certain behavior was not acceptable.

Although the civil jury is of course an organ of government, it nonetheless has an anti-statist quality because it allows the people to decide matters differently than the other institutions of government might wish. Both in the civil and criminal spheres, this is no mere theoretical matter, as demonstrated by the debate over jury nullification, the sometimes-claimed power of the jury to ignore the law as a way of "doing justice" that continues to the present.[77]

The jury's connection to American individualism is not as obvious as its egalitarian and populist qualities. In some sense it is anti-individualist because the jury operates as a collectivity. Moreover, people do not volunteer to serve as jurors but are compelled by force of law to do so. On the other hand, the role of the individual is apparent because the number of persons on each jury is small, twelve or less, and as few as six in some jurisdictions. Where, as is traditional, a verdict depends on unanimity, a single

73. Federal Rule Civil Proc. 50(a). The judge can also set the verdict aside if it is "against the weight of the evidence," but in such case there is a new trial before a new jury.

76. Curriden, *Power of 12*, ABA Journal 36 (August 2000).

77. Jeffrey Abramson, We, the Jury (1994) at 57–95. Several examples of juries' refusal to convict despite overwhelming evidence of guilt are presented.

hold-out can abort the trial and effectively command a new one.[78] But the American individualism as a value that underlies the civil jury is better appreciated when we introduce the point of view of the litigants. For the individual citizen whose liberty or property is in its hands, the jury is seen as a protector of the rights in a way that the judge, an official of the state, is not.

The synchronic development of an egalitarian American ethos and the jury as a device for protecting individual rights exemplifies the reciprocally constitutive role of cultural values and dispute institutions. The iconic status of the jury in American life emerged at the same time as the American people took on their "exceptionalist" values. It was in the period around the time of the American revolution that the jury became "so deeply embedded in American democratic ethos."[79] By the mid-eighteenth century, as Americans increasingly distinguished themselves as a separate people, juries had become a means of resisting the Crown's control over colonial affairs and British attempts to circumscribe jury powers were seen as a further cause of grievance. Tales of courageous jurors who stood up to tyrannical English government have ever since been an important part of the American self-image: "Most American history books hail the trial of [John Peter] Zenger for seditious libel in 1735 as the leading case for freedom of the press and as an example of a victory of the people over an aristocracy." Zenger, the publisher of a New York newspaper, was prosecuted because of the journal's sharp criticism of the appointed English governor of the colony. Andrew Hamilton, who defended Zenger, wove together a substantive claim—the right of the people to criticize their government—and the procedural point that the jurors had the power to protect that right.

> Jurymen are to see with their own eyes, to hear with their own ears, and to make use of their own consciences and understandings in judging of the lives, liberties or estates of their fellow subjects.[82]

Although the hagiography surrounding the Zenger case has arguably idealized the participants, the case did help to establish unique American views on the jury and its place between law and those governed. The jury's continuing role in the construction of the American ethos was observed by Jefferson, who called jury service the "school by which [the] people learn the exercise of civic duties as well as rights" and by Tocqueville: "The jury, and more especially the civil jury, ... is the soundest preparation for free

---

78. Unanimity is not required in all jurisdictions. In New York, for example, a verdict of five-sixths is sufficient in civil cases, see N.Y. Civil Practice Law and Rules 4113(a).

79. Valerie P. Hans & Neil Vidmar, Judging the Jury (1986) at 32.

82. Id. at 34.

institutions...." Modern scholars contend that the jury continues to serve as an influence on the moral reasoning of participants. A recent example of the jury/values connection is provided by the acquittal of John DeLorean, the entrepreneur who claimed that police entrapment had led to the charge of drug-dealing. One juror explained the verdict: "... there is a message here.... It's that our citizens will not let our government go too far.... It was like the book Nineteen Eighty–Four. They set one trap after another for DeLorean...."

It is telling that George Priest links the right to vote and the jury trial as the two institutions of American democracy that it "seems simply unthinkable to criticize."[88] Both are icons of American values. The attachment to the jury is not, *pace* Professor Priest, shared by all Americans, and its place in the legal system is not static.[89] Like the culture in which it is found, it is contested and dynamic; its powers have ebbed and flowed in response to changes in social life. In one sense the story has been one of diminution, both in the frequency in which civil cases are tried to a jury and in its power in respect to the judge.[90] In another, as we have seen, jurors are currently willing and eager to exercise their broad powers when they have a chance. Whether the American civil jury will, like its British ancestor, atrophy to irrelevance depends in large part on the continued viability of those ingredients of the collective American psyche that have sustained it so far.[92] Surveys of attorneys, judges, and the general public show that the civil jury continues to enjoy very wide support in the United States.[93]

---

88. See Faces of Justice, at 20–21.

89. A thoughtful critical assessment of the civil jury was made by Jerome Frank in Courts on Trial 110–25 (1949). For an argument that the popular conception of the jury in America has undergone changes over the life of the country, see Abramson, *The Jury and Popular Culture*, 50 DePaul L. Rev. 497 (2000).

90. Valerie P. Hans & Neil Vidmar, Judging the Jury (1986) at 31–46. In 1999, less than two percent of all civil actions brought in federal courts were resolved by a jury trial, see New York Times, March 2, 2001, p. 1.

92. Stephen Yeazell argues that the different fates of the British and American juries reflect more pervasive differences between the two cultures, most notably different attitudes about the concentration of governmental power: "The persistence of the civil jury in the United States reflects a distrust of concentrated governmental power." Yeazell, *The New Jury and the Ancient Jury Conflict*, 1990 U. Chi. Law Forum 87, 106 (1990).

93. See the surveys collected in Hans, *Attitudes Toward the Civil Jury: A Crisis of Confidence?*, in Verdict (Robert E. Litan ed., 1993) at 248. An "ambitious national survey" conducted in 1978 found that eighty per cent of the respondents rated the right of trial by jury as "extremely important" and most of the others rated it as "important." Id. at 255.

Notes

5–1. Do you agree with Professor Chase that the civil jury "continues to enjoy very wide support in the United States"?

5–2. The Preface to the Transnational Rules of Civil Procedure includes the following statement: "We conclude that a system of procedure acceptable generally throughout the world could not require a jury trial. . . . This in turn has led us to conclude that the scope of the proposed Transnational Civil Rules and Principles is limited to commercial disputes and excludes categories of litigation such as personal-injury and wrongful death actions, because barring jury trial in such cases would be unacceptable in the United States." Why would the elimination of jury trials in commercial cases be more acceptable than the elimination of jury trials in tort cases? (Can you use the five values—liberty, egalitarianism, individualism, populism, and laissez-faire—to explain this?)

Chapter 6

PERSONAL JURISDICTION

A. SUING FOREIGN DEFENDANTS IN U.S. COURTS

The constitutional limits on a court's authority to assert personal jurisdiction are likely very familiar. The Supreme Court has determined that a court has general jurisdiction over a defendant who maintains a systematic and continuous presence in the forum state, and has specific jurisdiction over a defendant who has minimum contacts provided those contacts are sufficiently related to the claim. The due process clause further demands that the exercise of jurisdiction not offend traditional notions of fair play and substantial justice.

Foreign defendants in United States courts enjoy the same constitutional protections as United States defendants. And the remoteness of a foreign defendant makes the motion to dismiss for lack of personal jurisdiction an extremely powerful tool in the context of transnational litigation. Indeed, unlike a purely domestic litigation matter where the plaintiff must refile in another *state* when the court lacks personal jurisdiction over the defendant, the plaintiff must commence litigation in another *country*. Dreading the inconvenience or fearing the unfamiliar, that case may simply never be pursued elsewhere once the action is dismissed in the United States.

One issue that arises frequently, although not exclusively, in transnational litigation is the attribution of contacts of an agent or affiliate. For example, the foreign parent of a domestic corporation might be the more attractive defendant. (E.g., the domestic corporation may be defunct, inadequately insured, or otherwise judgment-proof. Or in employment cases, a worker's compensation scheme might preclude suit against the employer-subsidiary but not the parent.) But if the foreign corporation has no presence or contacts in the forum state other than this subsidiary, can the court assert personal jurisdiction? Of course a related question is whether that foreign corporation could be *substantively* liable for the acts of its subsidiary, but the plaintiff's lawyer will worry about that later. Indeed, if the plaintiff's lawyer can establish personal jurisdiction, she may be able to negotiate a settlement rather quickly from a foreign defendant who may be a reluctant litigant. The *Telcordia* case below discusses personal jurisdiction in the context of the attribution of contacts of a corporate subsidiary.

Occasionally foreign defendants can be reached pursuant to FRCP 4(k)(2), the so-called "federal long-arm statute." This provision was added to the Federal Rules in 1993 to correct a gap in the enforcement of federal law.

> Under the former rule, a problem was presented when the defendant was a non-resident of the United States having contacts with the United States sufficient to justify the application of United States law and to satisfy federal standards of forum selection, but having insufficient contact with any single state to support jurisdiction under state long-arm legislation or meet the requirements of the Fourteenth Amendment limitation on state court territorial jurisdiction. In such cases, the defendant was shielded from the enforcement of federal law by the fortuity of a favorable limitation on the power of state courts, which was incorporated into the federal practice by [the principle now reflected in FRCP 4(k)(1)(A).]

> There remain constitutional limitations on the exercise of territorial jurisdiction by federal courts over persons outside the United States. These restrictions arise from the Fifth Amendment rather than from the Fourteenth Amendment ... The Fifth Amendment requires that any defendant have affiliating contacts with the United States sufficient to justify the exercise of personal jurisdiction over that party. There may also be a further Fifth Amendment constraint in that a plaintiff's forum selection might be so inconvenient to a defendant that it would be a denial of "fair play and substantial justice" required by the due process clause, even though the defendant had significant affiliating contacts with the United States.

1993 Adv. Comm. Note to Rule 4. The *Telcordia* case also addresses this theory for establishing personal jurisdiction.

TELCORDIA TECH., INC. v. ALCATEL S.A. AND ALCATEL USA, INC.

2005 WL 1268061 (D. Del.2005)

Sleet, J.:

On July 16, 2004, the plaintiff, Telcordia Technologies, Inc. ("Telcordia"), filed this patent infringement action against Alcatel

S.A. ("Alcatel S.A.") and Alcatel USA, Inc. ("Alcatel USA"). Presently before the court is Alcatel S.A.'s motion to dismiss for lack of personal jurisdiction. For the following reasons, the court will grant the motion.

Alcatel S.A. is a French corporation with its principal place of business in Paris, France. Alcatel S.A. is the parent company of Alcatel USA, a Delaware corporation with its principal place of business in Plano, Texas. [Alcatel S.A.] is a holding company that does not manufacture, sell, advertise, offer to sell, trade or import any goods or services in the United States or anywhere in the world. It does not maintain any offices or other facilities in Delaware, or the United States. It neither owns nor leases any real property in Delaware or the United States, but it does own United States patents. Alcatel S.A. does not maintain any bank accounts in Delaware and has never contracted to supply services or things in Delaware or the United States.

Telcordia, a Delaware Corporation with its principal place of business in Piscataway, New Jersey, is the assignee and owner of the patent-in-suit, U.S. Patent No. 4,893,306 (the " '306 patent"). The '306 patent relates to a method and apparatus for multiplexing circuit and packet traffic.... The complaint alleges that Alcatel S.A. and Alcatel USA have infringed, induced infringement of, and/or contributorily infringed one or more claims of the '306 patent by making, using, offering for sale, selling and/or importing into the United States communication network products embodying the patented invention....

A. DELAWARE'S LONG–ARM STATUTE

The first step in the court's analysis is to determine whether any of the provisions of Delaware's long-arm statute, Del. Code Ann. Tit. 10 § 3104, warrant the exercise of jurisdiction over Alcatel S.A. Alcatel S.A. contends that the court has no basis to assert jurisdiction, while Telcordia maintains that the conduct of Alcatel S.A. satisfies the requirements of subsections (c)(1) and (c)(3) of the long-arm statute.

Under subsection (c)(1), the court may exercise jurisdiction over a nonresident or agent of a nonresident who "transacts any business or performs any character of work or service in the State." Subsection (c)(3) gives the court the authority to exercise jurisdiction over a nonresident or agent of a nonresident who "causes tortious injury in the State by an act or omission in this State." Delaware courts construe the long-arm statute broadly to confer jurisdiction to the maximum extent possible so as to "provide residents a means of redress against those not subject to personal service within the state." *Boone v. Oy Partek Ab,* 724 A.2d 1150, 1156–57 (Del. Super. 1997). The Delaware Supreme Court has interpreted subsections (c)(1) and (c)(3) as specific jurisdiction provisions that require a "nexus" between the plaintiff's cause of action and the conduct of the defendant that is used as a basis for jurisdiction. In order to meet the requirements of subsections (c)(1) and (c)(3), Alcatel S.A.'s actions must be directed at residents of Delaware and the protection of Delaware laws.

Telcordia asserts that the court should exercise jurisdiction under § 3104(c)(1) and/or (c)(3) because Alcatel S.A.'s contacts with Delaware are attributable to its subsidiary, Alcatel USA, under the principles of agency.[2] The principles of agency allow a court to establish jurisdiction over the parent based upon its jurisdiction over a subsidiary. Under the agency theory, "the court may attribute the actions of a subsidiary company to its parent where the subsidiary acts on the parent's behalf or at the parent's direction." *C.R. Bard Inc. v. Guidant Corp.,* 997 F.Supp. 556, 559 (D. Del. 1998). Thus, the agency theory "examines the degree of control which the parent exercises over the subsidiary." *Applied Biosystems, Inc. v. Cruachem, Ltd.,* 772 F.Supp. 1458, 1463 (D. Del. 1991). The factors relevant to the court's examination include: (1) "the extent of overlap of officers and directors"; (2) "methods of financing"; (3) "the division of responsibility for day-to-day management"; and (4) "the process by which each corporation obtains its business. No one factor is either necessary or determinative; rather it is the specific combination of elements which is significant." *Id.* If the court determines that an agency relationship exists, it may attribute certain actions of the subsidiary, Alcatel USA, to the parent corporation, Alcatel S.A., in assessing whether Telcordia has satisfied the requirements of the long-arm statute. However, the mere existence of an agency relationship is not sufficient to confer jurisdiction. The court must still apply the Delaware long-arm statute. *See id.* at 1465 ("[A] finding of agency does not render the long-arm statute inapplicable, but simply implicates its 'or through an agent' provision.")

Telcordia contends that Alcatel S.A. should be subject to jurisdiction under the agency theory because "Alcatel S.A. and Alcatel

2. Delaware law provides two theories that allow a court to exercise jurisdiction over a parent corporation based on its jurisdiction over a subsidiary: the alter ego theory and the agency theory. Under the alter ego theory, the party showing jurisdiction must show fraud or inequity in the use of the corporate form for a court to "pierce the corporate veil," or attribute the actions of a subsidiary to the parent corporation. Telcordia has neither asserted the existence of any fraud in the corporate structure of Alcatel S.A. and Alcatel USA nor introduced evidence that would support a finding of fraud. Accordingly, the court will not address this jurisdictional theory.

USA are closely knit together, effectively operating as one." Telcordia alleges the following to support its contention of an agency theory of jurisdiction: (1) Alcatel S.A. makes it abundantly clear that the United States market is very important to it and raises funds in the United States; (2) it owns patents, *i.e.* property, in the United States; (3) it fails to distinguish among its multinational subsidiaries—that is, it consolidates descriptions of its activities with those of its subsidiaries; (4) it chose to incorporate Alcatel USA in Delaware; (5) its Senior Vice President, Mike Quigley is the CEO of Alcatel USA; and (6) its website solicits requests for information concerning its products, including allegedly infringing products from Delaware residents. Telcordia further contends that, "at the very least," Alcatel USA has offered to sell in Delaware products accused of infringing the '306 patent and, therefore, transacts business in the state. In addition, because Alcatel USA committed these acts as Alcatel S.A.'s agent, they are attributable to Alcatel S.A.

Before the court can determine whether it should attribute Alcatel USA's alleged acts in Delaware to Alcatel S.A., it must determine whether an agency relationship exists between the two corporations. As previously stated, in order to make this determination, the court must consider the extent of overlap of officers and directors between Alcatel USA and Alcatel S.A., the methods of financing with respect to the two corporations, the division of responsibility for day-to-day management between the two, and the process by which each corporation obtains its business. After having considered these factors, the court concludes that Telcordia has not carried its burden. As to the first factor, Telcordia points to one overlap in officers between the two corporations: Quigley is Senior Executive Vice President of Alcatel S.A. and CEO of Alcatel USA. According to Alcatel S.A., there is a second overlap between the two corporations: its President and COO, Philippe Germond, is a member of the Board of Directors of Alcatel USA. This minor overlap, however, is not dispositive, as "it is entirely appropriate for directors of a parent corporation to serve as directors of a subsidiary, and that fact alone may not serve to expose the parent corporation to liability for its subsidiary's acts." *United States v. Bestfoods,* 524 U.S. 51, 69 (1998) (noting that it is "well established principle . . . that directors and officers holding positions with a parent and its subsidiary can and do 'change hats' to represent the two corporations separately, despite their common ownership"). As such, this factor does not weigh in favor of a finding of agency.

Likewise, the remaining factors do not weigh in favor of applying the agency theory in the present case. First, Alcatel S.A. is merely a holding company that does not manufacture, sell, or advertise in the United States, or anywhere in the world. Thus, this is not a case in which Alcatel S.A. manufactures a product and uses an independent distributor to sell its product. In addition, Alcatel USA maintains its own executive team, which is responsible for the day-to-day management of Alcatel USA, and no employee of Alcatel S.A. is a member of the executive team of Alcatel USA. It also maintains its own financial statements, separate from those kept by Alcatel S.A. Alcatel USA files a consolidated United States federal income tax return that is separate from tax returns filed by Alcatel S.A. Alcatel USA finances its day-to-day activities through funds generated from its business activities, including the manufacture, marketing and distribution of the accused infringing products. Accordingly, the court finds that while there is a minor overlap of officers and directors between the parent and subsidiary, Telcordia has not produced sufficient evidence for the court to conclude that the specific combination of agency factors militates in favor of a finding that Alcatel USA was acting as Alcatel S.A.'s agent. Thus, sections (c)(1) and (c)(3) do not warrant the exercise of jurisdiction over Alcatel S.A.[3]

B. Federal Rule of Civil Procedure 4(k)(2)

Telcordia next asserts that, even if the Delaware long-arm statute does not apply in the present case, the court should not grant Alcatel S.A.'s motion to dismiss because it has the authority to exercise personal jurisdiction over Alcatel S.A. pursuant to Rule 4(k)(2) of the Federal Rules of Civil Procedure.... In order to establish jurisdiction pursuant to Rule 4(k)(2), (1) Telcordia's claim must arise under federal law; (2) Alcatel S.A. must lack sufficient contacts with any state to subject it to personal jurisdiction; and (3) Alcatel S.A. must have sufficient contacts with the United States as a whole to satisfy due process. *See BP Chems. Ltd. v. Formosa Chem. & Fibre Corp.,* 229 F.3d 254, 258–59 (3d Cir. 2000). Telcordia contends that all three requirements of Rule 4(k)(2) are satisfied. The court disagrees.

First, the parties do not dispute, nor could they, that Telcordia's claims arise under federal law. The complaint alleges that Alcatel S.A. has infringed, induced infringement of, and/or contributorily infringed the '306 patent. Patents and the protection of patent rights are the subject of Title 35 of the United States Code. 35 U.S.C. § 271 specifically provides the elements of patent infringement. Additionally, 28 U.S.C. § 1338 gives district courts original jurisdiction over patent actions. A patent infringement

---

3. The court need not address whether jurisdiction in Delaware comports with the requirements of the Due Process Clause because it has no statutory authority under the Delaware long-arm statute to exercise jurisdiction over Alcatel S.A.

action, therefore, is one that arises under federal law. Telcordia has thus satisfied the first requirement of Rule 4(k)(2).

Having found that the first requirement of Rule 4(k)(2) is satisfied, the court next must determine whether Alcatel S.A. is not subject to jurisdiction in any state.... [I]t appears that the Third Circuit has not yet addressed whether the plaintiff or defendant bears the burden of proving that the defendant is beyond the jurisdictional reach of any state court of general jurisdiction, or what is known as the negation requirement.... The court agrees with the Third Circuit district courts that have addressed the negation requirement and concludes that Telcordia bears the burden of demonstrating that Alcatel S.A. is not subject to jurisdiction in any state.

Here, Telcordia addresses the negation requirement only by asserting that, based on the information provided by Alcatel S.A. in its opening brief and the publicly available information regarding Alcatel S.A., an analysis of whether any other state has personal jurisdiction over Alcatel S.A. would not be "significantly different" from the analysis regarding Alcatel S.A.'s personal jurisdiction under the Delaware long-arm statute. According to Telcordia, if the court cannot exercise jurisdiction over Alcatel S.A. pursuant to the Delaware long-arm statute then Rule 4(k)(2) applies. The court is not persuaded by this argument, however, and concludes that Telcordia's conclusory statement does not support a finding that Alcatel S.A. lacks sufficient contacts with any state to subject it to personal jurisdiction. Thus, Telcordia has not satisfied the second requirement of Rule 4(k)(2).

Even assuming Telcordia was able to show that Alcatel S.A. was not subject to jurisdiction in any other state, it cannot satisfy the third requirement of Rule 4(k)(2) because the record evidence demonstrates that Alcatel S.A. lacks sufficient contacts with the United States as a whole to satisfy due process. The Due Process Clause requires that, in order to subject a defendant who is "not present within the territory of the forum" to personal jurisdiction, the court must first make sure that the party "ha[s] certain minimum contacts with [the forum] such that the maintenance of the suit does not offend traditional notions of justice and fair play." *See International Shoe Co. v. Washington,* 326 U.S. 310, 316 (1945). In order for the court to find that Alcatel S.A. has "minimum contacts" with the United States, Telcordia must demonstrate either specific or general personal jurisdiction. *Helicopteros Nacionales de Colombia v. Hall,* 466 U.S. 408, 414 (1984). The court can assert specific jurisdiction over a nonresident defendant that has "purposefully directed his activities at residents of the forum and the litigation results from alleged injuries that 'arise out of or [are] related to' those activities." *Burger King,* 471 U.S. at 472. The court can assert general jurisdiction over a defendant when its contacts with the forum, regardless of their relation to the litigation, are "continuous and systematic." *Helicopteros Nacionales,* 466 U.S. at 416. The court will address the reasons it cannot exercise specific or general jurisdiction over Alcatel S.A. in turn.

When determining whether a defendant's contacts give rise to specific jurisdiction, "[i]t is essential in each case that there be some act by which the defendant purposely avails itself of the privilege of conducting activities within the forum ... thus invoking the benefits and protections of its laws." *BP Chems.,* 229 F.3d at 259 (quoting *World-Wide Volkswagen Corp. v. Woodson,* 444 U.S. 286 (1980)). In other words, the defendant's contact must be of the nature that would cause it to reasonably foresee that it might be "haled before a court" in the forum as a result of its conduct. *See World–Wide Volkswagen Corp.,* 444 U.S. at 297. Thus, a court usually must determine the character of the defendant's activity in the forum, and whether the plaintiff's claim arises out of or has a substantial connection with that activity. *See Burger King,* 471 U.S. at 475–76. In the present case, however, the court need not make this determination because Telcordia bases its argument on the specific jurisdiction subsections of the Delaware long-arm statute which ... do not warrant the exercise of jurisdiction over Alcatel S.A. because Alcatel USA is not its United States agent.

The court also concludes that Alcatel S.A.'s contacts with the United States that are unrelated to the present litigation are not "continuous and systematic" so as to give rise to general jurisdiction. Telcordia contends that general jurisdiction exists because there is "ample evidence of Alcatel S.A.'s contacts with the United States." According to Telcordia, this evidence includes the following: (1) Alcatel S.A. is listed on the New York Stock Exchange; (2) Alcatel S.A. owns property in the United States, specifically hundreds of patents; (3) Alcatel S.A.'s website fails to distinguish among its multinational subsidiaries and uses its name in the name of its subsidiaries; (4) Alcatel S.A.'s website describes its worldwide activities, including its activities in the United States, but never discloses that its United States activities are performed by one of its subsidiaries; and (5) Alcatel S.A. incorporated its subsidiary, Alcatel USA in Delaware. The court does not find the evidence sufficient to support Telcordia's assertion.

First, as previously discussed, Alcatel S.A. is a French holding company that does not make, sell, export or import any products into the United States. Alcatel S.A. does not maintain any offices in the United States, or lease or own any real property in the United States. It does not maintain any bank accounts in Delaware and has never contracted to supply services or things in Delaware or the

United States. Alcatel S.A.'s employees also all reside outside of the United States.

Moreover, while Alcatel S.A. is listed on the New York Stock Exchange as an American Depository Receipt, this factor alone does not justify the exercise of jurisdiction. *See Doe v. Unocal Corp.*, 248 F.3d 915, 922 (9th Cir. 2001) ("'[T]he Court is not persuaded that Congress intended for the courts to assert jurisdiction under Rule 4(k)(2) whenever a corporation lists its stock on a United States exchange.'"). Likewise, "[o]wnership of a United States patent, without more, cannot support the assertion of personal jurisdiction over a foreign patentee in any state besides the District of Columbia." *Advanced Cardiovascular Sys., Inc. v. Medtronic, Inc.*, No. C–95–3577 DLJ, 1996 WL 467293, at *6 n.5 (N.D. Cal. July 24, 1996) (citing 35 U.S.C. § 293). Furthermore, incorporating a subsidiary in the United States does not give rise to jurisdiction unless the litigation is related to the act of incorporation and, here, it is not related. *See Applied Biosystems*, 772 F.Supp. at 1468. Additionally, "the mere operation of a commercially interactive web site should not subject the operator to jurisdiction anywhere in the world. Rather, there must be evidence that the defendant 'purposefully availed' itself of conduct activity in the forum, knowingly interacting with residents of the forum state via its web site." *Toys "R" Us, Inc. v. Step Two, S.A.*, 318 F.3d 446, 454 (3d Cir. 2003). Here, Telcordia has not adduced evidence to support a finding that Alcatel S.A.'s web site was intended to reach customers in Delaware, or any other state in the United States.[5]

The court also disagrees with Telcordia's assertion that Alcatel's website "never discloses that its United States activities are performed by some entity (or entities) other than Alcatel S.A." First, when one enters the Alcatel website and clicks on "United States" as its country/region the web address changes from "www.alcatel.com" to "www.usa.alcatel.com." Further, when one clicks on the "About Alcatel" dropdown menu and selects "Alcatel in the U.S.A.," he or she is provided with information regarding Alcatel USA, including its business locations. Moreover, the web page states "[i]t is the policy of *Alcatel USA* to satisfy the expectation of our customers." www.usa.alcatel.com/company/ausa_info.jhtml (last visited May 23, 2005) (emphasis added).

---

5. Telcordia asserts that there can be "no question that Alcatel S.A.'s website solicits requests for information concerning its products (including allegedly infringing products) from Delaware residents, pointing to a "website page concerning the possible purchase of Alcatel products" with Delaware chosen as the potential buyer's state. Telcordia misses the point, however, as the record does not support any documented sales to persons in Delaware (or any other state in the United States). Nor does it support any interaction between Alcatel S.A. and Delaware residents, as the web site page, in Telcordia's own words, demonstrates only the *possible* purchase of Alcatel products.

Thus, the Alcatel web site does distinguish Alcatel S.A. from Alcatel USA. This fact does not support the exercise of jurisdiction over Alcatel S.A. Accordingly, Alcatel S.A.'s alleged contacts with the United States do not provide a basis for the court to conclude that it has a "continuous and systematic" presence in the United States.

Nor does the combination of Alcatel S.A.'s alleged contacts with the United States provide the court with a sufficient basis to conclude that the requirements for general jurisdiction are met. *BP Chemicals Ltd. v. Formosa Chemical & Fibre Corp.*, 229 F.3d 254 (3d Cir. 2000) is instructive on this point. In *BP Chemicals,* the Third Circuit found that a foreign defendant did not have sufficient contacts with the United States as a whole to justify the exercise of Rule 4(k)(2) jurisdiction, even though the defendant exported its products to the United States, held a small ownership interest in a Delaware corporation, and entered into contracts requiring its personnel to travel to the United States for training. *Id.* at 263. The Court of Appeals also found that the cumulative effect of the defendants contacts did not meet the requirements for general jurisdiction. In the present case, Alcatel S.A.'s alleged contacts fall short of those alleged by the plaintiff in *BP Chemicals.* As such, the court finds that there is no basis for exercising Rule 4(k)(2) jurisdiction over Alcatel S.A.

C.   JURISDICTIONAL DISCOVERY

Lastly, Telcordia asserts that if the court does not conclude that Alcatel S.A. "is subject to personal jurisdiction under the *Delaware long-arm statute,*" it should permit limited jurisdictional discovery rather than granting Alcatel S.A.'s motion to dismiss. Telcordia asserts that its claims against Alcatel S.A. are not clearly frivolous, and that discovery is necessary due to the "limited publicly available information" that it has gathered without discovery. Telcordia further asserts that the case will not be delayed as a result of any discovery on the personal jurisdiction issue....

"Although the plaintiff bears the burden of demonstrating facts that support personal jurisdiction, courts are to assist the plaintiff by allowing jurisdictional discovery unless the plaintiff's claim is clearly frivolous." *Toys "R" Us, Inc. v. Step Two, S.A.*, 318 F.3d 446, 456 (3d Cir. 2003). Thus, resolution of Telcordia's request "begins with the presumption in favor of allowing discovery to establish personal jurisdiction." *Hansen v. Neumueller GmbH,* 163 F.R.D. 471, 474 (D. Del. Oct. 5, 1995). However, "[t]he court must be satisfied that there is some indication that this particular defendant is amenable to suit in this forum." *Id.* at 475. For example, "a plaintiff may not rely on the bare allegations in his complaint to warrant further discovery." *Id.* at 476. Likewise, "a mere unsupported allegation that [a] defendant transacts business in an area is clearly frivolous." *Mass. Sch. of Law at Andover, Inc. v. Am. Bar Ass'n,* 107 F.3d 1026, 1042 (3d Cir. 1997); *see B.L. Poe v. Babcock Int'l,* 662 F.Supp. 4, 7 (M.D. Pa. Mar. 14, 1985) ("Since plaintiff has met defendants' affidavit evidence with mere speculation, plaintiff's request for an opportunity to conduct discovery on the matter must be denied. It would be inappropriate for this court to allow plaintiff to conduct a fishing expedition in order to construct a basis for jurisdiction."). Rather, "there must be *some* competent evidence to demonstrate that personal jurisdiction over [a] defendant might exist before allowing discovery to proceed." *Hansen,* 163 F.R.D. at 475. Furthermore, "[w]hen the lack of personal jurisdiction is clear, ... further discovery serves no purpose and should be denied." *Hockerson-Halberstadt, Inc. v. Propet USA, Inc.,* 62 Fed.Appx. 322, 338 (Fed. Cir. 2003) (unpublished).

Here, ... the record evidence regarding Telcordia's agency theory of specific jurisdiction is insufficient to support the conclusion that Alcatel USA was acting as Alcatel S.A.'s agent. In addition, Telcordia did not assert that the court could exercise personal jurisdiction over Alcatel S.A. based on the general jurisdiction subsection of the Delaware long-arm statute. For these reasons, the court believes it is clear that it may not exercise personal jurisdiction over Alcatel S.A. pursuant to the Delaware long-arm statute. Thus, further discovery would not be worthwhile. In other words, granting Telcordia's request for jurisdictional discovery would amount to allowing it to conduct a fishing expedition in order to form a basis for jurisdiction. The court, therefore, will deny Telcordia's request for jurisdictional discovery.

Notes

6–1.   Judge Sleet concluded that the court did not have personal jurisdiction under FRCP 4(k)(1)(A) nor under 4(k)(2). Imagine that you represent Telcordia on appeal. Page limits on briefs and time limits on oral argument might require you to emphasize one of these arguments for jurisdiction over the other. Which of these two arguments is stronger?

6–2.   How should Telcordia have established "control" by Alcatel S.A. of Alcatel USA? What jurisdictional discovery might have been pursued to demonstrate this? (Why did the district court judge deny jurisdictional discovery?)

6–3.   How does one satisfy the second part of the test under FRCP 4(k)(2) (i.e., that the defendant lacks sufficient contacts with any state to subject it to personal jurisdiction)? Judge Sleet assigns this burden to which party?

6–4. Under FRCP 4(k)(2), Telcordia needed to demonstrate an aggregation of contacts with the United States as a whole to satisfy due process. Why is the court demanding systematic and continuous contacts rather than minimum contacts?

B. FOREIGN FORUM SELECTION CLAUSES

Often the issue of jurisdiction will be addressed by the parties long before any dispute has developed. Indeed, provisions limiting the place or court in which an action may be brought are commonplace in a variety of contracts—and especially those with multinational connections. Courts typically uphold these clauses by drawing from a well of principles that include the right to contract, efficiency and cost savings for contracting parties, and the expeditious resolution by courts of a threshold issue. In both domestic and transnational actions, forum selection clauses are presumptively valid and enforceable. Only where enforcement would be "unreasonable and unjust" or the clause is invalid for fraud or overreaching should a clause be invalidated. *The Bremen v. Zapata Off–Shore Co.,* 407 U.S. 1 (1973). In *Carnival Cruise Lines, Inc. v. Shute,* 499 U.S. 585 (1991), the Court determined that it could also consider the "fundamental fairness" of the clause. In *Richards* the Ninth Circuit had to reconcile those well-settled principles with a pre-determined Congressional mandate that appears to prohibit the enforcement of forum selection clauses in cases seeking enforcement of federal securities laws.

RICHARDS v. LLOYD'S OF LONDON

135 F.3d 1289 (9th Cir.), *cert. denied* 525 U.S. 943 (1998)

GOODWIN, CIRCUIT JUDGE:

The primary question this case presents is whether the anti-waiver provisions of the Securities Act of 1933 and the Securities Exchange Act of 1934 void choice of law and choice of forum clauses in an international transaction. The district court found that they do not.... [W]e affirm the district court.

Appellants, all citizens or residents of the United States, are more than 600 "Names" who entered into underwriting agreements. The Names sued four defendants: the Corporation of Lloyd's, the Society of Lloyd's, the Council of Lloyd's, (collectively, "Lloyd's") and Lloyd's of London, (the "unincorporated association").

Lloyd's is a market in which more than three hundred Underwriting Agencies compete for underwriting business. Pursuant to the Lloyd's Act of 1871–1982, Lloyd's oversees and regulates the competition for underwriting business in the Lloyd's market. The market does not accept premiums or insure risks. Rather, Underwriting Agencies, or syndicates, compete for the insurance business. Each Underwriting Agency is controlled by a Managing Agent who is responsible for the financial status of its agency. The Managing Agent must attract not only underwriting business from brokers but also the capital with which to insure the risks underwritten.

The Names provide the underwriting capital. The Names become Members of the Society of Lloyd's through a series of agreements, proof of financial means, and the deposit of an irrevocable letter of credit in favor of Lloyd's. To become a Name, one must travel to England to acknowledge the attendant risks of participating in a syndicate and sign a General Undertaking. The General Undertaking is a two page document containing choice of forum and choice of law clauses (collectively the "choice clauses"), which form the basis for this dispute. The choice clauses read:

2.1 The rights and obligations of the parties arising out of or relating to the Member's membership of, and/or underwriting of insurance business at, Lloyd's and any other matter referred to in this Undertaking shall be governed by and construed in accordance with the laws of England.

2.2 Each party hereto irrevocably agrees that the courts of England shall have exclusive jurisdiction to settle any dispute and/or controversy of whatsoever nature arising out of or relating to the Member's membership of, and/or underwriting of insurance business at, Lloyd's. . . .

By becoming a Member, the Names obtain the right to participate in the Lloyd's Underwriting Agencies. The Names, however, do not deal directly with Lloyd's or with the Managing Agents. Instead, the Names are represented by Members' Agents who, pursuant to agreement, stand in a fiduciary relationship with their Names. Upon becoming a Name, an individual selects the syndicates in which he wishes to participate. In making this decision, the individual must rely to a great extent on the advice of his Members' Agent. The Names generally join more than one underwriting agency in order to spread their risks across different types of insurance. When a Name undertakes an underwriting obligation, that Name is responsible only for his share of an agency's losses; however, his liability is unlimited for that share.

In this case, the risk of heavy losses has materialized and the Names now seek shelter under United States securities laws and the Racketeer Influenced and Corrupt Organizations Act ("RICO"), 18 U.S.C. § 1961 et seq. The Names claim that Lloyd's actively sought the investment of United States residents to fill an urgent need to build up capital. According to the Names, Lloyd's concealed information regarding the possible consequences of the risks under-

taken and deliberately and disproportionately exposed the Names
to massive liabilities for which sufficient underwriting capital or
reinsurance was unavailable. . . .

I

We analyze the validity of the choice clause under *The Bremen
v. Zapata Off–Shore Co.*, 407 U.S. 1 (1972), where the Supreme
Court stated that courts should enforce choice of law and choice of
forum clauses in cases of "freely negotiated private international
agreement[s]." *Bremen*, 407 U.S. at 12–13.

A

The Names dispute the application of *Bremen* to this case.
They contend that *Bremen* does not apply to cases where Congress
has spoken directly to the immediate issue—as they claim the
antiwaiver provisions do here.

The Securities Act of 1933 provides that:

Any condition, stipulation, or provision binding any person
acquiring any security to waive compliance with any provision
of this subchapter or of the rules and regulations of the
Commission shall be void.

15 U.S.C. § 77n. The 1934 Securities Exchange Act contains a
substantially similar provision. 15 U.S.C. § 78cc(a). The Names
seize on these provisions and claim that they void the choice clauses
in their agreement with Lloyd's.

Certainly the antiwaiver provisions are worded broadly enough
to reach this case. They cover *"any* condition, stipulation, or
provision binding *any* person acquiring *any* security to waive compliance with *any* provision of this subchapter. . . ." Indeed, this
language is broad enough to reach any offer or sale of anything that
could be alleged to be a security, no matter where the transaction
occurs.

Nevertheless, this attempt to distinguish *Bremen* fails. In *Bremen* itself, the Supreme Court contemplated that a forum selection
clause may conflict with relevant statutes. *Bremen*, 407 U.S. at 15
("A contractual choice-of-forum clause should be held unenforceable if enforcement would contravene a strong public policy of the
forum in which suit is brought, whether declared *by statute* or by
judicial decision.") (emphasis added).

Moreover, in *Scherk v. Alberto–Culver Co.*, 417 U.S. 506 (1974),
the Supreme Court explicitly relied on *Bremen* in a case involving a
securities transaction. Echoing the language of *Bremen*, the Court
found that "[a] contractual provision specifying in advance the
forum in which disputes shall be litigated and the law to be applied

is ... an almost indispensable precondition to achievement of the orderliness and predictability essential to any international business transaction." *Id.* at 516. *See Bremen*, 407 U.S. at 13–14 ("[A]greeing in advance on a forum acceptable to both parties is an indispensable element in international trade, commerce, and contracting."). ...

Indeed, were we to find that *Bremen* did not apply, the reach of United States securities laws would be unbounded. The Names simply prove too much when they assert that "*Bremen's* judicially-created policy analysis under federal common law is *not* controlling when Congress has expressed its will in a statute." This assertion, if true, expands the reach of federal securities law to any and all such transactions, no matter how remote from the United States. We agree with the Fifth Circuit that "we must tread cautiously before expanding the operation of U.S. securities law in the international arena." *Haynsworth v. The Corporation*, 121 F.3d 956, 966 (5th Cir. 1997).

B

Having determined that *Bremen* governs international contracts specifying forum and applicable law, we turn to the question whether the contract between Lloyd's and the Names is international. Not surprisingly, the Names contend that these were purely domestic securities sales. They claim that Lloyd's solicited the Names in the United States and that the trip the Names made to England was a mere ritual without legal significance.

We disagree. The Names signed a contract with English entities to participate in an English insurance market and flew to England to consummate the transaction. That the Names received solicitations in the United States does not somehow erase these facts. Moreover, Lloyd's insistence that individuals travel to England to become a Name does not strike us as mere ritual. Lloyd's likely requires this precisely so that those who choose to be the Names understand that English law governs the transaction. Entering into the Lloyd's market in the manner described is plainly an international transaction.

II

We now apply *Bremen* to this case. *Bremen* emphasized that "in the light of present-day commercial realities and expanding international trade we conclude that the forum clause should control absent a strong showing that it should be set aside." *Bremen*, 407 U.S. at 15. The Court reasoned that "[t]he elimination of all [ ] uncertainties [regarding the forum] by agreeing in advance ... is an indispensable element in international trade, commerce, and contracting." *Id.* at 13–14. Thus, "absent some compelling and countervailing reason [a forum selection clause] should be honored by the parties and enforced by the courts." *Id.* at 12. The party seeking to avoid the forum selection clause bears "a heavy burden of proof." *Id.* at 17.

The Supreme Court has identified three grounds for repudiating a forum selection clause: first, if the inclusion of the clause in the agreement was the product of fraud or overreaching; second, if the party wishing to repudiate the clause would effectively be deprived of his day in court were the clause enforced; and third, "if enforcement would contravene a strong public policy of the forum in which suit is brought." *Id.* at 12–13, 15, 18. The Names contend that the first and third grounds apply in this case.

A

The Names' strongest argument for escaping their agreement to litigate their claims in England is that the choice clauses contravene a strong public policy embodied in federal and state securities law and RICO. *See Bonny v. Society of Lloyd's,* 3 F3d 156, 160–61 (7th Cir. 1993) (expressing "serious concerns" that the choice clauses offend public policy but ultimately ruling in Lloyd's favor), *cert. denied,* 510 U.S. 1113; *Roby v. Corporation of Lloyd's,* 996 F.3d 1353, 1364–66 (2nd Cir.) (substantially the same), *cert. denied,* 510 U.S. 945 (1993).

We follow our six sister circuits that have ruled to enforce the choice clauses. *See Haynsworth,* 121 F.3d 956; *Allen v. Lloyd's of London,* 94 F.3d 923 (4th Cir. 1996); *Shell v. R.W. Sturge, Ltd.,* 55 F.3d 1227 (6th Cir. 1995); *Bonny,* 3 F.3d 156; *Roby,* 996 F.2d 1353; and *Riley v. Kingsley Underwriting Agencies, Ltd.,* 969 F.2d 953 (10th Cir.), *cert. denied,* 506 U.S. 1021 (1992). We do so because we apply *Scherk* and because English law provides the Names with sufficient protection.

In *Scherk,* the Supreme Court was confronted with a contract that specified that all disputes would be resolved in arbitration before the International Chamber of Commerce in Paris, France. *Scherk,* 417 U.S. at 508. The arbitrator was to apply the law of the state of Illinois. *Id.* The Court enforced the forum selection clause despite then hostile precedent.[4] *Id.* at 520–21. *See Wilko v. Swan,* 346 U.S. 427 (1953), *overruled by Rodriguez de Quijas v. Shearson/American Express, Inc.,* 490 U.S. 477, 485 (1989).

The Court's treatment of *Wilko* leaves little doubt that the choice clauses in this case are enforceable. In *Wilko,* the Supreme Court ruled that "the right to select the judicial forum is the kind of 'provision' that cannot be waived under § 14 of the Securities

---

4. The court recognized that an agreement to arbitrate "is, in effect, a specialized kind of forum-selection clause." *Scherk,* 417 U.S. at 519.

Act." *Wilko,* 346 U.S. at 435. In *Scherk,* the Court had before it a case where both the District Court and the Seventh Circuit found a forum selection clause invalid on the strength of *Wilko. Scherk,* 417 U.S. at 510.

In distinguishing *Wilko,* the Supreme Court stated that there were "significant and, we find, crucial differences between the agreement involved in *Wilko* and the one signed by the parties here." *Scherk,* 417 U.S. at 515. The first and primary difference that the Court relied upon was that "Alberto–Culver's contract . . . was a truly international agreement." *Id.* The Court reasoned that such a contract needs, as "an almost indispensable precondition," a "provision specifying in advance the forum in which disputes shall be litigated *and the law to be applied.*" *Id.* at 516 (emphasis added).

Moreover, the Supreme Court has explained that, in the context of an international agreement, there is "no basis for a judgment that only United States laws and United States courts should determine this controversy in the face of a solemn agreement between the parties that such controversies be resolved elsewhere." *Id.* at 517 n. 11. To require that " 'American standards of fairness' must . . . govern the controversy demeans the standards of justice elsewhere in the world, and unnecessarily exalts the primacy of United States law over the laws of other countries." *Id.*

These passages from *Scherk,* we think, resolve the question whether public policy reasons allow the Names to escape their "solemn agreement" to adjudicate their claims in England under English law. *Scherk* involved a securities transaction. *Id.* at 514 n. 8. The Court rejected *Wilko*'s holding that the antiwaiver provision of the '34 Act prohibited choice clauses. *Id.* at 515–16. It also recognized that enforcing the forum selection clause would, in some cases, have the same effect as choosing foreign law to apply. *Id.* at 516, 517 n. 11. Yet the Court did not hesitate to enforce the forum selection clauses. It believed that to rule otherwise would "reflect a 'parochial concept that all disputes must be resolved under our laws and in our courts.' " *Id.* at 519 (quoting *Bremen,* 407 U.S. at 9). As the Supreme Court has explained, " '[w]e cannot have trade and commerce in world markets and international waters exclusively on our terms, governed by our laws, and resolved in our courts.' " *Id.* (quoting *Bremen,* 407 U.S. at 9).

Relying on *Mitsubishi Motors Corp. v. Soler Chrysler–Plymouth, Inc.,* 473 U.S. 614, 634 (1985), the Names argue that federal and state securities laws are of "fundamental importance to American democratic capitalism." They claim that enforcement of the choice clauses will deprive them of important remedies provided by our securities laws. The Supreme Court disapproved of such an outcome, the Names contend, when it stated that "in the event the choice-of-forum and choice-of-law clauses operated in tandem as a prospective waiver of a party's right to pursue statutory remedies for antitrust violations, we would have little hesitation in condemning the agreement as against public policy." *Id.* at 637 n. 19.

Without question this case would be easier to decide if this footnote in *Mitsubishi* had not been inserted. Nevertheless, we do not believe dictum in a footnote regarding antitrust law outweighs the extended discussion and holding in *Scherk* on the validity of clauses specifying the forum and applicable law. The Supreme Court repeatedly recognized in *Scherk* that parties to an international securities transaction may choose law other than that of the United States, *Scherk,* 417 at 516, 517 n. 11, 519 n. 13, yet it never suggested that this affected the validity of a forum selection clause. *See also Bremen,* 407 U.S. at 13 n.15 (recognizing that a forum selection clause also acts to select applicable law); *Milanovich v. Costa Crociere, S.p.A.,* 954 F.2d 763, 767 n.7 (D.C. Cir. 1992) (*"The Bremen* involved a choice-of-forum clause, but the Supreme Court recognized that enforcing the provision would have the effect of subjecting the contract to foreign law.").

B

Of course, were English law so deficient that the Names would be deprived of any reasonable recourse, we would have to subject the choice clauses to another level of scrutiny. *See Carnival Cruise Lines, Inc. v. Shute,* 499 U.S. 585, 595 (1991) ("It bears emphasis that forum-selection clauses contained in form passage contracts are subject to judicial scrutiny for fundamental fairness."). In this case, however, there is no such danger. *See Haynsworth,* 121 F.3d at 969 ("English law provides a variety of protections for fraud and misrepresentations in securities transactions."). *Cf. British Midland Airways Ltd. v. International Travel, Inc.,* 497 F.2d 869, 871 (9th Cir. 1974) (This court is "hardly in a position to call the Queen's Bench a kangaroo court.").

We disagree with the dramatic assertion that "[t]he available English remedies are not adequate substitutes for the firm shields and finely honed swords provided by American securities law." *Richards v. Lloyd's of London,* 107 F.3d 1422, 1430 (9th Cir. 1997). The Names have recourse against both the Member and Managing Agents for fraud, breach of fiduciary duty, or negligent misrepresentation. Indeed, English courts have already awarded substantial judgments to some of the other Names. *See Arubuthnott v. Fagan and Feltrim Underwriting Agencies Ltd.,* 3 Re LR 145 (H.L. 1994)....[6]

---

6. The Names complain that the Member and Managing Agents are insolvent. If so, this is truly unfortunate. It does not, however, affect our analysis of the adequacy of English law.

While it is true that the Lloyd's Act immunizes Lloyd's from many actions possible under our securities laws, Lloyd's is not immune from the consequences of actions committed in bad faith, including fraud. The Names contend that entities using the Lloyd's trade name willfully and fraudulently concealed massive long tail liabilities in order to induce them to join syndicates. If so, we have been cited to no authority that Lloyd's partial immunity would bar recovery.

C

... The Names also argue that the choice clauses were the product of fraud. They claim that at the time of signing the General Undertaking, Lloyd's knew that the Names were effectively sacrificing valid claims under United States law by signing the choice clauses and concealed this fact from the Names. Had the Names known this fact, they contend, they never would have agreed to the choice clauses. The Names never allege, however, that Lloyd's misled them as to the legal effect of the choice clauses. Nor do they allege that Lloyd's fraudulently inserted the clauses without their knowledge. Accordingly, we view the allegations made by the Names as going only to the contract as a whole, with no allegations as to the inclusion of the choice clauses themselves.

Absent such allegations, these claims of fraud fail. The Supreme Court has noted that simply alleging that one was duped into signing the contract is not enough. *Scherk,* 417 U.S. at 519 n.14 (The fraud exception in *Bremen* "does not mean that any time a dispute arising out of a transaction is based upon an allegation of fraud ... the clause is unenforceable."). For a party to escape a forum selection clause on the grounds of fraud, it must show that "the *inclusion of that clause in the contract* was the product of fraud or coercion." *Id.* (citing *Prima Paint Corp. v. Flood & Conklin Mfg. Co.,* 388 U.S. 395 (1967)) (emphasis in original). *See also Prima Paint,* 388 U.S. at 404 ("[T]he statutory language [of the United States Arbitration Act] does not permit the federal court to consider claims of fraud in the inducement of the contract generally."). . . .

Notes

6–5. In *Richards,* the Ninth Circuit enforced the forum selection clause, emphasizing the need for "orderliness and predictability" in international business transactions. Is the need for orderliness and predictability less compelling in domestic transactions? (Would the clause have been enforced if this had been a domestic transaction and a domestic forum selected by the parties?)

6–6.   How does the court distinguish *Mitsubishi*?

6–7.   If the principal defendants are insolvent (*see* note 6 of the opinion), how will the plaintiffs obtain an adequate remedy in England? (How might the remedy differ if the litigation proceeded in the United States?)

6–8.   The *Richards* opinion was a decision upon rehearing by the Ninth Circuit *en banc*. In the earlier decision, a three-judge panel of the Ninth Circuit had reversed the trial court and held that the clause was invalidated by the anti-waiver provision of the securities law. Judge Goodwin dissented from that original panel decision and, ultimately, wrote the majority opinion for a court divided 8–3 on rehearing. Was it a tactical mistake for the Names' lawyers to have filed this suit in the United States?

C. EUROPEAN PERSPECTIVES

In most countries, the doctrine of personal jurisdiction is derived not from constitutional theory, as it is in the United States, but rather from a pragmatic search for a stable and certain solution to an administrative problem. Generally speaking the rest of the world has managed to avoid doctrines founded on conceptual vessels such as "minimum contacts" and "traditional notions of fair play and substantial justice" that are, on one hand, empty phrases without any obvious meaning, yet on the other, also overflowing with meaning. Instead codes that purport to be relatively simple and straightforward enumerate the permissible bases for exercise of a court's authority over a defendant.

In contract cases, for example, codes in the European countries provide that their national courts may exercise territorial authority over the case provided that the forum was the:

- place of formation (per Italy);
- place of payment (per Luxembourg);
- place of past performance (per Germany); and/or
- place of anticipated future performance (per Belgium).

Mechanical rules that can easily be applied to the facts increase predictability and minimize controversy. Of course under such codes, parties in a multinational transaction still might still dispute whether a contract's "place of formation" is traceable to where it was signed first, signed last, or where an amendment was executed, but—the thinking goes—even in circumstances such as these, the resolution of that narrow issue will also resolve the issue of territorial authority.

In these countries, separate code provisions address each of the various categories of substantive law. In tort cases, for example, the codes may authorize the exercise of jurisdiction where the forum was:

- the place of the harm (per Austria); and/or
- the place of the allegedly wrongful conduct (per France).

Satisfaction of the factual condition, in turn, resolves the issue of territorial authority.

Although it is often repeated that the European approach to personal jurisdiction is much more restrained than the American approach, such generalities oversimplify. For example, in *World-Wide Volkswagen Corp. v. Woodson*, 444 U.S. 286 (1980), the Supreme Court held unconstitutional the exercise of jurisdiction by an Oklahoma court over a New York retailer. Pursuant to the approach of certain European codes, however, the location of the accident could have authorized the exercise of jurisdiction by an Oklahoma court.

Cases involving multiple defendants are another area where the European approach to personal jurisdiction may be more expansive than the American approach. The constitutional foundation of personal jurisdiction doctrine in the United States requires separate analyses for each defendant in a case. Thus, in *World-Wide Volkswagen*, the court had personal jurisdiction over the manufacturer and the importer, but not also over the regional distributor or the retailer. European codes, however, can be drafted to reach co-defendants, third party defendants, and necessary parties. A court with authority to assert jurisdiction over one defendant, may then exercise territorial authority over all of the defendants in related claims.

All of the European codes have, at their foundation, the principle that a defendant may be sued in the place of his or her domicile. Article 126 of the Dutch Code of Civil Procedure, for example, provides:

> (1) In civil matters, the territorially competent court is that of the place where the defendant is domiciled.
>
> (2) If the defendant does not have a domicile he may be sued before the court within whose jurisdiction the factual residence is located.

Individuals thus can be sued where they habitually reside, and corporations can be sued where they have their corporate seat. Since this exercise of jurisdiction requires no reference to the nature of the underlying cause of action, this corresponds loosely to the American concept of "general jurisdiction." Domicile is the core concept of jurisdiction under the European codes and, historically speaking, the only authoritative basis for the exercise of a court's authority. All of the previously-mentioned grounds for jurisdiction, often called "special" exercises, have been a slow evolution away from that core principle derivative of Roman law.

Many Europeans are quick to emphasize, however, that their exercise of territorial authority typically does not extend to transient jurisdiction over individuals who may be served while in the jurisdiction. Nor does it extend to corporations that are "doing business" in the jurisdiction. Instead, European codes are drafted to focus on the domicile of the defendant, the place of incorporation of a corporate defendant, or the location of the incidents at issue in the litigation. Some Europeans have been outraged by American courts' willingness to assert authority over foreign defendants:

> [I]t is not surprising that in the small European country where the author of this contribution lives, [the court's decision in *In re Ski Train Fire in Kaprun, Austria on Nov. 11, 2000,* 230 F.Supp.2d 392, 395 (S.D.N.Y. 2002), has] given rise to harsh criticism and bewilderment. The claims were raised by relatives of eight United States citizens who had been killed in a ski train fire in the Austrian Alps and were advanced against two foreign companies that had been involved in the installation of the electric equipment of a ski train which burst into flames on the underground transportation line in an Austrian ski resort killing 155 people. Jurisdiction was affirmed on the grounds that the defendants were "doing business" in the United States.

> A court in a Member State of the European Union would not find international jurisdiction on such grounds. . . . Only if the cause of the accident alleged to be a product manufactured by the defendant within the borders of that state would there be ... jurisdiction at the forum in the place of manufacture, because the "harmful event" is deemed to have occurred there as well.

Willibald Posch, *Resolving Business Disputes Through Litigation or Other Alternatives: The Effects of Jurisdictional Rules and Recognition Practice*, 26 Hous. J. Int'l L. 363, 370–71 (2004).

Again, however, it would be an oversimplification to suggest that the exercise of territorial authority by European courts is *always* narrower than that exercised by United States courts or even to suggest that *all* European countries would be equally offended. In the ski train fire case, the Southern District of New York used a theory of "doing business" jurisdiction, but the transparent motive was to provide a forum to a United States citizen. In comparison, some civil codes have authorized their national courts to adjudicate cases based principally upon the domicile of the plaintiff. Most notoriously, Article 14 of the French Civil Code provides:

> An alien, even though not residing in France, may be summoned before the French courts for the fulfillment of obligations contracted by him in France with a French national; he may be brought before the French courts for obligations contracted by him in a foreign country toward a French national.

Luxembourg, Belgium, Greece, and The Netherlands are among the countries that codified similar provisions. And in acts of retaliation to those codes authorizing exorbitant jurisdiction, the countries of Italy, Belgium, and Portugal adopted codes that likewise provided a forum for their own citizens against foreign defendants, but limited the exercise of that exorbitant jurisdiction to situations where the foreign defendant was in a country that would assert jurisdiction if the roles were reversed. Countries that once followed the French approach have since largely abandoned it. Even in France, this exercise of exorbitant jurisdiction has been somewhat curtailed.

Similarly, several European countries have experimented with codes that authorize the exercise of jurisdiction based solely on the fact that the defendant has property in the forum. For example, Article 23 of the German Code of Civil Procedure provides:

> For actions asserting pecuniary claims against a person who has no domicile within the country, the court of the district within which this person has property, or within which the subject of the action is situated, has jurisdiction. . . .

Sweden and Denmark have similar provisions. And importantly, unlike the American doctrine of *quasi in rem* jurisdiction, the exercise of the court's jurisdiction pursuant to these codes is not necessarily limited to the extent or value of the assets within the jurisdiction. (Scotland, Belgium, and The Netherlands recognize similar limitations; but other countries do not.) "The danger of leaving one's umbrella in Sweden is known the world over. For if a non-resident leaves his umbrella in Sweden, he creates the authority for a Swedish court to cast him in a personal judgment for a debt obligation in any amount."*

Variations among the codes of the various European countries created tension, and also interfered with the free movement of people, goods, services, and capital. An effort by the six founding members of the European Community (Belgium, France, Germany, Holland, Italy and Luxembourg) to reduce the barriers and to

* Hans Smit, *Common and Civil Law Rules of In Personam Adjudicatory Au-* *thority: An Analysis of Underlying Policies*, 21 Int'l & Comp. L. Q. 335 (1972).

harmonize national laws on a broader scale led to the Brussels Convention on Jurisdiction and the Recognition and Enforcement of Judgments, which was ratified in 1973.** Other countries joined upon their accession to the European Community. A parallel convention, called the Lugano Convention, expanded the reach to Member States of the European Free Trade Association. Accession to the Conventions required sacrifice by the parliaments of the ratifying states. To implement uniform rules for the exercise of jurisdiction in countries throughout the European Community, countries had to abandon those forms of jurisdiction that were not part of the common ground set forth in the Conventions. These Conventions, in turn, were incorporated into the Council Regulation on Jurisdiction and the Recognition and Enforcement of Judgments in Civil and Commercial Matters which came into effect on March 1, 2002 (the "Brussels I Regulation"). The Brussels I Regulation, excerpted below, is binding on all Member States (except Denmark, which is bound by the Brussels Convention).

Council Regulation (EC) No 44/2001 of 22 December 2000 on Jurisdiction and the Recognition and Enforcement of Judgments in Civil and Commercial Matters

Whereas:

... (11) The rules of jurisdiction must be highly predictable and founded on the principle that jurisdiction is generally based on the defendant's domicile and jurisdiction must always be available on this ground save in a few well-defined situations in which the subject-matter of the litigation or the autonomy of the parties warrants a different linking factor. The domicile of a legal person must be defined autonomously so as to make the common rules more transparent and avoid conflicts of jurisdiction....

(13) In relation to insurance, consumer contracts and employment, the weaker party should be protected by rules of jurisdiction more favourable to his interests than the general rules provide for.

(14) The autonomy of the parties to a contract, other than an insurance, consumer or employment contract, where only limited autonomy to determine the courts having jurisdiction is allowed, must be respected subject to the exclusive grounds of jurisdiction laid down in this Regulation....

** This harmonization effort was consistent and largely coincident with similar multilateral reforms. *See, e.g.,* Chapter 4, *supra* (discussing the Hague Convention on the Taking of Evidence Abroad in Civil and Commercial Matters (1970)); Chapter 7, *infra* (discussing the Hague Convention on the Service Abroad of Judicial and Extrajudicial Documents in Civil or Commercial Matters (1965)).

CHAPTER I: SCOPE

Article 1

1. This Regulation shall apply in civil and commercial matters whatever the nature of the court or tribunal. It shall not extend, in particular, to revenue, customs or administrative matters.

2. The Regulation shall not apply to:

(a) the status or legal capacity of natural persons, rights in property arising out of a matrimonial relationship, wills and succession;

(b) bankruptcy, proceedings relating to the winding-up of insolvent companies or other legal persons, judicial arrangements, compositions and analogous proceedings;

(c) social security;

(d) arbitration.

3. In this Regulation, the term 'Member State' shall mean Member States with the exception of Denmark.

CHAPTER II: JURISDICTION

Section 1: General provisions

Article 2

1. Subject to this Regulation, persons domiciled in a Member State shall, whatever their nationality, be sued in the courts of that Member State.

2. Persons who are not nationals of the Member State in which they are domiciled shall be governed by the rules of jurisdiction applicable to nationals of that State.

Article 3

1. Persons domiciled in a Member State may be sued in the courts of another Member State only by virtue of the rules set out in Sections 2 to 7 of this Chapter.

2. In particular the rules of national jurisdiction set out in Annex I shall not be applicable as against them.

Article 4

1. If the defendant is not domiciled in a Member State, the jurisdiction of the courts of each Member State shall, subject to Articles 22 and 23, be determined by the law of that Member State.

2. As against such a defendant, any person domiciled in a Member State may, whatever his nationality, avail himself in that State of the rules of jurisdiction there in force, and in particular

those specified in Annex I, in the same way as the nationals of that State.

Section 2: Special jurisdiction

Article 5

A person domiciled in a Member State may, in another Member State, be sued:

1. (a) in matters relating to a contract, in the courts for the place of performance of the obligation in question;

(b) for the purpose of this provision and unless otherwise agreed, the place of performance of the obligation in question shall be:

— in the case of the sale of goods, the place in a Member State where, under the contract, the goods were delivered or should have been delivered,

— in the case of the provision of services, the place in a Member State where, under the contract, the services were provided or should have been provided,

(c) if subparagraph (b) does not apply then subparagraph (a) applies;

2. in matters relating to maintenance, in the courts for the place where the maintenance creditor is domiciled or habitually resident or, if the matter is ancillary to proceedings concerning the status of a person, in the court which, according to its own law, has jurisdiction to entertain those proceedings, unless that jurisdiction is based solely on the nationality of one of the parties;

3. in matters relating to tort, delict or quasi-delict, in the courts for the place where the harmful event occurred or may occur;

4. as regards a civil claim for damages or restitution which is based on an act giving rise to criminal proceedings, in the court seised of those proceedings, to the extent that that court has jurisdiction under its own law to entertain civil proceedings;

5. as regards a dispute arising out of the operations of a branch, agency or other establishment, in the courts for the place in which the branch, agency or other establishment is situated;

6. as settlor, trustee or beneficiary of a trust created by the operation of a statute, or by a written instrument, or created orally and evidenced in writing, in the courts of the Member State in which the trust is domiciled;

7. as regards a dispute concerning the payment of remuneration claimed in respect of the salvage of a cargo or freight, in the court under the authority of which the cargo or freight in question:

(a) has been arrested to secure such payment, or

(b) could have been so arrested, but bail or other security has been given;

provided that this provision shall apply only if it is claimed that the defendant has an interest in the cargo or freight or had such an interest at the time of salvage.

Article 6

A person domiciled in a Member State may also be sued:

1. where he is one of a number of defendants, in the courts for the place where any one of them is domiciled, provided the claims are so closely connected that it is expedient to hear and determine them together to avoid the risk of irreconcilable judgments resulting from separate proceedings;

2. as a third party in an action on a warranty or guarantee or in any other third party proceedings, in the court seised of the original proceedings, unless these were instituted solely with the object of removing him from the jurisdiction of the court which would be competent in his case;

3. on a counter-claim arising from the same contract or facts on which the original claim was based, in the court in which the original claim is pending;

4. in matters relating to a contract, if the action may be combined with an action against the same defendant in matters relating to rights in rem in immovable property, in the court of the Member State in which the property is situated....

Section 3: Jurisdiction in matters relating to insurance

Article 8

In matters relating to insurance, jurisdiction shall be determined by this Section, without prejudice to Article 4 and point 5 of Article 5....

Article 12

1. ...[A]n insurer may bring proceedings only in the courts of the Member State in which the defendant is domiciled, irrespective of whether he is the policyholder, the insured or a beneficiary....

Section 4: Jurisdiction over consumer contracts

Article 15

1. In matters relating to a contract concluded by a person, the consumer, for a purpose which can be regarded as being outside his trade or profession, jurisdiction shall be determined by this Section, without prejudice to Article 4 and point 5 of Article 5, if:

> (a) it is a contract for the sale of goods on instalment credit terms; or

> (b) it is a contract for a loan repayable by instalments, or for any other form of credit, made to finance the sale of goods; or

> (c) in all other cases, the contract has been concluded with a person who pursues commercial or professional activities in the Member State of the consumer's domicile or, by any means, directs such activities to that Member State or to several States including that Member State, and the contract falls within the scope of such activities.

2. Where a consumer enters into a contract with a party who is not domiciled in the Member State but has a branch, agency or other establishment in one of the Member States, that party shall, in disputes arising out of the operations of the branch, agency or establishment, be deemed to be domiciled in that State.

3. This Section shall not apply to a contract of transport other than a contract which, for an inclusive price, provides for a combination of travel and accommodation.

Article 16

1. A consumer may bring proceedings against the other party to a contract either in the courts of the Member State in which that party is domiciled or in the courts for the place where the consumer is domiciled.

2. Proceedings may be brought against a consumer by the other party to the contract only in the courts of the Member State in which the consumer is domiciled. . . .

Article 17

The provisions of this Section may be departed from only by an agreement:

1. which is entered into after the dispute has arisen; or

2. which allows the consumer to bring proceedings in courts other than those indicated in this Section; or

3.   which is entered into by the consumer and the other party to the contract, both of whom are at the time of conclusion of the contract domiciled or habitually resident in the same Member State, and which confers jurisdiction on the courts of that Member State, provided that such an agreement is not contrary to the law of that Member State.

Section 5: Jurisdiction over individual contracts of employment

Article 18

1.   In matters relating to individual contracts of employment, jurisdiction shall be determined by this Section, without prejudice to Article 4 and point 5 of Article 5.

2.   Where an employee enters into an individual contract of employment with an employer who is not domiciled in a Member State but has a branch, agency or other establishment in one of the Member States, the employer shall, in disputes arising out of the operations of the branch, agency or establishment, be deemed to be domiciled in that Member State.

Article 19

An employer domiciled in a Member State may be sued:

1.   in the courts of the Member State where he is domiciled; or

2.   in another Member State:

(a) in the courts for the place where the employee habitually carries out his work or in the courts for the last place where he did so, or

(b) if the employee does not or did not habitually carry out his work in any one country, in the courts for the place where the business which engaged the employee is or was situated.

Article 20

1.   An employer may bring proceedings only in the courts of the Member State in which the employee is domiciled.

2.   The provisions of this Section shall not affect the right to bring a counter-claim in the court in which, in accordance with this Section, the original claim is pending.

Article 21

The provisions of this Section may be departed from only by an agreement on jurisdiction:

1.   which is entered into after the dispute has arisen; or

2.   which allows the employee to bring proceedings in courts other than those indicated in this Section.

Section 6: Exclusive jurisdiction

Article 22

The following courts shall have exclusive jurisdiction, regardless of domicile:

1.   in proceedings which have as their object rights in rem in immovable property or tenancies of immovable property, the courts of the Member State in which the property is situated. . . .

2.   in proceedings which have as their object the validity of the constitution, the nullity or the dissolution of companies or other legal persons or associations of natural or legal persons, or of the validity of the decisions of their organs, the courts of the Member State in which the company, legal person or association has its seat. In order to determine that seat, the court shall apply its rules of private international law; . . .

4.   in proceedings concerned with the registration or validity of patents, trade marks, designs, or other similar rights required to be deposited or registered, the courts of the Member State in which the deposit or registration has been applied for, has taken place or is under the terms of a Community instrument or an international convention deemed to have taken place.

Without prejudice to the jurisdiction of the European Patent Office under the Convention on the Grant of European Patents, signed at Munich on 5 October 1973, the courts of each Member State shall have exclusive jurisdiction, regardless of domicile, in proceedings concerned with the registration or validity of any European patent granted for that State;

5.   in proceedings concerned with the enforcement of judgments, the courts of the Member State in which the judgment has been or is to be enforced.

Section 7: Prorogation of jurisdiction

Article 23

1.   If the parties, one or more of whom is domiciled in a Member State, have agreed that a court or the courts of a Member State are to have jurisdiction to settle any disputes which have arisen or which may arise in connection with a particular legal relationship, that court or those courts shall have jurisdiction. Such jurisdiction shall be exclusive unless the parties have agreed otherwise. Such an agreement conferring jurisdiction shall be either:

(a) in writing or evidenced in writing; or

(b) in a form which accords with practices which the parties have established between themselves; or

(c) in international trade or commerce, in a form which accords with a usage of which the parties are or ought to have been aware and which in such trade or commerce is widely known to, and regularly observed by, parties to contracts of the type involved in the particular trade or commerce concerned.

2. Any communication by electronic means which provides a durable record of the agreement shall be equivalent to "writing".

3. Where such an agreement is concluded by parties, none of whom is domiciled in a Member State, the courts of other Member States shall have no jurisdiction over their disputes unless the court or courts chosen have declined jurisdiction....

Section 9: Lis pendens—related actions

Article 27

1. Where proceedings involving the same cause of action and between the same parties are brought in the courts of different Member States, any court other than the court first seised shall of its own motion stay its proceedings until such time as the jurisdiction of the court first seised is established.

2. Where the jurisdiction of the court first seised is established, any court other than the court first seised shall decline jurisdiction in favour of that court.

Article 28

1. Where related actions are pending in the courts of different Member States, any court other than the court first seised may stay its proceedings.

2. Where these actions are pending at first instance, any court other than the court first seised may also, on the application of one of the parties, decline jurisdiction if the court first seised has jurisdiction over the actions in question and its law permits the consolidation thereof.

3. For the purposes of this Article, actions are deemed to be related where they are so closely connected that it is expedient to hear and determine them together to avoid the risk of irreconcilable judgments resulting from separate proceedings....

CHAPTER V: GENERAL PROVISIONS

Article 59

1. In order to determine whether a party is domiciled in the Member State whose courts are seised of a matter, the court shall apply its internal law.

2. If a party is not domiciled in the Member State whose courts are seised of the matter, then, in order to determine whether the party is domiciled in another Member State, the court shall apply the law of that Member State.

Article 60

1. For the purposes of this Regulation, a company or other legal person or association of natural or legal persons is domiciled at the place where it has its:

    (a) statutory seat, or

    (b) central administration, or

    (c) principal place of business. . . .

Notes

6–9. The Regulation framework contemplates nine steps of inquiry:

First, Scope. Does Article 1 exclude the fact situation?

Second, Member Status. Is the defendant domiciled in any Member State? (Article 4)

Third, Domicile. Is there general jurisdiction in the forum because the defendant is domiciled there? (Articles 2 & 59–61)

Fourth, Special Jurisdiction. Is there jurisdiction in the forum pursuant to the special rules of Article 5?

Fifth, Additional Parties or Claims. Are these additional parties or claims over which there is jurisdiction pursuant to Article 6?

Sixth, Special Rules. Are special rules implicated because this is an insurance, consumer contract or employment matter? (Articles 8–14; 15–17; and 18–21)

Seventh, Exclusive Jurisdiction. Is jurisdiction invalidated by the exclusive jurisdiction of another court? (Article 22)

Eighth, Prorogation. Is there an enforceable forum selection clause that invalidates the jurisdiction of this court? (Articles 23 & 24)

Ninth, Lis pendens. Is the same cause of action pending in the court of another Member State? (Articles 27–30)

6–10. A useful exercise to advance your understanding of the Regulation is to use familiar American cases to explore the framework.

    It is interesting to think about the leading United States Supreme Court decision, *Asahi Metal Industry Co. v. Superior Court* in this context. In *Asahi*, the California plaintiff was injured in California as the result of a motorcycle accident, which was attributed to a defective motorcycle tire. Zurcher, the plaintiff, sued the manufacturer of the cycle (Honda), the manufacturer of the tire (Dunlop), and the Taiwanese manufacturer of the tire tube (Cheng Shin), but not the Japanese manufacturer of the valve assembly (Asahi). Cheng Shin then filed an indemnification claim against Asahi, joining Asahi as a third-party defendant. Notwithstanding the fact that the main claim had been settled, the California courts exercised jurisdiction over Asahi. The United States Supreme Court reversed in a confusing decision. The Court was divided (4–4–1) on the question of whether putting a product into the stream of commerce establishes sufficient minimum contacts for jurisdiction. Despite this disagreement, eight justices joined an opinion holding that the exercise of jurisdiction over an indemnification claim between two foreign companies was unreasonable.

If the facts of *Asahi* arose within the framework of the Brussels Convention, the outcome would be different from that reached by the United States Supreme Court. For this purpose, assume that the principal defendants are from one state in the European Community, such as the Netherlands, the third-party defendant is from another Community state, such as [Spain], and the accident occurred in a third Community state, such as Italy. Jurisdiction in Italy under the provisions of the Brussels Convention would extend to claims asserted against the principal defendants (on the basis of the injury) as well as claims by those defendants against the third-party defendant (either on the basis of the injury or the special provision for third-party proceedings).

Note that the jurisdictional provisions of the Brussels Convention apply only to Community domiciliaries and do not necessarily apply to defendants domiciled outside the European Community. Jurisdiction with respect to defendants not domiciled within the Community will therefore depend upon national law. A number of European countries would appear to take jurisdiction over an indemnification claim against a non-Community (e.g. Japanese) third-party defendant (on *Asahi*-type facts) on the basis of "place of the tort" or "more than one defendant" provisions. Italy, for example, appears to authorize jurisdiction in these circumstances under its domestic rules, and England's provision for jurisdiction over additional parties seems to fit such facts. Perhaps more surprisingly, the Japanese Code of Civil Procedure, which provides for jurisdiction at the "place of the tort," also seems to authorize jurisdiction over American defendants who put products into the stream of commerce, thereby reaching a United States third-party defendant in a mirror situation of Asahi.

Linda J. Silberman, *Judicial Jurisdiction in the Conflict of Laws Course: Adding a Comparative Dimension*, 28 Vand. J. Transnat'l L. 389 (1995).

6–11.   As emphasized in Article 4, the Regulation openly discriminates against outsiders. Why include this provision?

6–12.   As already mentioned, the foundational principle of the exercise of jurisdiction under the Regulation is that a person domiciled in a Member States shall be sued in that country. *See* Article 3 (Derogations from that principle are limited to the rules set forth in the Regulation.) Note that the principle is tied to domicile, not nationality.

6–13.   Insurance, consumer contracts and employment cases enjoy particularized jurisdiction rules. Are these three the only categories that deserve such treatment? If the United States were to articulate special jurisdiction rules for particular categories of cases, what would be preferred?

6–14.   Article 24 authorizes a court to assert territorial authority based on the defendant's appearance and consent. If this provision were not included in the Regulation, would courts have the inherent authority to exercise jurisdiction on this basis?

6–15.   Article 3(2) emphasizes that certain rules of national jurisdiction will not be applicable in litigation involving persons domiciled in Member States. Annex I, then, provides a list of each country's exorbitant grounds—the so-called "umbrella provisions" granting jurisdiction based on the presence of property in the forum, the provisions granting jurisdiction based on the domicile of the plaintiff, and others.

6–16.   Article 23 demonstrates the Regulation's respect for forum selection clauses. Strict limitations on the use of forum selection clauses in the context of insurance, consumer contracts, and employment cases are set forth in Articles 13, 17 and 21, respectively.

6–17.   The need for uniform interpretation of the Brussels Convention led to a 1971 Protocol that made it possible for national courts to refer questions of interpretation to the Court of Justice of the European Communities (ECJ). The ECJ will likewise ensure uniformity by interpreting provisions of the Brussels I Regulation, which applies only to cases filed on or after March 1, 2002. In *Gruber*, which follows, the ECJ is applying provisions of the Brussels Convention rather than the Regulation. The relevant text of the Convention is reprinted in the court's judgment, but the most relevant sections of the consumer contract provisions of both the Convention and the Regulation are reprinted below for comparison and reference.

Brussels Convention Article 13

In proceedings concerning a contract concluded by a person for a purpose which can be regarded as being outside his trade or profession, hereinafter called "the consumer," jurisdiction shall be determined by this Section, if it is:
(1) a contract for the sale of goods on instalment credit terms; or
(2) a contract for a loan repayable by instalments, or for any other form of credit, made to finance the sale of goods; or

EC (Brussels I) Regulation Article 15

In matters relating to a contract concluded by a person, the consumer, for a purpose which can be regarded as being outside his trade or profession, jurisdiction shall be determined by this Section, if:
(a) it is a contract for the sale of goods on instalment credit terms; or
(b) it is a contract for a loan repayable by instalments, or for any other form of credit, made to finance the sale of goods; or

(3) any other contract for the supply of goods or a contract for the supply of services, and (a) in the State of the consumer's domicile the conclusion of the contract was preceded by a specific invitation addressed to him by advertising; and (b) the consumer took in that State the steps necessary for the conclusion of the contract...

(c) in all other cases, the contract has been concluded with a person who pursues commercial or professional activities in the Member State of the consumer's domicile or, by any means, directs such activities to that Member State or to several States including that Member State, and the contract falls within the scope of such activities....

GRUBER v. BAY WA AG

[2005] ECJ C–464/01

Reference for a preliminary ruling under the Protocol of 3 June 1971 on the interpretation by the Court of Justice of the Convention of 27 September 1968 on Jurisdiction and the Enforcement of Judgments in Civil and Commercial Matters, from the Oberster Gerichtshof (Austria).

THE COURT (SECOND CHAMBER), COMPOSED OF C.W.A. TIMMERMANS, PRESIDENT OF THE CHAMBER, C. GULMANN, R. SCHINTGEN (RAPPORTEUR), G. ARESTIS AND J. KLUKA, JUDGES.

1. This reference for a preliminary ruling concerns the interpretation of the first paragraph of Article 13 of the Convention of 27 September 1968 on Jurisdiction and the Enforcement of Judgments in Civil and Commercial Matters (OJ 1978 L 304, p. 36), as amended....

2. The reference was made in the course of proceedings between Mr Gruber, domiciled in Austria, and Bay Wa AG (Bay Wa), a company incorporated under German law, established in Germany, on account of the alleged defective performance of a contract that Mr Gruber had concluded with Bay Wa.

LEGAL BACKGROUND

3. The rules on jurisdiction laid down by the Brussels Convention are set out in Title II thereof, which consists of Articles 2 to 24.

4. The first paragraph of Article 2 of the Brussels Convention, which forms part of Title II, Section 1, entitled General Provisions, sets out the basic rule in the following terms:

Subject to the provisions of this Convention, persons domiciled in a Contracting State shall, whatever their nationality, be sued in the courts of that State.

5. The first paragraph of Article 3 of the Brussels Convention, which appears in the same section, provides:

Persons domiciled in a Contracting State may be sued in the courts of another Contracting State only by virtue of the rules set out in Sections 2 to 6 of this Title.

6.   Articles 5 to 18 of the Brussels Convention, which make up Sections 2 to 6 of Title II thereof, lay down rules governing special, mandatory or exclusive jurisdiction.

7.   Article 5(1) of the Brussels Convention, which is part of Title II, Section 2, entitled Special jurisdiction, provides:

A person domiciled in a Contracting State may, in another Contracting State, be sued:

(1) in matters relating to a contract, in the courts for the place of performance of the obligation in question; . . . .

8.   Section 4, entitled "Jurisdiction over consumer contracts," in Title II of the Brussels Convention, consists of Articles 13 to 15.

9.   Article 13 of the Brussels Convention is worded as follows:

In proceedings concerning a contract concluded by a person for a purpose which can be regarded as being outside his trade or profession, hereinafter called the consumer, jurisdiction shall be determined by this Section . . . if it is:

1.   a contract for the sale of goods on instalment credit terms; or

2.   a contract for a loan repayable by instalments, or for any other form of credit, made to finance the sale of goods; or

3.   any other contract for the supply of goods or a contract for the supply of services, and

(a) in the State of the consumer's domicile the conclusion of the contract was preceded by a specific invitation addressed to him or by advertising; and

(b) the consumer took in that State the steps necessary for the conclusion of the contract. . . .

10.   The first paragraph of Article 14 of the Brussels Convention provides:

A consumer may bring proceedings against the other party to a contract either in the courts of the Contracting State in which that party is domiciled or in the courts of the Contracting State in which he is himself domiciled.

11.   That rule of jurisdiction may be departed from only if the conditions laid down in Article 15 of the Brussels Convention are complied with.

DISPUTE IN THE MAIN PROCEEDINGS AND THE QUESTIONS
REFERRED FOR A PRELIMINARY RULING

12.   According to the documents in the main proceedings Mr Gruber, a farmer, owns a farm building constructed around a

square (Vierkanthof), situated in Upper Austria, close to the German border. He uses about a dozen rooms as a dwelling for himself and his family. In addition over 200 pigs are kept there, and there are fodder silos and a large machine room. Between 10% and 15% of the total fodder necessary for the farm is also stored there. The area of the farm building used for residential purposes is slightly more than 60% of the total floor area of the building.

13.   Bay Wa operates a number of separately managed businesses in Germany. In Pocking (Germany), not far from the Austrian border, it has a building materials business and a DIY [Do–It–Yourself–ed.] and garden centre. The latter published brochures which were also distributed in Austria.

14.   Wishing to replace the roof tiles of his farm building, Mr Gruber became aware of those advertising brochures, which were sent out with the Braunauer Rundschau, a local periodical distributed to households. The tiles offered for sale by Bay Wa's building materials department in Pocking did not feature in those brochures.

15.   Mr Gruber made several telephone enquiries to an employee of Bay Wa concerning the different types of tiles and the prices, stating his name and address but not mentioning the fact that he was a farmer. The employee made him an offer by telephone but Mr Gruber wished to inspect the tiles on site. On his visit to Bay Wa's premises, he was given by the employee a written quotation dated 23 July 1998. During that meeting Mr Gruber told Bay Wa's employee that he had a farm and wished to tile the roof of the farm building. He stated that he also owned ancillary buildings that were used principally for the farm, but did not expressly state whether the building to be tiled was used mainly for business or for private purposes. The following day, Mr Gruber called the employee, from Austria, to say that he accepted Bay Wa's quotation. Bay Wa then faxed a confirmation of the order to Mr Gruber's bank in Austria. [Mr Gruber picked up the tiles at Bay Wa in Germany.]

16.   [After installing the tiles on his farm building, Mr Gruber found] significant variations in colour despite the warranty that the colour would be uniform. As a result the roof would have to be re-tiled. He therefore decided to bring proceedings on the basis of the warranty together with a claim for damages, seeking reimbursement of the cost of the tiles (ATS 258 123) [approximately (US) $20,000–ed.] and of the expense of removing them and re-tiling the roof (ATS 141 877) [approximately (US) $11,000–ed.] and a declaration of liability for any future expenses.

17.   For that purpose, Mr Gruber commenced proceedings on 26 May 1999 before the Landesgericht Steyr (Austria), designated as the competent court in Austria by the Oberster Gerichtshof in

accordance with Paragraph 28 of the Law of 1 August 1895 on the allocation of jurisdiction and the territorial jurisdiction of the ordinary courts in civil matters (Jurisdiktionsnorm, RGBl. 111).

18.   By judgment of 29 November 2000, the Landesgericht (Regional Court) Steyr dismissed Bay Wa's objection of lack of jurisdiction and ruled that it was competent to hear the dispute.

19.   According to the Landesgericht Steyr, the conditions for the application of Article 13 of the Brussels Convention are satisfied. Where a contract has a dual purpose, the predominant purpose, whether private or business, must be ascertained. Since the dividing line between private and business supplies is difficult to distinguish in the case of agricultural enterprises, the court found that the seller had had no way of ascertaining objectively whether one or other purpose predominated at the time when the contract was concluded so that, given the uncertainty, the contract was to be regarded as a consumer contract. Furthermore, in the context of Article 13(3)(a) of the Brussels Convention it mattered little whether the product ultimately bought by the consumer had itself been advertised. It was sufficient that there had been advertisements drawing attention to a particular undertaking. It was thanks to that advertising that Bay Wa was able to conclude a contract with Mr Gruber, even though it came from a department other than the one which supplied the goods. Finally, the condition that there be a specific invitation by the seller within the meaning of that provision was satisfied in this case, since Mr Gruber had received an offer by telephone. Whether that offer was accepted was irrelevant.

20.   By judgment of 1 February 2001 the Oberlandesgericht (Higher Regional Court) Linz (Austria) upheld Bay Wa's appeal, however, and dismissed Mr Gruber's claim on the ground that the Austrian courts do not have jurisdiction to hear the dispute.

21.   According to the Oberlandesgericht Linz, for there to be a consumer contract within the meaning of Article 13 of the Brussels Convention the contract must constitute an act attributable to a purpose outside the trade or profession of the person concerned. In order to identify that purpose the intention of the recipient of the service is irrelevant. What matters are the circumstances of the supply which could be objectively ascertained by the other party to the contract. Articles 13 to 15 of the Brussels Convention are applicable only if the person concerned has acted predominantly outside his trade or profession and if the other party to the contract knew or should have been aware of the fact at the time when the contract was concluded, the existence of such knowledge being determined on the basis of all the objective evidence.

22.   On the basis of the facts which could be objectively ascertained by Bay Wa, the supply at issue had at least essentially a

business purpose. The purchase of tiles by a farmer to tile the roof of his farm building is, prima facie, connected with his agricultural business. In the case of an agricultural enterprise, the farm building is by nature business premises which also, but not primarily, serve as a residence for the farmer and his family. Living on a farm is usually a consequence of carrying on agricultural activities and thus has a particular connection with them; for a large majority of the population, it is the farmer's place of work. When Mr Gruber stated that he owned an agricultural enterprise and wished to replace the tiles on the roof of his farm building Bay Wa was led, rightly, to assume that he was acting essentially for business purposes. The findings as to the floor areas used for private and for business purposes respectively cannot invalidate that conclusion, since those facts were not made known to Bay Wa. The seller had no reason to believe that Mr Gruber would use the tiles exclusively or principally for private purposes. Finally, from the seller's point of view, the large quantities purchased, 24 000 tiles in total, could reasonably constitute a decisive factor for concluding that the building was used essentially for business purposes.

23.   Mr Gruber then brought an appeal before the Oberster Gerichtshof (Supreme Court) against the judgment of 1 February 2001 of the Oberlandesgericht Linz.

24.   In support of his appeal, Mr Gruber claims that in order for him to be regarded as a consumer within the meaning of Article 13 of the Convention the private purpose of the supply must predominate. In this case, the private use of the farm building is greater than the business use thereof. The other party to the contract is under an obligation to make enquiries and to advise the client in that regard and bears the risk of any mistake. Mr Gruber argues that in this case Bay Wa had sufficient reason to consider that the farm building was used essentially for private purposes, and in case of doubt it should have made enquiries of the purchaser about this. Furthermore, the sale of the tiles was preceded by an advertisement circulated in Austria by Bay Wa which led Mr Gruber to deal with it, whereas before that advertisement he was unaware of that company. Finally, all the preparatory steps for the conclusion of the contract were taken by Mr Gruber in Austria.

25.   Bay Wa replies that in an agricultural enterprise the farm building is above all a place of work, and that in general supplies relating to it cannot be made on the basis of consumer contracts. In this case, the private use was in any event secondary and Bay Wa was unaware of such use. The consumer should clearly state in which capacity he is acting where, as in this case, it is possible to suppose, prima facie, that he is acting for a business purpose. The other party to the contract has no obligation to make enquiries in that respect. Where there is doubt as to whether a party is a

consumer the Brussels Convention rules of jurisdiction on consumer contracts should not be applied. Furthermore, Bay Wa's building materials department, from which the tiles were ordered, did not benefit from the advertising by brochure, and its DIY and garden centres, for whose benefit the advertising was undertaken, do not sell roof tiles. In any event there was no advertising for the tiles. The steps necessary for the conclusion of the contract were not taken in Austria but in Germany, as, under German law, the statement of acceptance of the quotation by telephone constitutes evidence of intention requiring an acknowledgement, and the confirmation of the order by the seller was made by fax from Germany. Where offer and acceptance are not simultaneous, which is the case where the order is made by telephone on the basis of an earlier quotation, the contract is deemed to have been concluded in the place where the defendant is domiciled.

26.   The Oberster Gerichtshof observes that whilst it follows from the case-law of the Court that the jurisdictional rules on consumer contracts in the Brussels Convention constitute a derogation from the principle that the courts of the Contracting State where the defendant is domiciled should have jurisdiction, so that the concept of consumer must be given a strict interpretation, the Court has not yet ruled on some of the conditions for the application of Article 13 of the Brussels Convention which are at issue in the case before it.

27.   Taking the view that in those circumstances the resolution of the dispute before it depends on the interpretation of the Brussels Convention, the Oberster Gerichtshof decided to stay the proceedings and to refer the following questions to the Court of Justice for a preliminary ruling:

1.   Where the purposes of a contract are partly private, does the status of consumer for the purposes of Article 13 of the Convention depend on which of the private and the trade or professional purposes is predominant, and what criteria are to be applied in determining which of the private and the trade or professional purposes predominates?

2.   Does the determination of the purpose depend on the circumstances which could be objectively ascertained by the other party to the contract with the consumer?

3.   In case of doubt, is a contract which may be attributed both to private and to trade or professional activity to be regarded as a consumer contract?

4.   Is the conclusion of a contract preceded by advertising within the meaning of Article 13(3)(a) of the Convention where the other party to the subsequent contract with the consumer advertised his products by brochure in the Contracting State of

the consumer but did not advertise the products the consumer subsequently bought in it?

5.   Is there a consumer contract within the meaning of Article 13 of the Convention where the seller makes an offer by telephone from his own State to the buyer who lives in a different State, and the offer is not accepted but the buyer subsequently buys the product thus offered in response to a written offer?

6.   Does the consumer take the steps necessary for the conclusion of the contract in his own State within the meaning of Article 13(3)(b) of the Convention where an offer is made to him in the State of his contracting partner and he accepts that offer by telephone from his own State?

THE FIRST THREE QUESTIONS

28.   By its first three questions, which it is appropriate to consider together, the national court asks, essentially, whether the rules of jurisdiction laid down by the Brussels Convention must be interpreted as meaning that a contract of the kind at issue in the main proceedings, which relates to activities which are partly business and partly private, must be regarded as having been concluded by a consumer for the purposes of the first paragraph of Article 13 of the Convention.

29.   As is clear from the order for reference, the Oberster Gerichtshof wishes to know essentially whether, and if so in what circumstances, a contract which has a dual purpose, such as the contract that Mr Gruber concluded with Bay Wa, is covered by the special rules of jurisdiction laid down in Articles 13 to 15 of the Brussels Convention. More specifically, the national court asks for clarification as to the circumstances of which it must take account in order to classify such a contract, the relevance of whether the contract was made predominantly for private or for business purposes, and the effect of knowledge of the party to the contract other than the party served by those purposes of either the purpose of the contract or the circumstances in which it was concluded.

30.   As a preliminary point, it must be recalled that Title II, Section 4, of the Brussels Convention lays down the rules of jurisdiction for consumer contracts. The notion of a consumer contract is defined, as shown by the wording of the first paragraph of Article 13 of the Convention, as a contract concluded by a person for a purpose which can be regarded as being outside his trade or profession.

31.   According to settled case-law, the concepts used in the Brussels Convention—which include, in particular, that of consumer for the purposes of Articles 13 to 15 of that Convention—must

be interpreted independently, by reference principally to the scheme and purpose of the Convention, in order to ensure that it is uniformly applied in all the Contracting States....

32. First of all, within the scheme of the Brussels Convention, the jurisdiction of the courts of the Contracting State in which the defendant is domiciled constitutes the general principle enshrined in the first paragraph of Article 2, and it is only by way of derogation from that principle that the Convention provides for an exhaustive list of cases in which the defendant may or must be sued before the courts of another Contracting State. As a consequence, the rules of jurisdiction which derogate from that general principle are to be strictly interpreted, so that they cannot give rise to an interpretation going beyond the cases envisaged by the Convention (see, in particular, Case 150/77 *Bertrand* [1978] ECR 1431, paragraph 17; Case C–89/91 *Shearson Lehman Hutton* [1993] ECR I–139, paragraphs 14, 15 and 16; Case C269/95 *Benincasa* [1997] ECR I–3767, paragraph 13; and Case C–99/96 *Mietz* [1999] ECR I2277, paragraph 27).

33. That interpretation must apply a fortiori with respect to a rule of jurisdiction, such as that contained in Article 14 of the Convention, which allows a consumer, within the meaning of the first paragraph of Article 13 of the Convention, to sue the defendant in the courts of the Contracting State in which the claimant is domiciled. Apart from the cases expressly provided for, the Convention does not appear to favour the attribution of jurisdiction to the courts of the claimant's domicile....

34. Second, the Court has repeatedly held that the special rules introduced by the provisions of Title II, Section 4, of the Brussels Convention, which derogate from the general rule laid down in the first paragraph of Article 2, and from the rules of special jurisdiction for contracts in general enshrined in Article 5(1) of the Convention, serve to ensure adequate protection for the consumer as the party deemed to be economically weaker and less experienced in legal matters than the other, commercial, party to the contract, who must not therefore be discouraged from suing by being compelled to bring his action before the courts in the Contracting State in which the other party to the contract is domiciled (see in particular, *Shearson Lehman Hutton*, paragraph 18 ...).

35. From the scheme of the rules of jurisdiction put in place by the Brussels Convention, as well as the rationale of the special rules introduced by the provisions of Title II, Section 4, the Court has concluded that those provisions only cover private final consumers, not engaged in trade or professional activities, as the benefit of those provisions must not be extended to persons for whom special protection is not justified (see to that effect *inter alia*

Bertrand, paragraph 21; *Shearson Lehman Hutton*, paragraphs 19 and 22 ...).

36.   In paragraphs 16 to 18 of the judgment in *Benincasa* the Court stated in that respect that the concept of consumer for the purposes of the first paragraph of Article 13 and the first paragraph of Article 14 of the Brussels Convention must be strictly construed, reference being made to the position of the person concerned in a particular contract, having regard to the nature and aim of that contract and not to the subjective situation of the person concerned, since the same person may be regarded as a consumer in relation to certain supplies and as an economic operator in relation to others. The Court held that only contracts concluded outside and independently of any trade or professional activity or purpose, solely for the purpose of satisfying an individual's own needs in terms of private consumption, are covered by the special rules laid down by the Convention to protect the consumer as the party deemed to be the weaker party. Such protection is unwarranted in the case of contracts for the purpose of a trade or professional activity.

37.   It follows that the special rules of jurisdiction in Articles 13 to 15 of the Brussels Convention apply, in principle, only where the contract is concluded between the parties for the purpose of a use other than a trade or professional one of the relevant goods or services.

38.   It is in the light of those principles that it is appropriate to examine whether and to what extent a contract such as that at issue in the main proceedings, which relates to activities of a partly professional and partly private nature, may be covered by the special rules of jurisdiction laid down in Articles 13 to 15.

39.   In that regard, it is already clearly apparent from the purpose of Articles 13 to 15 of the Brussels Convention, namely to properly protect the person who is presumed to be in a weaker position than the other party to the contract, that the benefit of those provisions cannot, as a matter of principle, be relied on by a person who concludes a contract for a purpose which is partly concerned with his trade or profession and is therefore only partly outside it. It would be otherwise only if the link between the contract and the trade or profession of the person concerned was so slight as to be marginal and, therefore, had only a negligible role in the context of the supply in respect of which the contract was concluded, considered in its entirety.

40.   [I]nasmuch as a contract is entered into for the person's trade or professional purposes, he must be deemed to be on an equal footing with the other party to the contract, so that the

special protection reserved by the Brussels Convention for consumers is not justified in such a case.

41.   That is in no way altered by the fact that the contract at issue also has a private purpose, and it remains relevant whatever the relationship between the private and professional use of the goods or service concerned, and even though the private use is predominant, as long as the proportion of the professional usage is not negligible.

42.   Accordingly, where a contract has a dual purpose, it is not necessary that the purpose of the goods or services for professional purposes be predominant for Articles 13 to 15 of the Convention not to be applicable.

43.   That interpretation is supported by the fact that the definition of the notion of consumer in the first paragraph of Article 13 of the Brussels Convention is worded in clearly restrictive terms, using a negative turn of phrase ("contract concluded . . . for a purpose . . . outside [the] trade or profession"). Moreover, the definition of a contract concluded by a consumer must be strictly interpreted as it constitutes a derogation from the basic rule of jurisdiction laid down in the first paragraph of Article 2, and confers exceptional jurisdiction on the courts of the claimant's domicile (see paragraphs 32 and 33 of the present judgment).

44.   That interpretation is also dictated by the fact that classification of the contract can only be based on an overall assessment of it, since the Court has held on many occasions that avoidance of multiplication of bases of jurisdiction as regards the same legal relationship is one of the main objectives of the Brussels Convention. . . .

45.   An interpretation which denies the capacity of consumer, within the meaning of the first paragraph of Article 13 of the Brussels Convention, if the link between the purpose for which the goods or services are used and the trade or profession of the person concerned is not negligible is also that which is most consistent with the requirements of legal certainty and the requirement that a potential defendant should be able to know in advance the court before which he may be sued, which constitute the foundation of that Convention. . . .

46.   Having regard to the normal rules on the burden of proof, it is for the person wishing to rely on Articles 13 to 15 of the Brussels Convention to show that in a contract with a dual purpose the business use is only negligible, the opponent being entitled to adduce evidence to the contrary.

47.   In the light of the evidence which has thus been submitted to it, it is therefore for the court seised to decide whether the

contract was intended, to a non-negligible extent, to meet the needs of the trade or profession of the person concerned or whether, on the contrary, the business use was merely negligible. For that purpose, the national court should take into consideration not only the content, nature and purpose of the contract, but also the objective circumstances in which it was concluded.

48. Finally, as regards the national court's question as to whether it is necessary for the party to the contract other than the supposed consumer to have been aware of the purpose for which the contract was concluded and the circumstances in which it was concluded, it must be noted that, in order to facilitate as much as possible both the taking and the evaluation of the evidence, it is necessary for the court seised to base its decision mainly on the evidence which appears, de facto, in the file.

49. If that evidence is sufficient to enable the court to conclude that the contract served to a non-negligible extent the business needs of the person concerned, Articles 13 to 15 of the Brussels Convention cannot be applied in any event because of the status of those provisions as exceptions within the scheme introduced by the Convention. There is therefore no need to determine whether the other party to the contract could have been aware of the business purpose.

50. If, on the other hand, the objective evidence in the file is not sufficient to demonstrate that the supply in respect to which a contract with a dual purpose was concluded had a non-negligible business purpose, that contract should, in principle, be regarded as having been concluded by a consumer within the meaning of Articles 13 to 15, in order not to deprive those provisions of their effectiveness.

51. However, having regard to the fact that the protective scheme put in place by Articles 13 to 15 of the Brussels Convention represents a derogation, the court seised must in that case also determine whether the other party to the contract could reasonably have been unaware of the private purpose of the supply because the supposed consumer had in fact, by his own conduct with respect to the other party, given the latter the impression that he was acting for business purposes.

52. That would be the case, for example, where an individual orders, without giving further information, items which could in fact be used for his business, or uses business stationery to do so, or has goods delivered to his business address, or mentions the possibility of recovering value added tax.

53. In such a case, the special rules of jurisdiction for matters relating to consumer contracts enshrined in Articles 13 to 15 of the Brussels Convention are not applicable even if the contract does not

as such serve a non-negligible business purpose, and the individual must be regarded, in view of the impression he has given to the other party acting in good faith, as having renounced the protection afforded by those provisions.

54.   In the light of all the foregoing considerations, the answer to the first three questions must be that the rules of jurisdiction laid down by the Brussels Convention are to be interpreted as follows:

— a person who concludes a contract for goods intended for purposes which are in part within and in part outside his trade or profession may not rely on the special rules of jurisdiction laid down in Articles 13 to 15 of the Convention, unless the trade or professional purpose is so limited as to be negligible in the overall context of the supply, the fact that the private element is predominant being irrelevant in that respect;

— it is for the court seised to decide whether the contract at issue was concluded in order to satisfy, to a non-negligible extent, needs of the business of the person concerned or whether, on the contrary, the trade or professional purpose was negligible;

— to that end, that court must take account of all the relevant factual evidence objectively contained in the file. On the other hand, it must not take account of facts or circumstances of which the other party to the contract may have been aware when the contract was concluded, unless the person who claims the capacity of consumer behaved in such a way as to give the other party to the contract the legitimate impression that he was acting for the purposes of his business.

THE LAST THREE QUESTIONS

55.   Since the last three questions were referred only if the capacity of consumer within the meaning of the first paragraph of Article 13 of the Brussels Convention was established, and in view of the answer given in that respect to the first three questions, there is no longer any need to answer the last three questions, relating to the other conditions for the application of that provision.

———

Notes

6–18.   Would the ECJ have reached a different result in *Gruber* if the Regulation were applicable, instead of the Convention? (Do the textual changes affect the scope of whether the contract regards one's "trade or profession"?)

6–19.   Would there have been personal jurisdiction if Mr. Gruber had added a claim for fraud, an intentional tort?

6–20.   Many thoughtful commentators question the level of certainty accomplished by the Regulation and even by codes generally. Can codes remove ambiguity and complexity? Is there such thing as "mechanical application" where the stakes of litigation are often very high and creative lawyering rewarded so handsomely? Moreover, life is complicated, and the unimaginable is inevitable: how can codes contemplate the endless number of scenarios that might be presented?

6–21.   How would a case with these facts have been decided by a United States court under a Fourteenth Amendment Due Process analysis? Substitute New Jersey for Germany, and New York for Austria; and assume a long-arm statute that extends to the constitutional limits.

6–22.   Consider the methodology and structure of the ECJ opinion. In what ways is the opinion similar to the American common law model? And how does it differ? (Consider the invocation of precedent, the method of statutory interpretation, the use of dicta, writing style and organization.)

D.   FORUM NON CONVENIENS

In most common law countries the doctrine of forum non conveniens is an important part of the jurisdictional analysis. A plaintiff in a given case may be able to persuade the court that it would not violate due process for the court to exercise personal jurisdiction over the defendant, yet the defendant can get the case dismissed nevertheless by persuading the court that there is a more appropriate forum for the litigation. Over time, this doctrinal analysis has evolved from a more rigid form applicable only in exceptional cases where the suit is vexatious or oppressive to a much more fluid form that requires a balancing of various interests and factors.

Yet the civil law systems generally have no such mechanism. Is this because the discretionary decline of jurisdiction is a bad idea? Do the more focused jurisdictional rules of the civil law tradition obviate the need for such a doctrine? The following case stands at the intersection of the civil law and common law traditions. Although English courts have long recognized the doctrine of forum non conveniens, the doctrine is not codified in the Brussels Regulation. The Regulation does not apply in purely domestic cases, however. Accordingly, whether an English judge has the discretionary authority to decline to hear a case can depend on whether the case falls outside or inside the scope of the Regulation. In the case that follows, an English plaintiff is pursuing claims against English and Jamaican defendants. Of course, Jamaica is not a Member State of the European Union. The issue before the ECJ is whether the English court has the authority to decline jurisdiction on grounds of forum non conveniens. Again the ECJ is applying the Brussels Convention; the corresponding provisions of the Regulation are substantially similar.

OWUSU v. JACKSON ET AL.

[2005] ECJ C–281/02

Reference for a preliminary ruling under the Protocol of 3 June 1971 on the interpretation by the Court of Justice of the Convention of 27 September 1968 on Jurisdiction and the Enforcement of Judgments in Civil and Commercial Matters by the Court of Appeal (England and Wales) Civil Division (United Kingdom)....

THE COURT (GRAND CHAMBER), COMPOSED OF P. JANN, PRESIDENT OF THE FIRST CHAMBER, ACTING FOR THE PRESIDENT, C.W.A. TIMMERMANS AND A. ROSAS, PRESIDENTS OF CHAMBERS, C. GULMANN, J.-P. PUISSOCHET, R. SCHINTGEN (RAPPORTEUR), N. COLNERIC, S. VON BAHR AND J.N. CUNHA RODRIGUES, JUDGES.

1.   This reference for a preliminary ruling concerns the interpretation of Article 2 of the Convention of 27 September 1968 on Jurisdiction and the Enforcement of Judgments in Civil and Commercial Matters (OJ 1978 L 304, p. 36), as amended.

2.   The reference was made in the course of proceedings brought by Mr Owusu against Mr Jackson, trading as Villa Holidays Bal–Inn Villas, and several companies governed by Jamaican law, following an accident suffered by Mr Owusu in Jamaica.

LEGAL BACKGROUND

The Brussels Convention

3.   According to its preamble the Brussels Convention is intended to facilitate the reciprocal recognition and enforcement of judgments of courts or tribunals, in accordance with Article 293 EC, and to strengthen in the Community the legal protection of persons therein established. The preamble also states that it is necessary for that purpose to determine the international jurisdiction of the courts of the contracting States.

4.   The provisions relating to jurisdiction appear in Title II of the Brussels Convention. According to Article 2 of the Convention:

> Subject to the provisions of this Convention, persons domiciled in a Contracting State shall, whatever their nationality, be sued in the courts of that State.

> Persons who are not nationals of the State in which they are domiciled shall be governed by the rules of jurisdiction applicable to nationals of that State.

5. However, Article 5(1) and (3) of that convention provides that a defendant may be sued in another Contracting State, in matters relating to a contract, in the courts for the place of performance of the obligation in question, and, in matters relating to tort, delict or quasi-delict, in the courts for the place where the harmful event occurred.

6. The Brussels Convention is also intended to prevent conflicting decisions. Thus, according to Article 21, which concerns lis pendens:

Where proceedings involving the same cause of action and between the same parties are brought in the courts of different Contracting States, any court other than the court first seised shall of its own motion stay its proceedings until such time as the jurisdiction of the court first seised is established.

Where the jurisdiction of the court first seised is established, any court other than the court first seised shall decline jurisdiction in favour of that court.

7. Article 22 of the Convention provides:

Where related actions are brought in the courts of different Contracting States, any court other than the court first seised may, while the actions are pending at first instance, stay its proceedings.

A court other than the court first seised may also, on the application of one of the parties, decline jurisdiction if the law of that court permits the consolidation of related actions and the court first seised has jurisdiction over both actions.

For the purposes of this article, actions are deemed to be related where they are so closely connected that it is expedient to hear and determine them together to avoid the risk of irreconcilable judgments resulting from separate proceedings.

National law

8. According to the doctrine of forum non conveniens, as understood in English law, a national court may decline to exercise jurisdiction on the ground that a court in another State, which also has jurisdiction, would objectively be a more appropriate forum for the trial of the action, that is to say, a forum in which the case may be tried more suitably for the interests of all the parties and the ends of justice (1986 judgment of the House of Lords, in *Spiliada Maritime Corporation v Cansulex Ltd* [1987], AC 460, particularly at p. 476).

9. An English court which decides to decline jurisdiction under the doctrine of forum non conveniens stays proceedings so that the proceedings which are thus provisionally suspended can be

resumed should it prove, in particular, that the foreign forum has no jurisdiction to hear the case or that the claimant has no access to effective justice in that forum.

THE MAIN PROCEEDINGS AND THE QUESTIONS
REFERRED FOR A PRELIMINARY RULING

10.   On 10 October 1997, Mr Owusu (the claimant), a British national domiciled in the United Kingdom, suffered a very serious accident during a holiday in Jamaica. He walked into the sea, and when the water was up to his waist he dived in, struck his head against a submerged sand bank and sustained a fracture of his fifth cervical vertebra which rendered him tetraplegic.

11.   Following that accident, Mr Owusu brought an action in the United Kingdom for breach of contract against Mr Jackson, who is also domiciled in that State. Mr Jackson had let to Mr Owusu a holiday villa in Mammee Bay (Jamaica). Mr Owusu claims that the contract, which provided that he would have access to a private beach, contained an implied term that the beach would be reasonably safe or free from hidden dangers.

12.   Mr Owusu also brought an action in tort in the United Kingdom against several Jamaican companies, namely Mammee Bay Club Ltd (the third defendant), the owner and occupier of the beach at Mammee Bay which provided the claimant with free access to the beach, The Enchanted Garden Resorts & Spa Ltd (the fourth defendant), which operates a holiday complex close to Mammee Bay, and whose guests were also licensed to use the beach, and Town & Country Resorts Ltd (the sixth defendant), which operates a large hotel adjoining the beach, and which has a licence to use the beach, subject to the condition that it is responsible for its management, upkeep and control.

13.   According to the file, another English holidaymaker had suffered a similar accident two years earlier in which she, too, was rendered tetraplegic. The action in tort against the Jamaican defendants therefore embraces not only a contention that they failed to warn swimmers of the hazard constituted by the submerged sand bank, but also a contention that they failed to heed the earlier accident.

14.   The proceedings were commenced by a claim form issued out of Sheffield District Registry of the High Court (England and Wales) Civil Division on 6 October 2000. They were served on Mr Jackson in the United Kingdom and, on 12 December 2000, leave was granted to the claimant to serve the proceedings on the other defendants in Jamaica. Service was effected on the third, fourth and sixth defendants, but not on Mammee Bay Resorts Ltd or Consulting Services Ltd.

15.   Mr Jackson and the third, fourth and sixth defendants applied to that court for a declaration that it should not exercise its jurisdiction in relation to the claim against them both. In support of their applications, they argued that the case had closer links with Jamaica and that the Jamaican courts were a forum with jurisdiction in which the case might be tried more suitably for the interests of all the parties and the ends of justice.

16.   By order of 16 October 2001, the Judge sitting as Deputy High Court Judge in Sheffield (United Kingdom) held that it was clear from Case C–412/98 *UGIC v Group Josi* [2000] ECR I–5925, paragraphs 59 to 61, that the application of the jurisdictional rules in the Brussels Convention to a dispute depended, in principle, on whether the defendant had its seat or domicile in a Contracting State, and that the Convention applied to a dispute between a defendant domiciled in a Contracting State and a claimant domiciled in a non-Contracting State. In those circumstances the decision of the Court of Appeal in *In re Harrods (Buenos Aires) Ltd* [1992] Ch 72, which accepted that it was possible for the English courts, applying the doctrine of forum non conveniens, to decline to exercise the jurisdiction conferred on them by Article 2 of the Brussels Convention, was bad law.

17.   Taking the view that he had no power himself under Article 2 of the Protocol of 3 June 1971 to refer a question to the Court of Justice for a preliminary ruling to clarify this point, the Judge sitting as Deputy High Court Judge held that, in the light of the principles laid down in *Group Josi*, it was not open to him to stay the action against Mr Jackson since he was domiciled in a Contracting State.

18.   Notwithstanding the connecting factors that the action brought against the other defendants might have with Jamaica, the judge held that he was also unable to stay the action against them, in so far as the Brussels Convention precluded him from staying proceedings in the action against Mr Jackson. Otherwise, there would be a risk that the courts in two jurisdictions would end up trying the same factual issues upon the same or similar evidence and reach different conclusions. He therefore held that the United Kingdom, and not Jamaica was the State with the appropriate forum to try the action and dismissed the applications for a declaration that the court should not exercise jurisdiction.

19.   Mr Jackson and the third, fourth and sixth defendants appealed against that order. The Court of Appeal (England and Wales) Civil Division states that, in this case, the competing jurisdictions are a Contracting State and a non-Contracting State. If Article 2 of the Brussels Convention is mandatory, even in this context, Mr Jackson would have to be sued in the United Kingdom

before the courts of his domicile and it would not be open to the claimant to sue him under Article 5(3) of the Brussels Convention in Jamaica, where the harmful event occurred, because that State is not another Contracting State. In the absence of an express derogation to that effect in the Convention, it is therefore not permissible to create an exception to the rule in Article 2. According to the referring court, the question of the application of forum non conveniens in favour of the courts of a non-Contracting State, when one of the defendants is domiciled in a Contracting State, is not a matter on which the Court of Justice has ever given a ruling.

20.   According to the claimant, Article 2 of the Brussels Convention is of mandatory application, so that the English courts cannot stay proceedings in the United Kingdom against a defendant domiciled there, even though the English court takes the view that another forum in a non-Contracting State is more appropriate.

21.   The referring court points out that if that position were correct it might have serious consequences in a number of other situations concerning exclusive jurisdiction or lis pendens. It adds that a judgment delivered in England, deciding the case, which was to be enforced in Jamaica, particularly as regards the Jamaican defendants, would encounter difficulty over certain rules in force in that country on the recognition and enforcement of foreign judgments.

22.   Against that background, the Court of Appeal decided to stay its proceedings and to refer the following questions to the Court for a preliminary ruling:

> 1.   Is it inconsistent with the Brussels Convention ... , where a claimant contends that jurisdiction is founded on Article 2, for a court of a Contracting State to exercise a discretionary power, available under its national law, to decline to hear proceedings brought against a person domiciled in that State in favour of the courts of a non-Contracting State:
>
> > (a) if the jurisdiction of no other Contracting State under the 1968 Convention is in issue;
> >
> > (b) if the proceedings have no connecting factors to any other Contracting State?
>
> 2.   If the answer to question 1(a) or (b) is yes, is it inconsistent in all circumstances or only in some and if so which?

ON THE QUESTIONS REFERRED

The first question

23.   In order to reply to the first question it must first be determined whether Article 2 of the Brussels Convention is applica-

ble in circumstances such as those in the main proceedings, that is to say, where the claimant and one of the defendants are domiciled in the same Contracting State and the case between them before the courts of that State has certain connecting factors with a non-Contracting State, but not with another Contracting State. Only if it is will the question arise whether, in the circumstances of the case in the main proceedings, the Brussels Convention precludes the application by a court of a Contracting State of the forum non conveniens doctrine where Article 2 of that convention would permit that court to claim jurisdiction because the defendant is domiciled in that State.

The applicability of Article 2 of the Brussels Convention

24.   Nothing in the wording of Article 2 of the Brussels Convention suggests that the application of the general rule of jurisdiction laid down by that article solely on the basis of the defendant's domicile in a Contracting State is subject to the condition that there should be a legal relationship involving a number of Contracting States.

25.   Of course, as is clear from the Jenard report on the Convention (OJ 1979 C 59, pp. 1, 8), for the jurisdiction rules of the Brussels Convention to apply at all the existence of an international element is required.

26.   However, the international nature of the legal relationship at issue need not necessarily derive, for the purposes of the application of Article 2 of the Brussels Convention, from the involvement, either because of the subject-matter of the proceedings or the respective domiciles of the parties, of a number of Contracting States. The involvement of a Contracting State and a non-Contracting State, for example because the claimant and one defendant are domiciled in the first State and the events at issue occurred in the second, would also make the legal relationship at issue international in nature. That situation is such as to raise questions in the Contracting State, as it does in the main proceedings, relating to the determination of international jurisdiction, which is precisely one of the objectives of the Brussels Convention, according to the third recital in its preamble....

34.   [T]he uniform rules of jurisdiction contained in the Brussels Convention are not intended to apply only to situations in which there is a real and sufficient link with the working of the internal market, by definition involving a number of Member States. Suffice it to observe in that regard that the consolidation as such of the rules on conflict of jurisdiction and on the recognition and enforcement of judgments, effected by the Brussels Convention in respect of cases with an international element, is without doubt

intended to eliminate obstacles to the functioning of the internal market which may derive from disparities between national legislations on the subject (see, by analogy, as regards harmonisation directives based on Article 95 EC intended to improve the conditions for the establishment and working of the internal market, Joined Cases C–465/00, C138/01 and C–139/01 *Osterreichischer Rundfunk and Others* [2003] ECR I4989, paragraphs 41 and 42).

35.   It follows from the foregoing that Article 2 of the Brussels Convention applies to circumstances such as those in the main proceedings, involving relationships between the courts of a single Contracting State and those of a non-Contracting State rather than relationships between the courts of a number of Contracting States.

36.   It must therefore be considered whether, in such circumstances, the Brussels Convention precludes a court of a Contracting State from applying the forum non conveniens doctrine and declining to exercise the jurisdiction conferred on it by Article 2 of that Convention.

The compatibility of the forum non conveniens doctrine with the Brussels Convention

37.   It must be observed, first, that Article 2 of the Brussels Convention is mandatory in nature and that, according to its terms, there can be no derogation from the principle it lays down except in the cases expressly provided for by the Convention (see, as regards the compulsory system of jurisdiction set up by the Brussels Convention, Case C–116/02 *Gasser* [2003] ECR I–0000, paragraph 72, and Case C–159/02 *Turner* [2004] ECR I–0000, paragraph 24). It is common ground that no exception on the basis of the forum non conveniens doctrine was provided for by the authors of the Convention, although the question was discussed when the Convention of 9 October 1978 on the Accession of Denmark, Ireland and the United Kingdom was drawn up, as is apparent from the report on that Convention by Professor Schlosser (OJ 1979 C 59, p. 71, paragraphs 77 and 78).

38.   Respect for the principle of legal certainty, which is one of the objectives of the Brussels Convention (see, inter alia, Case C–440/97 *GIE Groupe Concorde and Others* [1999] ECR I6307, paragraph 23, and Case C–256/00 *Besix* [2002] ECR I1699, paragraph 24), would not be fully guaranteed if the court having jurisdiction under the Convention had to be allowed to apply the forum non conveniens doctrine.

39.   According to its preamble, the Brussels Convention is intended to strengthen in the Community the legal protection of persons established therein, by laying down common rules on jurisdiction to guarantee certainty as to the allocation of jurisdic-

tion among the various national courts before which proceedings in a particular case may be brought (*Besix*, paragraph 25).

40.   The Court has thus held that the principle of legal certainty requires, in particular, that the jurisdictional rules which derogate from the general rule laid down in Article 2 of the Brussels Convention should be interpreted in such a way as to enable a normally well-informed defendant reasonably to foresee before which courts, other than those of the State in which he is domiciled, he may be sued (*GIE Groupe Concorde and Others*, paragraph 24, and *Besix*, paragraph 26).

41.   Application of the forum non conveniens doctrine, which allows the court seised a wide discretion as regards the question whether a foreign court would be a more appropriate forum for the trial of an action, is liable to undermine the predictability of the rules of jurisdiction laid down by the Brussels Convention, in particular that of Article 2, and consequently to undermine the principle of legal certainty, which is the basis of the Convention.

42.   The legal protection of persons established in the Community would also be undermined. First, a defendant, who is generally better placed to conduct his defence before the courts of his domicile, would not be able, in circumstances such as those of the main proceedings, reasonably to foresee before which other court he may be sued. Second, where a plea is raised on the basis that a foreign court is a more appropriate forum to try the action, it is for the claimant to establish that he will not be able to obtain justice before that foreign court or, if the court seised decides to allow the plea, that the foreign court has in fact no jurisdiction to try the action or that the claimant does not, in practice, have access to effective justice before that court, irrespective of the cost entailed by the bringing of a fresh action before a court of another State and the prolongation of the procedural time-limits.

43.   Moreover, allowing forum non conveniens in the context of the Brussels Convention would be likely to affect the uniform application of the rules of jurisdiction contained therein in so far as that doctrine is recognised only in a limited number of Contracting States, whereas the objective of the Brussels Convention is precisely to lay down common rules to the exclusion of derogating national rules.

44.   The defendants in the main proceedings emphasise the negative consequences which would result in practice from the obligation the English courts would then be under to try this case, inter alia as regards the expense of the proceedings, the possibility of recovering their costs in England if the claimant's action is dismissed, the logistical difficulties resulting from the geographical distance, the need to assess the merits of the case according to

Jamaican standards, the enforceability in Jamaica of a default judgment and the impossibility of enforcing cross-claims against the other defendants.

45. In that regard, genuine as those difficulties may be, suffice it to observe that such considerations, which are precisely those which may be taken into account when forum non conveniens is considered, are not such as to call into question the mandatory nature of the fundamental rule of jurisdiction contained in Article 2 of the Brussels Convention, for the reasons set out above.

46. In the light of all the foregoing considerations, the answer to the first question must be that the Brussels Convention precludes a court of a Contracting State from declining the jurisdiction conferred on it by Article 2 of that convention on the ground that a court of a non-Contracting State would be a more appropriate forum for the trial of the action even if the jurisdiction of no other Contracting State is in issue or the proceedings have no connecting factors to any other Contracting State.

The second question

47. By its second question, the referring court seeks essentially to know whether, if the Court takes the view that the Brussels Convention precludes the application of forum non conveniens, its application is ruled out in all circumstances or only in certain circumstances.

48. According to the order for reference and the observations of the defendants in the main proceedings and of the United Kingdom Government, that second question was asked in connection with cases where there were identical or related proceedings pending before a court of a non-Contracting State, a convention granting jurisdiction to such a court or a connection with that State of the same type as those referred to in Article 16 of the Brussels Convention. . . .

51. In the present case, it is common ground that the factual circumstances described in paragraph 48 of this judgment are not the same as those of the main proceedings.

52. Accordingly there is no need to reply to the second question.

––––––––

Notes

6–23. The ECJ emphasizes the importance of the principle of certainty. (*See* paragraphs 38–41 of the opinion) Are common law systems that recognize the doctrine of forum non conveniens less committed to the principle of certainty? What principles are advanced by the doctrine of forum non conveniens? Are these principles more compelling than the principle of certainty?

6–24. The Brussels I Regulation and some civil codes recognize a related doctrine, lis pendens, that authorizes a stay of an action in favor of a similar action that is already pending in the court of another state. Note that the court issues a stay instead of a dismissal. Understand also that a similar action must be pending to justify the stay. In situations where related actions are pending, Article 27 of the Brussels I Regulation assigns the case to the court that first exercised jurisdiction.

Chapter 7

SERVICE UPON FOREIGN DEFENDANTS

The service of a summons and complaint formally notifies the defendant of the filing of an action. Service is also an exercise of the authority of the court, because process demands a response from the defendant. Federal Rule 4 details the provisions regarding service of various types of defendants and service in various locations. In most cases, service in a foreign country is facilitated by a Hague Convention that provides a uniform framework for serving process in civil or commercial cases upon defendants located in any of the dozens of Contracting States (including the United States).* The framework is relatively straightforward and the Convention is generally considered to have been a success.

HAGUE CONVENTION ON THE SERVICE ABROAD OF JUDICIAL AND EXTRAJUDICIAL DOCUMENTS IN CIVIL OR COMMERCIAL MATTERS

(1969)

Article 1

The present Convention shall apply in all cases, in civil or commercial matters, where there is occasion to transmit a judicial or extrajudicial document for service abroad.

This Convention shall not apply where the address of the person to be served with the document is not known.

---

* The Hague Conference on Private International Law maintains an excellent website, including a list of the contracting states to conventions such as the Convention on Service Abroad of Judicial and Extrajudicial Documents. *See* http://www.hcch.net (last visited October 1, 2005).

Article 2

Each Contracting State shall designate a Central Authority which will undertake to receive requests for service coming from other Contracting States and to proceed in conformity with the provisions of Articles 3 to 6.

Each State shall organise the Central Authority in conformity with its own law.

Article 3

The authority or judicial officer competent under the law of the State in which the documents originate shall forward to the Central Authority of the State addressed a request conforming to the model annexed to the present Convention, without any requirement of legalisation or other equivalent formality.

The document to be served or a copy thereof shall be annexed to the request. The request and the document shall both be furnished in duplicate.

Article 4

If the Central Authority considers that the request does not comply with the provisions of the present Convention it shall promptly inform the applicant and specify its objections to the request.

Article 5

The Central Authority of the State addressed shall itself serve the document or shall arrange to have it served by an appropriate agency, either—

a) by a method prescribed by its internal law for the service of documents in domestic actions upon persons who are within its territory, or

b) by a particular method requested by the applicant, unless such a method is incompatible with the law of the State addressed.

Subject to sub-paragraph (b) of the first paragraph of this Article, the document may always be served by delivery to an addressee who accepts it voluntarily.

If the document is to be served under the first paragraph above, the Central Authority may require the document to be written in, or translated into, the official language or one of the official languages of the State addressed.

That part of the request, in the form attached to the present Convention, which contains a summary of the document to be served, shall be served with the document.

Article 6

The Central Authority of the State addressed or any authority which it may have designated for that purpose, shall complete a certificate in the form of the model annexed to the present Convention.

The certificate shall state that the document has been served and shall include the method, the place and the date of service and the person to whom the document was delivered. If the document has not been served, the certificate shall set out the reasons which have prevented service.

The applicant may require that a certificate not completed by a Central Authority or by a judicial authority shall be countersigned by one of these authorities.

The certificate shall be forwarded directly to the applicant.

Article 7

The standard terms in the model annexed to the present Convention shall in all cases be written either in French or in English. They may also be written in the official language, or in one of the official languages, of the State in which the documents originate.

The corresponding blanks shall be completed either in the language of the State addressed or in French or in English.

Article 8

Each Contracting State shall be free to effect service of judicial documents upon persons abroad, without application of any compulsion, directly through its diplomatic or consular agents.

Any State may declare that it is opposed to such service within its territory, unless the document is to be served upon a national of the State in which the documents originate.

Article 9

Each Contracting State shall be free, in addition, to use consular channels to forward documents, for the purpose of service, to those authorities of another Contracting State which are designated by the latter for this purpose.

Each Contracting State may, if exceptional circumstances so require, use diplomatic channels for the same purpose.

Article 10

Provided the State of destination does not object, the present Convention shall not interfere with—

(a) the freedom to send judicial documents, by postal channels, directly to persons abroad,

(b) the freedom of judicial officers, officials or other competent persons of the State of origin to effect service of judicial documents directly through the judicial officers, officials or other competent persons of the State of destination,

(c) the freedom of any person interested in a judicial proceeding to effect service of judicial documents directly through the judicial officers, officials or other competent persons of the State of destination.

Article 11

The present Convention shall not prevent two or more Contracting States from agreeing to permit, for the purpose of service of judicial documents, channels of transmission other than those provided for in the preceding Articles and, in particular, direct communication between their respective authorities. . . .

Article 12

The service of judicial documents coming from a contracting State shall not give rise to any payment or reimbursement of taxes or costs for the services rendered by the State addressed. The applicant shall pay or reimburse the costs occasioned by—

(a) the employment of a judicial officer or of a person competent under the law of the state of destination,

(b) the use of a particular method of service.

Article 13

Where a request for service complies with the terms of the present Convention, the State addressed may refuse to comply therewith only if it deems that compliance would infringe its sovereignty or security.

It may not refuse to comply solely on the ground that, under its internal law, it claims exclusive jurisdiction over the subject-matter of the action or that its internal law would not permit the action upon which the application is based.

The Central Authority shall, in case of refusal, promptly inform the applicant and state the reasons for the refusal. . . .

Article 19

To the extent that the internal law of a Contracting State permits methods of transmission, other than those provided for in the preceding Articles, of documents coming from abroad, for service within its territory, the present Convention shall not affect such provisions.

Article 20

The present Convention shall not prevent an agreement between any two or more Contracting States to dispense with—

a) the necessity for duplicate copies of transmitted documents as required by the second paragraph of Article 3,

b) the language requirements of the third paragraph of Article 5 and Article 7,

c) the provisions of the fourth paragraph of Article 5,

d) the provisions of the second paragraph of Article 12.

———

Of course, not all countries where service needs to be effected are Contracting States. And even in federal litigation matters involving defendants in Contracting States, FRCP 4 contemplates methods of service other than the procedures outlined in the Convention. The *Brockmeyer* and *Prewitt Enterprises* opinions, reprinted below, discuss several methods of service upon foreign defendants.

BROCKMEYER v. MAY

383 F.3d 798 (9th Cir. 2004)

WILLIAM A. FLETCHER, CIRCUIT JUDGE:

Plaintiffs in this case attempted to serve process on an English defendant by using ordinary first class mail to send a summons and complaint from the United States to England. We join the Second Circuit in concluding that the Convention on the Service Abroad of Judicial and Extrajudicial Documents ("Hague Convention," or the "Convention") does not prohibit—or, in the words of the Convention, does not "interfere with"—service of process by international mail. But this conclusion tells us only that the Hague Convention does not prohibit such service. For service by international mail to be effective in federal court, it must also be affirmatively authorized by some provision in federal law.

Federal Rule of Civil Procedure 4 governs service of process in federal district court. In this case, after determining that the Hague

Convention does not prohibit service by international mail, the necessary next step is to analyze Rule 4(f) to determine whether it affirmatively authorizes such service. The plaintiffs' attempted service fails because they failed to follow the requirements of that rule. We therefore reverse and remand to the district court with instructions to vacate the judgment.

I.   BACKGROUND: PLAINTIFFS' ATTEMPTS TO SERVE PROCESS

Ronald B. Brockmeyer is the owner of the trademark <<O>>, under which he publishes and distributes adult entertainment media and novelties. On August 3, 1998, Brockmeyer and his company, Eromedia, filed suit against Marquis Publications, Ltd. ("Marquis") and several other defendants in federal district court in the Southern District of New York, alleging trademark infringement and various state-law causes of action. Marquis is a company registered under British law. Plaintiffs' counsel made two attempts to serve on Marquis.

Plaintiffs' counsel made his first attempt on October 7, 1998. He sent the summons and complaint, together with a request for waiver of service, by ordinary first class mail to a post office box in England. Marquis did not respond.

On April 5, 1999, the district court in New York transferred the suit to the Central District of California. On October 6, 1999, the district court in California entered an order to show cause ("OSC") why the suit should not be dismissed for lack of prosecution. Plaintiffs were required to respond to the OSC by October 25, 1999.

Plaintiffs' counsel made his second attempt at service four days before the OSC deadline, on October 21, 1999. This time, instead of sending the summons and complaint together with a request for waiver of service, he sent only the summons and complaint. He sent them by first class mail to the same post office box in England to which he had previously sent the request for waiver. Marquis still did not respond.

Default was entered by the court clerk against several defendants (not including Marquis) on November 24, 1999. Default was entered against Marquis a year later, on November 8, 2000. On February 22, 2002, the district court entered a default judgment of $410,806.12, plus attorneys' fees and costs, against Marquis and two German defendants.

The German defendants moved to set aside the default judgment against them. On June 6, 2002, the district court granted the motion on the ground that they had not been properly served under the Hague Convention and German law. The court ordered plaintiffs to serve the German defendants properly within 90 days or face dismissal. The district court subsequently gave plaintiffs a two-month extension until November 4, 2002. Seven days before the expiration of the extended deadline, plaintiffs' counsel finally submitted documents to the German Central Authority for service. The Central Authority rejected the documents the same day for failure to comply with German law. Almost two months later, plaintiffs' counsel resubmitted documents to the German Central Authority. Nothing in the record indicates whether these resubmitted documents complied with German law. On January 2, 2003, the district court dismissed the suit against the German defendants for failure to serve process within the time allowed under the extended deadline. Plaintiffs have not appealed that dismissal.

Marquis moved independently to set aside the default judgment against it. Among other things, Marquis contended that international mail service must be made by certified or registered mail. On June 26, 2002, the district court denied Marquis's motion, holding that plaintiffs' second attempt at service had been successful. It ruled that mail service is not forbidden by the Hague Convention, and that service on an English defendant by ordinary international first class mail is proper.

Marquis appeals the district court's denial of its motion to set aside plaintiffs' default judgment. We have jurisdiction pursuant to 29 U.S.C. § 1291. Once service is challenged, plaintiffs bear the burden of establishing that service was valid under Rule 4.

II. DISCUSSION

A. *The Hague Convention*

The resolution of this appeal depends on whether Marquis was properly served. Because service of process was attempted abroad, the validity of that service is controlled by the Hague Convention, to the extent that the Convention applies. *Volkswagenwerk Aktiengesellschaft v. Schlunk*, 486 U.S. 694, 705 (1988) ("[C]ompliance with the Convention is mandatory in all cases to which it applies.").

The Hague Convention, ratified by the United States in 1965, regularized and liberalized service of process in international civil suits. The primary means by which service is accomplished under the Convention is through a receiving country's "Central Authority." The Convention affirmatively requires each member country to designate a Central Authority to receive documents from another member country. *See* Hague Convention, art. 2. The receiving country can impose certain requirements with respect to those documents (for example, that they be translated into the language of that country). *See id.*, art. 5. If the documents comply with applicable requirements, the Convention affirmatively requires the

Central Authority to effect service in its country. *See id.*, arts. 4 & 5.

The Convention also provides that it does not "interfere with" other methods of serving documents. Article 10(a) of the Convention recites:

Provided the State of destination does not object, the present Convention shall *not interfere with*—

(a) the freedom to *send* judicial documents, by postal channels, directly to persons abroad.

(Emphasis added.) American courts have disagreed about whether the phrase "the freedom to *send* judicial documents" in Article 10(a) includes within its meaning the freedom to *serve* judicial documents.

One line of cases follows *Bankston v. Toyota Motor Corp.*, 889 F.2d 172, 173–74 (8th Cir. 1989). In *Bankston,* the Eighth Circuit held that the meaning of the word "send" in Article 10(a) does not include "serve"; that is, it held that "send" permitted the sending of judicial documents by mail, but only after service of process was accomplished by some other means. In *Nuovo Pignone v. Storman Asia M/V,* 310 F.3d 374, 384 (5th Cir. 2002), the Fifth Circuit similarly held that a strict reading of the Hague Convention did not permit an Italian plaintiff who filed suit in the United States to serve an Italian defendant in Italy by Federal Express.

A second line of cases follows *Ackermann v. Levine,* 788 F.2d 830, 838 (2d Cir. 1986), in which the Second Circuit approved a German plaintiff's service of process by mail, when the plaintiff filed suit in Germany and served by registered mail a defendant in the United States. *Ackermann* relied primarily on the purpose and history of the convention to interpret the word "send" in Article 10(a) to include the meaning "serve." *See id.*

Whether service by mail is permitted under the Hague Convention is an open question in our circuit. We briefly discussed Article 10(a) in *Lidas, Inc. v. United States,* 238 F.3d 1076, 1084 (9th Cir. 2001), but we did not confront the question whether Article 10(a) allows service by mail. District courts within our circuit are split. . . .

Today we join the Second Circuit in holding that the meaning of "send" in Article 10(a) includes "serve." *See Ackermann,* 788 F.2d at 838. In so doing, we also join the essentially unanimous view of other member countries of the Hague Convention. *See, e.g.,* Case C–412/97, *E.D. Srl. v. Italo Fenocchio,* 1999 E.C.R. I–3845, [2000] C.M.L.R. 855 (Court of Justice of the European Communities) ("Article 10(a) of [the Hague Convention] allows service by post."); *Integral Energy & Envtl. Eng'g Ltd. v. Schenker of Canada*

Ltd., (2001) 295 A.R. 233, 2001 WL 454163 (Alberta Queens Bench) ("Article 10(a) of the Hague Convention provides that if the state of destination does not object, judicial documents may be served by postal channels"), *rev'd on other grounds,* (2001) 293 A.R. 327; *R. v. Re Recognition of an Italian Judgment,* [2002] I.L.Pr. 15, 2000 WL 33541696 (Thessaloniki Court of Appeal, Greece) ("It should be noted that the possibility of serving judicial documents in civil and commercial cases through postal channels ... is envisaged in Article 10(a) of the Hague Convention.").

We agree with the Second Circuit that this holding is consistent with the purpose of the Convention to facilitate international service of judicial documents. *See* Hague Convention, art.1 ("[T]he present Convention shall apply in all cases, in civil or commercial matters, where there is occasion to transmit a judicial or extrajudicial document for *service* abroad.") (emphasis added); *see also* 1 Moore's Federal Practice § 4.52[2][d] (stating that "it comports with the broad purpose of the Hague Convention" to construe "send" to mean "serve").

Commentaries on the history of negotiations leading to the Hague Convention further indicate that service by mail is permitted under Article 10(a). According to the official Rapporteur's report, the first paragraph of Article 10 of the draft Convention, which "except for minor editorial changes" is identical to Article 10 of the final Convention, was intended to permit service by mail. *See* 1 Bruno A. Ristau, *International Judicial Assistance* § 4–3–5, at 204–05 (2000) (quoting the Service Convention Negotiating Document) (translated from French by Ristau). A "Handbook" published by the Permanent Bureau of the Hague Convention, which summarizes meetings of a "Special Commission of Experts," states that to interpret Article 10(a) not to permit service by mail would "contradict what seems to have been the implicit understanding of the delegates at the 1977 Special Commission meeting, and indeed of the legal literature on the Convention and its predecessor treaties." Permanent Bureau of the Hague Convention, *Practical Handbook on the Operation of the Hague Convention of 15 November 1965 on the Service Abroad of Judicial and Extrajudicial Documents in Civil or Commercial Matters* 44 (1992). As further evidence of the understanding of the parties at the time the Hague Convention was signed, the United States delegate to the Hague Convention reported to Congress that Article 10(a) permitted service by mail. *See* S. Exec. R. No. 6, at 13 (1967) (statement by Philip W. Amram).

The United States government, through the State Department, has specifically disapproved the Eighth Circuit's holding in *Bankston.* On March 14, 1991, the Deputy Legal Advisor of the State Department wrote a letter to the Administrative Office of the

United States Courts. After discussing Article 10(a) and noting that Japan did not object to the use of postal channels under Article 10(a), the letter concluded:

> We therefore believe that the decision of the Court of Appeals in *Bankston* is incorrect to the extent that it suggests that the Hague Convention does not permit as a method of service of process the sending of a copy of a summons and complaint by registered mail to a defendant in a foreign country.

The letter also emphasized that, "while courts in the United States have final authority to interpret international treaties for the purposes of their application as law of the United States, they give great weight to treaty interpretations made by the Executive Branch." *See also United States v. Lombera–Camorlinga,* 206 F.3d 882, 887 (9th Cir. 2000) (en banc).

State Department circulars also indicate that service by mail is permitted in international civil litigation. *See, e.g.,* U.S. Dep't of State, *Circular: Service of Process Abroad, in Selected Materials in Int'l Litig. and Arbitration,* 688 PLI/Lit. 777, 1021 (2003). The State Department circular tailored to the United Kingdom specifies that mail service by international registered mail is allowed. U.S. State Dep't, *Judicial Assistance in the United Kingdom (England, Scotland, Wales, and Northern Ireland), in Selected Materials in Int'l Litig. & Arbitration,* 689 PLI/Lit. 13, 325 (2003).

The purpose and history of the Hague Convention, as well as the position of the United States State Department, convince us that "send" in Article 10(a) includes "serve." We therefore hold that the Convention permits—or, in the words of the Convention, does not "interfere with"—service of process by international mail, so long as the receiving country does not object.

B.   Rule 4(f): "Service Upon Individuals in a Foreign Country"

Article 10(a) does not itself affirmatively authorize international mail service. It merely provides that the Convention "shall not interfere with" the "freedom" to use postal channels if the "State of destination" does not object to their use. As the Rapporteur for the Convention wrote in explaining Article 10(a), "It should be stressed that in permitting the utilization of postal channels, ... the draft convention did not intend to pass on the validity of this mode of transmission under the law of the forum state: *in order for the postal channel to be utilized, it is necessary that it be authorized by the law of the forum state.*" 1 Ristau § 4–3–5, at 205 (emphasis added) (quoting Service Convention Negotiating Document); *see also id.* at 162 ("Even though a contracting state may not object to methods of service of foreign judicial documents in its territory in a manner other than as provided for in the Convention ... *it is still necessary that the law of the state where the action is pending authorize the particular method of service employed.*") (emphasis added).

In other words, we must look outside the Hague Convention for affirmative authorization of the international mail service that is merely not forbidden by Article 10(a). Any affirmative authorization of service by international mail, and any requirements as to how that service is to be accomplished, must come from the law of the forum in which the suit is filed.

Fed. R. Civ. P. 4(h)(2) directs that service on a foreign corporation, if done outside of the United States, shall be effected "in any manner prescribed for individuals by subdivision [4](f) except personal delivery as provided in paragraph (2)(C)(i) thereof," unless a waiver of service has been obtained and filed. No waiver of service under Rule 4(d) was obtained in this case. To determine whether service of process was proper, we therefore look to Fed. R. Civ. P. 4(f). As will be seen, no part of Rule 4(f) authorizes service by ordinary international first class mail.

1.   Rule 4(f)(1)

Rule 4(f)(1) authorizes service by those methods of service authorized by international agreements, including the Hague Convention. It provides:

> (f) ... Unless otherwise provided by federal law, service upon an individual from whom a waiver has not been obtained and filed ... may be effected in a place not within any judicial district of the United States:
>
> > (1) by any internationally agreed means reasonably calculated to give notice, such as those means authorized by the Hague Convention on the Service Abroad of Judicial and Extrajudicial Documents[.]

The Hague Convention affirmatively authorizes service of process through the Central Authority of a receiving state. Rule 4(f)(1), by incorporating the Convention, in turn affirmatively authorizes use of a Central Authority. However, Rule 4(f)(1) does not go beyond means of service affirmatively authorized by international agreements. It is undisputed that Brockmeyer did not use either the Central Authority under the Hague Convention or any other internationally agreed means for accomplishing service. Rule 4(f)(1), therefore, does not provide a basis for service in this case.

2.   Rule 4(f)(2)(C)(ii)

Explicit, affirmative authorization for service by international mail is found only in Rule 4(f)(2)(C)(ii) (previously Rule 4(i)(1)(D)). This rule authorizes service abroad by mail for which a signed receipt is required, when such mail is addressed and mailed by the clerk of the federal district court in which the suit is filed. It provides:

(f) [S]ervice ... may be effected in a place not within any judicial district of the United States: ...

(2) if there is no internationally agreed means of service or the applicable international agreement allows other means of service, provided that service is reasonably calculated to give notice: ...

(C) unless prohibited by the law of the country, by ...

(ii) *any form of mail requiring a signed receipt, to be addressed and dispatched by the clerk of the court to the party to be served* [.]

(Emphasis added.)

It is undisputed that the plaintiffs in this case did not comply with the requirements of Rule 4(f)(2)(C)(ii), as notice was not sent by the clerk of the district court, nor by a form of mail requiring a signed receipt. Rule 4(f)(2)(C)(ii) therefore does not provide a basis for service in this case.

3.   Rule 4(f)(3)

Rule 4(f)(3) (previously Rule 4(i)(1)(E)) affirmatively authorizes the federal district court to direct any form of service that is not prohibited by an international agreement. It provides:

(f) [S]ervice ... may be effected in a place not within any judicial district of the United States: ...

(3) by other means not prohibited by international agreement as may be directed by the court.

(Emphasis added.)

The decision whether to allow alternative methods of serving process under Rule 4(f)(3) is committed to the "sound discretion of the district court." *Rio Props., Inc. v. Rio Int'l Interlink*, 284 F.3d 1007, 1016 (9th Cir. 2002) (permitting service on a foreign corporation by regular mail and by e-mail, when authorized by the district court). The classic case is *Levin v. Ruby Trading Corp.*, 248 F.Supp. 537 (S.D.N.Y. 1965), in which the court authorized service abroad by ordinary mail under previous Rule 4(i)(1)(E), which was identical to current Rule 4(f)(3). In *Levin*, the court contrasted Rule 4(i)(1)(D) (now Rule 4(f)(2)(C)(ii)) with Rule 4(i)(1)(E), observing that Rule 4(i)(1)(D) "authorizes service by mail without court supervision, and it is for this reason that the double safeguard of mailing by the clerk of the court and a signed receipt was set up." *Id.* at 540. The court held that it could nonetheless authorize service by ordinary mail under Rule 4(i)(1)(E), because "the necessary safeguards are determined by the court[,] which to assure adequacy of notice, may 'tailor the manner of service to fit the necessities of a particular case....' " *Id.* (quoting Fed. R. Civ. P. 4(i)(E) (1963) Advisory Committee Note). Other courts have widely accepted *Levin's* reasoning. *See, e.g., Rio Props.,* 284 F.3d at 1016 (citing *Levin*); *Int'l Controls Corp. v. Vesco,* 593 F.2d 166, 175 n.4 (2d Cir. 1979) (same).

Courts have authorized a variety of alternative methods of service abroad under current Rule 4(f)(3) and former Rule 4(i)(1)(E), including not only ordinary mail and e-mail but also publication and telex. *Rio Props.,* 284 F.3d at 1016 (citing *SEC v. Tome,* 833 F.2d 1086, 1094 (2d Cir. 1987) (affirming district court's authorization of service of process by publication); *Int'l Controls Corp.,* 593 F.2d at 176 (affirming district court's authorization of service of process by ordinary mail to last known address); *Forum Fin. Group v. President, Harvard Coll.,* 199 F.R.D. 22, 23–24 (D. Me. 2001) (authorizing service by certified mail to defendant's attorney); *Smith v. Islamic Emirate,* 2001 WL 1658211, at *2–*3 (S.D.N.Y. Dec. 26, 2001) (authorizing service of process by publication on Osama bin Laden and al-Qaeda); *Broadfoot v. Diaz (In re Int'l Telemedia Assoc.),* 245 B.R. 713, 719–20 (Bankr. N.D. Ga. 2000) (authorizing service via facsimile, ordinary mail, and email); *Levin,* 248 F.Supp. at 541–44 (employing service by ordinary mail)). However, in *Rio* (and in all the cases it cites as applying Rule 4(f)(3)), plaintiffs are required to take a step that the plaintiffs in this case failed to take: They must obtain prior court approval for the alternative method of serving process. Rule 4(f)(3) thus is of no use to plaintiffs in this case.

     4.   Rule 4(f)(2)(A)

Because it is undisputed in this case that the plaintiffs neither effected service under the Hague Convention or other international agreement in accordance with Rule 4(f)(1), nor effected service by registered mail by the clerk of the court in accordance with the requirements of Rule 4(f)(2)(C)(ii), nor obtained a court order in accordance with Rule 4(f)(3), the only remaining section on which plaintiffs can conceivably rely is Rule 4(f)(2)(A). Rule 4(f)(2)(A) (previously Rule 4(i)(1)(A)) affirmatively authorizes service by means used in the receiving country for service in an action in its courts of general jurisdiction. As we read Rule 4(f)(2)(A), such means do not include service by international mail.

Rule 4(f)(2)(A) provides:

     (f) [S]ervice ... may be effected in a place not within any judicial district of the United States: ...

(2) if there is no internationally agreed means of service or the applicable international agreement allows other means of service, provided that service is reasonably calculated to give notice:

(A) in the manner prescribed by the law of the foreign country for service in that country in an action in any of its courts of general jurisdiction [.]

(Emphasis added.) The district court held that service was proper because the United Kingdom allows service for domestic suits in that country by both ordinary and registered post. A number of factors counsel against reading Rule 4(f)(2)(A) to authorize service by international mail, however.

First, the common understanding of Rule 4(f)(2)(A) is that it is limited to personal service. A well-known example of service under Rule 4(f)(2)(A) is "substituted service in Italy by delivery to the concierge of the building where the person to be served lives, as long as the method of service is likely to give the actual notice required by United States due process concepts." Gary N. Horlick, *A Practical Guide to Service of United States Process Abroad*, 14 Int'l Law. 637, 640 (1980) (interpreting previous Rule 4(i)(1)(A) (1963)). Consistent with this example, courts have applied Rule 4(f)(2)(A) to approve personal service carried out in accordance with foreign law. . . .

Another reason to read Rule 4(f)(2)(A) not to authorize service by international mail is the explicit mention of international registered mail in Rule 4(f)(2)(C)(ii), considered above, and the absence of any such mention in Rule 4(f)(2)(A). Indeed, the Advisory Committee Note to Rule 4(i)(1)(D), Rule 4(f)(2)(C)(ii)'s nearly identical predecessor, stated that "service by mail is proper *only* when it is addressed to the party to be served and a form of mail requiring a signed receipt is used." Fed. R. Civ. P. 4(i)(1)(D) (1963) Advisory Committee Note (emphasis added).[2]

A further reason to read Rule 4(f)(2)(A) not to authorize service on foreign defendants by international mail to England—and, in particular, by ordinary international first class mail—is found in an exchange between the British government and the United States Department of State in 1991, in which the British objected to a then-proposed revision to Fed. R. Civ. P. 4. *See* 127 F.R.D. 266–84 (1989); 146 F.R.D. 515–16 (1992). As amended, this proposal eventually became what is now Rule 4(d), authorizing a plaintiff to request a waiver of service.

---

2. Rule 4(i)(1)(D) provided: "When service is to be effected upon the party in a foreign country, it is also sufficient if service of the summons and complaint is made ... (d) by any form of mail, requiring a signed receipt, to be addressed and dispatched by the clerk of the court to the party to be served."

Current Rule 4(d) allows a plaintiff to send a summons and complaint by ordinary first class mail, with a request for waiver of service. If the defendant agrees to waive service, the defendant's waiver has the same effect as actual service. Waiver of service under Rule 4(d) is valid for both domestic and foreign defendants. As originally proposed in 1989, Rule 4(d) would have assessed costs incurred in effecting service against all defendants who failed to waive service, including defendants outside the United States. *See* 127 F.R.D. 271–72. The British government strongly objected to assessment of costs against non-waiving defendants living in the United Kingdom. *See* Letter from Edwin D. Williamson, Legal Adviser, U.S. Dep't of State, to Chief Justice Rehnquist (April 19, 1991) ("Williamson letter"). The British Embassy transmitted to the State Department a diplomatic note expressing its objection, which the State Department in turn forwarded to Chief Justice Rehnquist.

The diplomatic note stated, in relevant part:

> The proposed new paragraph (d)(2) of Rule 4 would impose on a defendant who has received notice of the commencement of the action a duty to waive service of the summons. Inasmuch as this procedure, which would coerce a waiver of service of the summons, would be equally applicable to United Kingdom citizens resident in the United Kingdom, the British Government would object to it. The waiver system would conflict with the Hague Service Convention, and it would be oppressive, since agreement would be elicited under the threat of the proposed sanction in costs. . . .

> [T]he British Government would object to the proposed waiver system for commencing proceedings against those resident in the United Kingdom. The proposed system would, moreover, run contrary to the public policy of the United Kingdom, which is that litigation affecting persons resident in the United Kingdom and commenced in foreign jurisdictions should be properly documented in public form.

Williamson letter, at 2–3 (enclosing U.K. Embassy Note No. 63).

The Supreme Court returned the proposal to the Civil Rules Advisory Committee for further study "in the light of various comments that had been received, most notably from the British Embassy." 146 F.R.D. 515 (1992) (Excerpt from the Report of the Judicial Conference Committee on Rules of Practice and Procedure). In response, the Advisory Committee revised the proposed rule to eliminate the provision assessing costs of service against foreign defendants that decline to waive service. *See id.* at 515–16; *see also* Fed. R. Civ. P. 4(d)(2) (1993). The Committee specifically explained that its revision addressed concerns raised by the British government. *See* 146 F.R.D. 521 (Attachment B to letter to Hon. Robert E. Keeton, Chairman, May 1, 1992).

The objection of the British government to the proposed rule makes sense only if the British government understood Rule 4(f) not to permit service by ordinary, international first class mail against a defendant in England. This is so because if Rule 4(f)(2)(A) had authorized service by international first class mail, a plaintiff would never need to send a request for waiver of service by international first class mail. The plaintiff would simply *effect service* by international first class mail.

The purpose of Rule 4(f)(2)(A) supports our interpretation of the exchange between the British Embassy and the State Department and our conclusion that the rule does not authorize ordinary international mail service to England. According to the 1963 Committee Notes accompanying Rule 4(i)(1)(A), the predecessor to Rule 4(f)(2)(A), the purpose of the Rule is to provide an alternative method of service "that is likely to create least objection in the place of service." *See also* Ronan E. Degnan and Mary Kay Kane, *The Exercise of Jurisdiction Over and Enforcement of Judgments Against Alien Defendants,* 39 Hastings L.J. 799, 840 (1988) ("[T]he approach [of Rule 4(i)(1)(A)] assures that the receiving state can have no objection to the means of transmitting notice."). From the exchange, it is clear that an interpretation of Rule 4(f)(2)(A) permitting service of process on an English defendant by ordinary first class mail sent from the United States is not "likely to create least objection in the place of service." Rather, this exchange shows us that such an interpretation is likely to create a substantial objection.

Finally, we have found no cases upholding service of process by international mail under Rule 4(f)(2)(A). Rather, there are a number of cases *rejecting* service of process by international mail under that rule. . . . We therefore conclude, along with the other courts that have considered the question, that Rule 4(f)(2)(A) does not authorize service of process by ordinary first class international mail.

Conclusion

Today we join the Second Circuit in holding that the Hague Convention allows service of process by international mail. At the same time, we hold that any service by mail in this case was required to be performed in accordance with the requirements of Rule 4(f). Service by international mail is affirmatively authorized by Rule 4(f)(2)(C)(ii), which requires that service be sent by the clerk of the court, using a form of mail requiring a signed receipt. Service by international mail is also affirmatively authorized by

Rule 4(f)(3), which requires that the mailing procedure have been specifically directed by the district court. Service by international mail is not otherwise affirmatively authorized by Rule 4(f). Plaintiffs neither followed the procedure prescribed in Rule 4(f)(2)(C)(ii) nor sought the approval of the district court under Rule 4(f)(3). They simply dropped the complaint and summons in a mailbox in Los Angeles, to be delivered by ordinary, international first class mail. There is no affirmative authorization for such service in Rule 4(f). The attempted service was therefore ineffective, and the default judgment against Marquis cannot stand.

PREWITT ENTERPRISES, INC. v. ORGANIZATION OF PETROLEUM EXPORTING COUNTRIES

353 F.3d 916 (11th Cir. 2003)

BARKETT, CIRCUIT JUDGE:

Prewitt Enterprises, Inc. ("Prewitt") appeals from the dismissal of its complaint against the Organization of the Petroleum Exporting Countries ("OPEC") for insufficient service of process and from the denial of its motion for alternative service of process. Prewitt's complaint against OPEC alleged a violation of the Sherman Act, 15 U.S.C. § 1 for illegal price-fixing agreements on production and export of crude oil and claimed equitable relief pursuant to the Clayton Act, 15 U.S.C. § 26. Because OPEC initially did not respond to the complaint, the district court entered a default final judgment against OPEC enjoining it from entering into, implementing or enforcing any agreements to fix and control the production and export of crude oil for one year. OPEC then appeared and moved to vacate the default judgment and injunction on the grounds that OPEC had never been properly served with process, and thus, the court lacked jurisdiction over it. The district court concluded that, because OPEC resides in Austria and the applicable Austrian law prohibits service without OPEC's consent, Prewitt's complaint must be dismissed for lack of jurisdiction. We agree and affirm the dismissal of Prewitt's complaint for lack of jurisdiction because service of process on OPEC has not been effectuated. We also affirm the district court's denial of alternative service of process because, in this case, there are no means available for service upon OPEC under the Federal Rules of Civil Procedure.

I. BACKGROUND

Prewitt is a corporation organized and existing under the laws of Alabama with its principal place of business in Birmingham,

Alabama. Prewitt purchases substantial quantities of gasoline and other refined petroleum products for resale at its Eastwood Texaco Service Center gasoline station.

OPEC is an intergovernmental organization originally established in 1960 via resolutions promulgated at the Conference of the Representatives of the Governments of Iran, Iraq, Kuwait, Saudi Arabia and Venezuela in Baghdad, Iraq. The principal aim of OPEC is "the co-ordination and unification of the petroleum policies of Member Countries and the determination of the best means for safeguarding their interests, individually and collectively." OPEC Stat. art. 2(A) (2000). Presently, OPEC's membership consists of: Algeria, Indonesia, Iran, Iraq, Kuwait, Libya, Nigeria, Qatar, Saudi Arabia, the United Arab Emirates and Venezuela. Since September 1, 1965, OPEC has been headquartered in Vienna, Austria. Its relationship with the Austrian government is governed by the Agreement Between the Republic of Austria and the Organization of the Petroleum Exporting Countries Regarding the Headquarters of the Organization of the Petroleum Exporting Countries, February 18, 1974, *BGBL* 1974/382 ("Austrian/OPEC Headquarters Agreement" or "Headquarters Agreement").

Prewitt filed a complaint with the district court against OPEC on behalf of itself and as the representative of all persons or entities who have indirectly purchased petroleum or petroleum products in the United States since March 1999. Prewitt claimed that OPEC has been coordinating an international conspiracy through agreements among its Member States and non-OPEC members to limit the production and export of oil in order to fix world oil prices above competitive levels. Prewitt argued that these agreements constitute violations of United States antitrust laws, specifically the Sherman and Clayton Acts, and have resulted in a substantial and adverse impact on United States trade and commerce. Prewitt claimed that as a result of OPEC's illegal conduct, its own acquisition and inventory costs for gasoline have increased significantly. Consequently, Prewitt requested that the court declare the OPEC-coordinated agreements illegal under United States law, enjoin implementation of the agreements, grant any other appropriate equitable relief, and award costs of the suit against OPEC for injuries sustained by Prewitt.

Prewitt attempted service on OPEC by requesting that the trial court send a copy of the complaint to OPEC by international registered mail, return receipt requested. The court clerk did so, mailing Prewitt's summons and complaint to OPEC at its headquarters in Vienna. The pleadings were signed for, stamped "received" by OPEC's Administration and Human Resources Department, and forwarded to the Director of OPEC's Research Division as well as other departments including the Secretary General's office. Ultimately, the Secretary General decided that the OPEC Secretariat would not take any action with regard to the summons and complaint.

Without the participation of OPEC, the district court certified a class defined as all persons or entities who purchased refined petroleum products in the United States from March 1999 to the present and entered a default final judgment and order of injunction against OPEC. The court found that there was a conspiracy between OPEC, its Member States, and non-OPEC members, namely Norway, Mexico, the Russian Federation and Oman, to fix and control crude oil prices; that the agreements coordinated and implemented by OPEC were illegal under United States antitrust laws; that OPEC's illegal conduct has resulted in substantial and adverse impact on United States trade and commerce of approximately $80–120 million per day; and that OPEC and those acting in concert with OPEC should be enjoined from entering into, implementing, and enforcing any further oil price-fixing agreements for a period of twelve months. Copies of the court's orders were delivered to each of the United States embassies for the Member States of OPEC.

In response, OPEC made a special appearance and filed a motion to set aside the default judgment and stay its enforcement pursuant to Rule 60(b)(1), (4), (5) and (6) of the Federal Rules of Civil Procedure, which the district court granted, vacating the default judgment and injunction. OPEC then filed a motion to dismiss Prewitt's complaint on various grounds including insufficient service of process pursuant to Fed. R. Civ. P. 12(b)(5). The district court dismissed the case without prejudice, finding that Prewitt had failed to serve OPEC its summons and complaint properly under the Federal Rules. Prewitt then filed a motion to pursue alternative means of effecting service or to amend the judgment. The district court denied the motion finding that, in this case, OPEC cannot be effectively served with process.

II. DISCUSSION

We review the district court's grant of a motion to dismiss for insufficient service of process under Fed. R. Civ. P. 12(b)(5) by applying a *de novo* standard to the law and a clear error standard to any findings of fact. We generally review the district court's interpretation of Fed. R. Civ. P. 4 on service of process as a matter of law *de novo*. Likewise, the district court's interpretation of foreign law in determining sufficiency of service of process is subject to *de novo* review. However, we join our sister circuit in holding that the district court's denial of a motion for alternative service of process under Fed. R. Civ. P. 4(f)(3) is subject to an abuse of discretion standard because the plain language of the rule stipulates that the district court "may" direct alternative means of service. *Rio Properties, Inc. v. Rio Int'l Interlink,* 284 F.3d 1007, 1014 (9th Cir. 2002).

The threshold issue in this case is whether OPEC has been effectively served under the Federal Rules of Civil Procedure. If it has not, we must then determine whether extraterritorial service of process on OPEC may be effectuated at all under the circumstances here. By definition, "service of summons is the procedure by which a court having venue and jurisdiction of the subject matter of the suit asserts jurisdiction over the person of the party served." *Miss. Publ'g Corp. v. Murphree,* 326 U.S. 438, 444–45 (1946). A court is required to have personal jurisdiction under the Due Process Clauses of the Fifth and Fourteenth Amendments to the United States Constitution "as a matter of individual liberty" so that "the maintenance of the suit . . . [does] not offend 'traditional notions of fair play and substantial justice.'" *Ins. Corp. of Ir. v. Compagnie des Bauxites de Guinee,* 456 U.S. 694, 702–03 (1982) (quoting *Int'l Shoe Co. v. Washington,* 326 U.S. 310, 316 (1945)).

There are two rules of federal civil procedure that apply to service of process upon an international entity located outside of United States jurisdiction: Fed. R. Civ. P. 4(f) (Service Upon Individuals in a Foreign Country) and Fed. R. Civ. P. 4(h) (Service of Process Upon Corporations and Associations). The latter governs service on unincorporated associations located outside of the United States and provides that:

> Unless otherwise provided by federal law, service upon a[n] . . . unincorporated association that is subject to suit under a common name, and from which a waiver of service has not been obtained and filed, shall be effected: . . .
>
> (2) in a place not within any judicial district of the United States *in any manner prescribed for individuals by subdivision (f)* except personal delivery. . . .

Fed. R. Civ. P. 4(h)(2) (emphasis added). Thus, an "unincorporated association"[6] headquartered outside of the United States that is (1)

---

6. The district court treated OPEC as an unincorporated association pursuant to Fed. R. Civ. P. 17(b)(1). Under this Circuit's jurisprudence, an unincorporated association is defined as "a body of persons acting together, without a charter, but upon the methods and forms used by corporations, for the prosecution of some common enterprise." *Penrod Drilling Co. v. Johnson,* 414 F.2d 1217, 1222 (5th Cir. 1969) (holding that labor unions, agricultural societies, co-ops, banking associations, charitable associations, news associations, and religious societies may all be considered unincorporated associations). *But see Dean v. Barber,* 951 F.2d 1210, 1215 n.4 (11th Cir. 1992) (holding that a government unit, subdivision or agency may not be considered an unincorporated association). *Cf. Hennessey v. Nat'l Collegiate Athletic Ass'n,* 564 F.2d 1136 (5th Cir. 1977) (treating a college athletic association in an antitrust suit as an unincorporated association even where some of

subject to suit under a common name[7] and (2) has not waived service[8] may be served in any manner authorized under Fed. R. Civ. P. 4(f) for individuals in a foreign country except for personal delivery.

Turning to Fed. R. Civ. P. 4(f), the first relevant section provides that:

> Unless otherwise provided by federal law, service upon an individual from whom a waiver has not been obtained and filed, other than an infant or an incompetent person, may be effected in a place not within any judicial district of the United States:
>
> > (1) by any internationally agreed means reasonably calculated to give notice, such as those means authorized by the Hague Convention on the Service Abroad of Judicial and Extrajudicial Documents....

Fed. R. Civ. P. 4(f)(1). In this case, no other means of service has been "otherwise provided by federal law" nor is there an "internationally agreed means reasonably calculated to give notice such as those means authorized by the Hague Convention on the Service Abroad of Judicial and Extrajudicial Documents...." The federal laws pertaining to service of process on a foreign entity are codified in 28 U.S.C. §§ 1602 *et seq.*, the Foreign Sovereign Immunities Act ("FSIA"), and 22 U.S.C. §§ 288 *et seq.*, the International Organizations Immunities Act ("IOIA"). The parties agree that neither of these federal laws apply to OPEC in this case. The parties likewise agree that there is no international agreement that stipulates the appropriate means of service.[10]

---

its members were state institutions rather than individuals).

In this case, OPEC is an administrative body joined together for the common purpose of acting on behalf of the business and political interests of its members with regard to their petroleum resources. While its members are sovereign nation states rather than private individuals, OPEC is not a governmental unit or subdivision and is not incorporated under the laws of any one Member State. Thus, under the facts of this case, we agree that it is amenable to the designation of "unincorporated association." As the court in *Penrod* has found, the term unincorporated association is one that is "generic" and of "vague meaning" with few "sharp legal boundaries." *Penrod Drilling Co.,* 414 F.2d at 1222–23.

7. In this case, it is clear that suit was brought against OPEC, the common

name for this international organization of sovereign oil-producing foreign states.

8. No evidence has been presented by either party that any waiver of service was "obtained and filed" from OPEC.

10. The Hague Convention on the Service Abroad of Judicial and Extrajudicial Documents in Civil or Commercial Matters Done at The Hague, the Netherlands, November 15, 1965, 658 U.N.T.S. 163 ("Hague Service Convention"), provides rules governing service of process between signatory states. However, while the United States is party to the Hague Service Convention, Austria is not. Austria *is* party to the Hague Convention on Civil Procedure, entered into force March 1, 1954, 286 U.N.T.S. 265, 1 Am. J. Comp. L. 282 (1952) (translation), but the United States is not.

Thus, we must look to the remainder of Fed. R. Civ. P. 4(f), which provides for other methods by which an unincorporated association may be served in the absence of relevant federal law or international agreements:

(2) if there is no internationally agreed means of service or the applicable international agreement allows other means of service, provided that service is reasonably calculated to give notice:

(A) in the manner prescribed by the law of the foreign country for service in that country in an action in any of its courts of general jurisdiction; or

(B) as directed by the foreign authority in response to a letter rogatory or letter of request; or

(C) unless prohibited by the law of the foreign country, by

(i) delivery to the individual personally of a copy of the summons and the complaint; or

(ii) any form of mail requiring a signed receipt, to be addressed and dispatched by the clerk of the court to the party to be served; or

(3) by other means not prohibited by international agreement as may be directed by the court.

Fed. R. Civ. P. 4(f)(2) and (3).

Prewitt originally chose to attempt service of process on OPEC under Fed. R. Civ. P. 4(f)(C)(ii). However, the method set forth under that provision applies only if it is not prohibited by the law of the foreign country. Based on the evidence presented,[11] the district

---

11. Evidence on service of process in Austria under Austrian and international law was considered by the district court pursuant to Fed. R. Civ. P. 44.1 (Determination of Foreign Law), which provides that:

A party who intends to raise an issue concerning the law of a foreign country shall give notice by pleadings or other reasonable written notice. The court, in determining foreign law, may consider any relevant material or source, including testimony, whether or not submitted by a party or admissible under the Federal Rules of Evidence. The court's determination shall be treated as a ruling on a question of law.

The evidence before the district court included: sections of Austrian law from the Austrian Constitution, the Austrian Service Act, and the Austrian Code of Civil Procedure; articles of international treaties such as the Vienna Convention on the Law of Treaties, entered into force January 27, 1980, 1155 U.N.T.S. 331, and the Austrian/OPEC Headquarters Agreement; expert affidavits and testimony from Austrian lawyers and professors on Austrian law; correspondence between Austrian law experts; "Notes Verbales" between the Austrian Ministry of Foreign Affairs and OPEC; correspondence from the Austrian Embassy to the District Court for the Northern District of Alabama on service of process in Austria; the United States State Department circular on service of process abroad; the Austrian Foreign Ministry website on Austrian law; and

court correctly found that service on OPEC was prohibited by the law of Austria. Article 5(2) of the Austrian/OPEC Headquarters Agreement provides that: "the service of legal process ... shall not take place within the [OPEC] headquarters seat except with the express consent of, and under conditions approved by, the Secretary General."[12] Since the Headquarters Agreement was enacted into law by resolution of the Austrian Parliament and published in the Austrian Official Gazette pursuant to the Austrian Constitution, the district court found it to be an integral part of Austrian law. Thus, because service was prohibited by Austrian law, Prewitt could not have effectively served OPEC under Fed. R. Civ. P. 4(f)(2)(C)(ii).

Prewitt nonetheless suggests that we should liberally construe the formal requirements for service under the Federal Rules because OPEC received actual notice but simply chose to "ignore the whole thing." Br. of Appellant at 23. However, we find no support for such an argument.[14] Due process under the United States

---

academic treatises on transnational litigation.

12. As noted in some of the amicus curiae briefs submitted to this Court, this provision is commonly found in numerous other Headquarters Agreements between sovereign states and international organizations around the world. See e.g. Headquarters Agreement between the Organization of American States and the Government of the United States of America, signed May 14, 1992, art. IX, § 1, <http://www.oas.org/legal/english/docs/Bilateral-Agree/us/ sedeusa.htm> ("The service and execution of legal process ... may take place within the Headquarters only with the consent of and under conditions approved by the Secretary General."); Agreement Regarding the Headquarters of the Food and Agriculture Organization of the United Nations, signed October 31, 1950, art. III, § 7(a), 1409 U.N.T.S. 23602 ("The service of legal process ... may take place within the headquarters seat only with the consent of, and under conditions approved by, the Director–General."); and the Agreement Relating to the Headquarters of the International Bauxite Association between the International Bauxite Association and Jamaica, signed November 5, 1975, art. III, § 4, 1021 U.N.T.S. 15000 ("The service of legal process ... may take place within the Headquarters premises only with the express prior consent of and under conditions approved by the Secretary General.")

14. It is true that receipt of actual notice is an important factor in considering whether service of process is adequate. *Hanna v. Plumer,* 380 U.S. 460, 463 n.1 (1965) (dictum); *Milliken v. Meyer,* 311 U.S. 457, 463 (1940). However in all of the cases cited by Prewitt, the courts were careful to determine that service of process was in substantial compliance with the formal requirements of the Federal Rules; actual notice alone was not enough to allow the court personal jurisdiction over the defendant. *See Sanderford v. Prudential Ins. Co. of America,* 902 F.2d 897 (11th Cir. 1990) (holding that service of process was in substantial compliance with Fed. R. Civ. P. 4(b) even though it did not include a return date for the responsive pleading); *Direct Mail Specialists, Inc. v. Eclat Computerized Tech. Inc.,* 840 F.2d 685 (9th Cir. 1988) (finding that a corporation's receptionist had sufficient authority to receive service of process as a "managing or general agent" under Fed. R. Civ. P. 4(d)(3) and noting that the president of the company received actual notice of the summons and complaint a day later); *United Food & Commercial Workers Union v. Alpha Beta Co.,* 736 F.2d 1371 (9th Cir. 1984) (holding that service was effective under Fed. R. Civ. P. 4(b) even though the summons had a typographical error stating that the defendant had 10 rather than 20 days to answer the complaint); *Banco Latino, S.A.C.A. v. Gomez Lopez,*

Constitution requires that "before a court may exercise personal jurisdiction over a defendant, there must be *more than* notice to the defendant ... [t]here also must be a *basis* for the defendant's amenability to service of summons. Absent consent, this means there must be *authorization* for service of summons on the defendant." *Omni Capital Int'l v. Rudolf Wolff & Co.*, 484 U.S. 97, 104 (1987) (emphasis added). In other words, an individual or entity "is not obliged to engage in litigation unless [officially] notified of the action ... under a court's authority, by formal process." *Murphy Bros., Inc. v. Michetti Pipe Stringing, Inc.*, 526 U.S. 344, 347 (1999). In this case, Fed. R. Civ. P. 4(f)(2)(C)(ii) clearly states that service of process by registered mail is only authorized where it is not prohibited by foreign law. Here, the Headquarters Agreement constitutes Austrian law and, under Article 5(2), expressly prohibits all service of process upon OPEC within the headquarters seat that has not been consented to by its Secretary General. Thus, we agree with the district court that even though OPEC had actual notice of the filing of the suit, service of process was ineffective because it was clearly not in substantial compliance with the requirements of Fed. R. Civ. P. 4(f)(2)(C)(ii).

Alternatively, Prewitt argues that even if service failed under Fed. R. Civ. P. 4(f)(2)(C)(ii), service by registered mail upon OPEC nonetheless complied with Fed. R. Civ. P. 4(f)(2)(A), which permits service if it is effectuated "in the manner prescribed by the law of the foreign country for service in that country in an action in any of its courts of general jurisdiction." The provisions of Austrian law that Prewitt references from Austria's Civil Procedure Code and regulations for service of process by mail relate to service by Austrian courts on persons resident in Austria and abroad. None of these Austrian law provisions directly pertain to service mailed *from abroad* upon international organizations resident in Austria. Prewitt argues that we should look only to the approved "method" of service within the foreign jurisdiction and not to the substance of Austrian law. However, the substance of the law specifically relating to service of process cannot be divorced from the "method" of service. Indeed, §§ 12(1) and 11(2) of the Austrian Service Act specifically address service from authorities abroad upon residents in Austria and trump the more general provisions cited by Prewitt from the Austrian Code of Civil Procedure and regulations for service of process by Austrian courts on residents in Austria or abroad.[16] Moreover, the Regulation Regarding the Service of Pro-

---

53 F. Supp. 2d 1273 (S.D. Fla. 1999) (finding that personal delivery of service of process on the defendant in Spain was sufficient because it was authorized under Spanish law as required by the Hague Convention and Fed. R. Civ. P. 4(f)(1) and the defendant had actual no- tice even though he only received a copy of the summons and not the complaint because he departed hastily).

16. Expert Decl. Of Dr. Wolfgang Hahnkamper, Dist. Ct. Doc. 56, Exh. 8 at 4.

cess by Mail upon Persons Abroad in Civil Proceedings that Prewitt argues applies in this case specifically states that it *does not* apply to service on entities specified under § 11(2) of the Austrian Service Act. Dist. Ct. Doc. 87, Exh. 4B. Section 12(1) (as amended 1990) of the Austrian Service Act requires that:

> The service of documents generated by authorities abroad to recipients in Austria shall be carried out in accordance with the existing international conventions, *in the absence of which it has to be done in accordance with this law....* (emphasis added).

Section 11(2) (as amended 1998) of the Austrian Service Act directly addresses service from abroad upon international organizations such as OPEC requiring that:

> the mediation of the Federal Ministry for Foreign Affairs shall be enlisted in undertaking service of process on foreigners or international organizations that enjoy privileges and immunities under international law, regardless of their place of residence or headquarters.

There would be no way for Prewitt to serve OPEC under § 11(2) of the Austrian Service Act because we must assume that if it had gone to the Austrian Federal Ministry of Foreign Affairs, the Ministry would have applied the laws of its own country and obeyed the dictates of the Austrian/OPEC Headquarters Agreement prohibiting service without OPEC's consent.

In response, Prewitt again argues that actual notice can cure defective service of process pursuant to Section 7 of the Austrian Service Act, which provides:

> Should defects in service of process occur, service shall be deemed effectuated at the time when the document has actually reached the recipient designated by the authority.

Section 7 (as amended January 1, 1991) of the Austrian Service Act. However, this section has specifically been interpreted in Austria not to apply to defects in service of process that are in breach of the requirements for service under an international agreement such as the Austrian/OPEC Headquarters Agreement.[17]

---

17. The Austrian Administrative Court ("Verwaltungsgerichtshof") has held that a breach of a rule in an international agreement on service of process was not a "simple defect of service" that could be cured by Section 7 of the Austrian Service Act. The court stated the rule that: "[S]imple consideration of the generally acknowledged rules of public law, which apply according to Art. 9(1) B–VG [Federal Constitutional Act] as constituents of Federal law, and which include the principle that contracts are to be performed in good faith ... prohibits § 7 of the Service Act from being afforded the content that it should also reform breaches of explicit prohibitions on service contained in international agreements...." Verwaltungsgerichtshof [VwGH] Beschluï, December 18, 1997, No. 97/11/0274 (Aus.).

Moreover, Section 7 may not cure a failure to obtain OPEC's express consent because under the Austrian law of *lex specialis,* the more specific provision in the Headquarters Agreement for service of process upon OPEC takes precedence over the more general language of the Austrian Service Act. Expert Decl. of Dr. Wolfgang Hahnkamper, Dist. Ct. Doc. 80, Exh. 5 at 416–17, 420–21.[18] Finally, Prewitt contends that even if its service by registered mail on OPEC could not be effectuated pursuant to any of the provisions of Fed. R. Civ. P. 4(f)(2), the district court still had the discretion to order service of process pursuant to Fed. R. Civ. P. 4(f)(3), which provides that service may be effected "by *other means* not prohibited by international agreement as may be directed by the court." (emphasis added). We agree with Prewitt that a district court's denial of relief under 4(f)(3) is reviewed under an abuse of discretion standard. However, there is no abuse of discretion here; on the contrary, any circumvention of 4(f)(2)(C)(ii) by the district court in directing service again by registered mail would constitute such an abuse. On these facts, we cannot read 4(f)(3) as permitting that which has already been specifically prohibited under 4(f)(2).

Prewitt then argues that, even if service by registered mail is prohibited by 4(f)(2), other means of giving actual notice, such as fax or e-mail, that are not mentioned in the rule or prohibited by international agreement could be employed to serve OPEC under Fed. R. Civ. P. 4(f)(3), even if the service is contrary to the laws of Austria. However, the 1993 Advisory Committee Notes to Fed. R. Civ. P. 4(f)(3) instruct that:

> Paragraph (3) authorizes the court to approve other methods of service not prohibited by international agreements.... Inasmuch as our Constitution requires that reasonable notice be given, *an earnest effort* should be made to devise a method of communication that is *consistent with due process* and *minimizes offense to foreign law.*

(emphasis added). Rather than minimizing offense to Austrian law, the failure to obtain OPEC's consent would constitute a substantial affront to Austrian law. We can find no support permitting such a consequence in the face of Austria's direct prohibition of service on OPEC without its consent. The case relied upon as persuasive by

---

18. Prewitt similarly argues that because OPEC failed to immediately reject the pleadings sent to it by international registered mail, return them, or lodge diplomatic protests with the United States, its actual receipt of the pleadings constituted constructive consent or waiver of the protection under Article 5(2) of the Headquarters Agreement that OPEC may only be served where it has expressly consented to service of process. Br. of Appellant at 31 n.9. We reject this argument because Article 5(2) must be read together with Article 9 of the Headquarters Agreement, which provides that "OPEC ... shall enjoy immunity from *every form of legal process* except in so far as in any particular case OPEC shall have *expressly waived* its immunity ..." (emphasis added).

Prewitt, *Rio Properties, Inc. v. Rio Int'l Interlink,* 284 F.3d 1007, 1014 (9th Cir. 2002), is not at all applicable to the circumstances here. In *Rio,* the court held that the district court did not abuse its discretion by ordering service by email upon an international corporation based in Costa Rica. However, the primary issue in that case was whether Fed. R. Civ. P. 4(f) should be read to create a hierarchy of preferred methods of service of process, requiring a party to attempt service by the methods enumerated in Fed. R. Civ. P. 4(f)(2) before petitioning the court for alternative relief under Fed. R. Civ. P. 4(f)(3). More importantly, the facts supporting the district court's direction of alternative service in *Rio* are completely different from the facts here. In *Rio,* the court determined that the defendant, an international internet company doing business in the United States, had a viable presence in the United States; that physical personal service had been legally attempted by actually serving a legitimate agent of the defendant in the United States; and that the defendant had evaded the attempted service. The most important distinction, however, is that in *Rio,* there was no discussion of Costa Rican law at all, much less of any prohibitions relating to service of process and thus, no need to take into account the advisory note to Fed. R. Civ. P. 4(f)(3) directing that alternative service of process should minimize offense to foreign law.[21]

Austrian law clearly provides protection to OPEC as an international organization from all methods of service of process without its consent and also requires that any service of process from abroad be effected through Austrian authorities. In this case, OPEC has made clear that it refuses to consent expressly to service of process by Prewitt; thus, the district court did not abuse its discretion in denying Prewitt's motion to authorize alternative means of service.

III. Conclusion

Based on the foregoing, we affirm the district court's motion to dismiss this case for insufficient service of process and its denial of alternative service of process on OPEC.

———

Notes

7–1. The Hague Service Convention is generally thought to be a very successful framework. There has been some controversy, however,

---

21. We do not say that a district court *never* has discretion to direct service of process under Fed. R. Civ. P. 4(f)(3) that is in contravention of a foreign law. Rather, we are satisfied that under the facts and circumstances of this case, directing service of process would constitute a clear abuse of discretion.

about the extent to which the Convention is the exclusive framework for foreign service. In *Volkswagenwerk Aktiengesellschaft v. Schlunk,* 486 U.S. 694 (1988), the Court held that the defendant, although a German corporation, had enough of an agency relationship with its United States-based subsidiary that the subsidiary could be considered an agent of the foreign entity for purposes of service. Thus, even though the Convention is "mandatory," the Convention is mandatory only when it applies. Because service could be effected locally pursuant to state law (and without the need for the transmission of documents abroad), the Hague Service Convention did not apply.

7–2.   Service of process is an official act in many countries. Improper service not only creates needless international friction, it reduces the likelihood that any judgment obtained in the action will be enforceable, and it can even be a violation of the national law.

7–3.   Pursuant to Fed. R. Civ. P. 4(f)(3), courts have given their permission to use "a wide variety of alternative methods of service including publication, ordinary mail, mail to the defendant's last known address, delivery to the defendant's attorney, telex, and most recently, email." *Rio Props., Inc. v. Rio International Interlink,* 284 F.3d 1007, 1016 (9th Cir. 2002). "[W]hen faced with an international e-business scofflaw, playing hide-and-seek with the federal court, email may be the only means of effecting service of process." *Id.* As the opinions reprinted in this chapter emphasize, the use of this subparagraph of Rule 4(f) requires the court's advance permission.

Chapter 8

JURISDICTION OF CASES INVOLVING ALIENS

This chapter focuses on subject matter jurisdiction in American courts of cases involving aliens. Federal district courts are courts of limited subject matter jurisdiction that require statutory authority to hear any case. That limitation applies to Americans and aliens alike.

Certain statutes give federal courts original jurisdiction over claims by aliens filing certain types of claims. For example, the Alien Tort Claims Act provides:

> The district courts shall have original jurisdiction of any civil action by an alien for a tort only, committed in violation of the law of nations or a treaty of the United States.

28 U.S.C. § 1350. Aliens alleging a violation of customary international law (or the "law of nations") thus can invoke that statute. But, given limitations on federal subject matter jurisdiction, aliens (or Americans) alleging violations of some other law(s), must find statutory authority elsewhere.

Alien plaintiffs may invoke the original jurisdiction of the federal courts to adjudicate some violation of United States federal law. Section 1331 of Title 28 gives federal courts original jurisdiction over matters involving federal questions, and that statute makes no distinction between Americans and aliens. And, of course, pursuant to this same authority, federal courts may exercise original jurisdiction over claims against alien defendants for alleged violations of United States federal law.

Many claims filed by or against aliens, however, invoke claims only under state law. Resident aliens account for nearly 12 percent of the population of the United States (according to the Center for Immigration Studies). Millions more, of course, travel or do business in the United States. Aliens thus find themselves as plaintiffs and defendants in their share of tort, contract, property and other cases governed solely by state law. Under what circumstances can those claims be pursued in federal court?

Assuming satisfaction of the amount-in-controversy requirement, Section 1332 of Title 28 grants original subject matter jurisdiction over controversies between:

(1) citizens of different States;

(2) citizens of a State and citizens or subjects of a foreign state;

(3) citizens of different States and in which citizens or subjects of a foreign state are additional parties; and

(4) a foreign state, defined in section 1603(a) of this title, as plaintiff and citizens of a State or of different States.

However, not all issues regarding jurisdiction in cases involving aliens are clearly resolved within those paragraphs. A series of hypotheticals will explore the basic parameters of so-called "alienage jurisdiction." Each hypothetical presumes that there are no grounds other than Section 1332 upon which the district court's jurisdiction could be based.

#1: *French citizen v. Japanese citizen.* In cases involving a single alien plaintiff and a single alien defendant, there is no diversity jurisdiction. In Section 1332, the word "State," when capitalized, refers to one of the United States, the Territories, the District of Columbia, or Puerto Rico. References to "states," in lower case, include foreign countries. Because there is no grant of the federal court's limited subject matter jurisdiction to hear disputes between "citizens of different [foreign] states," this case could not be heard in federal court.

#2: *Texas citizen v. Japanese citizen.* In cases involving a citizen of a State and a citizen of a foreign state, there is jurisdiction under 28 U.S.C. § 1332(a)(2). Notice also that subparagraphs (1), (2) and (3) of Section 1332 make no distinction as to whether the alien is the plaintiff or the defendant. The roles of the Texas and the Japanese citizens in this hypothetical could be reversed, then, and the district court would still have subject matter jurisdiction under subparagraph (2).

#3: *Texas citizen + French citizen v. Florida citizen.* In cases involving actions between citizens of different States and in which a citizen or subject of a foreign state is joined as an additional party, there is jurisdiction under 28 U.S.C. § 1332(a)(3).

#4: *Texas citizen + French citizen v. Japanese citizen.* In this hypothetical, involving two plaintiffs (one American, one alien) suing an alien defendant, most courts have held that there is no diversity jurisdiction. This result is not obvious, since one could reasonably argue that this is a diversity alignment substantially similar to that in Hypothetical #2 which is authorized by 28 U.S.C. § 1332(a)(2). But that is *not* how the lower courts have viewed it. Instead they have viewed this situation as substantially similar to an action between two foreigners as in Hypothetical #1.

#5: *Texas citizen + French citizen v. Florida citizen + Japanese citizen.* In cases where there are United States citizens of different states on *both* sides of the lawsuit, courts have held that there is subject matter jurisdiction under 28 U.S.C. § 1332(a)(3). This hypothetical differs from Hypothetical #4 because there are United States citizens on *both sides* of the "v." This scenario tends to be viewed by courts as essentially a dispute between citizens of different (United) States.

————

An additional provision in Section 1332(a), added in 1988, also deserves attention:

> For the purposes of this section ... an alien admitted to the United States for permanent residence shall be deemed a citizen of the State in which such alien is domiciled.*

The amendment narrowed subject matter jurisdiction by denying a federal forum for controversies between permanent resident aliens and United States citizens domiciled in the same state. In other words, if the Japanese citizen in Hypothetical #2 had been admitted to the United States as a permanent resident *and* was domiciled in Texas, the district court would *not* have jurisdiction under Section 1332(a)(2) because of the "deeming" language in Section 1332(a).

This deeming language triggered by permanent residence has raised another possibility, however, that would *expand* jurisdiction. What if the French citizen in Hypothetical #1 had been admitted to the United States as a permanent resident and was domiciled in Texas? Whether the deeming language could be used to *create* subject matter jurisdiction is the subject of the *Singh* case, reprinted below.

Importantly, all of the hypotheticals above use Japan and France as examples of "foreign states." However, not all "foreign states" are so obvious. Countries that are not recognized by the

---

* Ed.'s Note: Lawful permanent residents are legally accorded the privilege of residing permanently in the United States. They may be issued immigrant visas by the Department of State overseas or adjusted to permanent resident status by the Immigration and Naturalization Service in the United States. This is a formal classification.

United States government as sovereign states may not be a "foreign state" within the meaning of 28 U.S.C. § 1332. Citizens of and corporations organized under those regimes may be "stateless" and thus unable to establish alienage jurisdiction. (An American citizen who has established a permanent residence in another country is similarly "Stateless" in a diversity jurisdiction analysis.)

Two more wrinkles of alienage jurisdiction are described in this excerpt from Professors Linda Silberman and Allan Stein:

> *Dual Nationals.* Dual nationals attempting to litigate in federal court have faced special problems. In *Sadat v. Mertes,* 615 F.2d 1176 (7th Cir. 1980), the plaintiff, a dual citizen of the United States and Egypt, was denied access to alienage diversity court because his American nationality was deemed to be "dominant." In *Risk v. Kingdom of Norway,* 707 F.Supp. 1159 (N.D. Cal. 1989), an American father brought an action on behalf of his children, who were dual nationals of Norway and the United States, against Norway and several Norwegian individuals. The court held that the children's dual nationality destroyed diversity—without addressing the issue of dominant nationality—explaining that the California children would be unlikely to suffer any local bias in the state courts....

> *Alien Corporations.* Foreign corporations are not specifically mentioned in 28 U.S.C. § 1332(c). Some courts have held that § 1332(c) is inapplicable to foreign corporations and that they should be considered citizens only of the state of their incorporation. *See, e.g., Eisenberg v. Commercial Union Assurance Co.,* 189 F.Supp. 500 (S.D.N.Y. 1960). Other courts have found that a foreign corporation whose world-wide principal place of business is in a state of the United States should be considered a citizen of that state as well.... Such a reading allowed a foreign corporation that had its principal place of business in the United States to sue another foreign corporation in federal court.... Some courts have suggested that foreign corporations be considered citizens both of their place of incorporation and of the state that is their principal place of business in the United States.... Is there any reason to treat a foreign corporation that has established a substantial presence in a state of the United States differently from a domestic corporation? On the other hand, does the fact that a foreign corporation has established a principal place of business in this country always negate the foreign relations concerns informing the establishment of alienage jurisdiction for foreign nationals?

> Related issues arise with respect to American corporations that have their principal place of business abroad. The Eleventh Circuit has held that when sued by an alien, such a

corporation would be deemed to be a citizen only of the state of the incorporation. *See Cabalceta v. Standard Fruit Co.,* 883 F.2d 1553 (11th Cir. 1989). The court was troubled that by giving effect to its foreign principal place of business, the firm would be deprived of access to a federal court. However, it is not clear from the standpoint either of the bias-avoidance policy of diversity jurisdiction or the foreign relations concerns of alienage jurisdiction, why the alien plaintiff's choice to sue in state court should have been overridden.

Linda J. Silberman & Allan R. Stein, Civil Procedure: Theory and Practice 371–73 (2001).

SINGH v. DAIMLER–BENZ AG

9 F.3d 303 (3d Cir. 1993)

SLOVITER, CHIEF JUDGE:

In this appeal we must determine, apparently for the first time by an appellate court, whether the amendment to the diversity jurisdiction statute defining a permanent resident alien as a citizen for diversity purposes gives a federal court subject matter jurisdiction over a case brought by a permanent resident alien against two defendants, one of whom is a nonresident alien. The district court saw no impediment to diversity jurisdiction, declined the plaintiff's motion to remand to state court, and ultimately entered judgment on a jury verdict for the defendants. Plaintiff's appeal is limited to the issue of the district court's subject matter jurisdiction.

I. FACTS AND PROCEDURAL HISTORY

Plaintiff Manjit Singh filed a products liability action individually and as administrator of the estate of his father, who died after suffering massive injuries when the Mercedes sedan he was driving slid off a snowy highway in Pennsylvania on November 22, 1989. The complaint alleges that there were design and manufacturing defects in the automobile which caused decedent's death. Singh is a citizen of India, admitted to the United States for permanent residence and domiciled in Virginia, as was his father. It is the decedent's residence and citizenship which control citizenship for diversity purposes. *See* 28 U.S.C. § 1332(c)(2) (1988). Singh's mother, with the same citizenship and residence, also was a plaintiff at the outset of this action, claiming for negligent infliction of emotional distress.

The defendants are the automobile's foreign manufacturer, Daimler–Benz, AG, a German corporation, and its American distributor, Mercedes–Benz of North America, Inc., a Delaware corporation with its principal place of business in New Jersey.

The action was originally filed in the Court of Common Pleas of Philadelphia County and was removed on the basis of diversity of citizenship. Plaintiffs moved to remand the case, arguing that there was not complete diversity of citizenship because the plaintiffs as well as the defendant Daimler–Benz are aliens. Defendants asserted federal jurisdiction based on the 1988 amendment to the diversity statute, which provides that a permanent resident alien of the United States is "deemed a citizen of the State in which such alien is domiciled." 28 U.S.C. § 1332(a)(1988).

The district court denied plaintiffs' motion to remand, noting that the states of domicile of the permanent resident alien plaintiffs (Virginia) and Mercedes, the citizen defendant, (Delaware and New Jersey), are not the same. The court declined to deviate from the plain language of section 1332(a) as amended, finding that "the best evidence of Congress' intent ... is found in the text of the statute itself." The court rejected the holding of the district court in *Arai v. Tachibana,* 778 F. Supp. 1535 (D. Haw. 1991), that there was no diversity jurisdiction where, as here, there were nonresident aliens and a resident alien as opposing parties. The district court then denied plaintiffs' motion to certify the question for an immediate appeal to this court.

After the individual claims by Manjit Singh and his mother were dismissed by stipulation, a jury trial was held on the representative claims asserted by Manjit Singh, and judgment was entered for the defendants. Singh appeals. Our review is plenary.

II. DISCUSSION

The Constitution provides that federal courts can have jurisdiction over suits "between a State, or the Citizens thereof, and foreign States, Citizens or Subjects." U.S. Const. art. III, § 2. The first Judiciary Act of 1789 implemented this authority by providing that federal courts have jurisdiction over suits "where ... an alien is a party, or the suit is between a citizen of the State where the suit is brought, and a citizen of another State." Act of Sept. 24, 1789, ch. 20, Sec. 11, 1 Stat. 73, 78. In an early interpretation of the diversity statute, the Court enunciated the requirement of complete diversity, i.e. that each plaintiff must be able to sue each defendant. *See Strawbridge v. Curtiss,* 7 U.S. (3 Cranch) 267 (1806). It has since clarified that the complete diversity requirement is statutory, because Article III only requires minimal diversity. *See State Farm Fire & Cas. Co. v. Tashire,* 386 U.S. 523, 531 (1967). Thus Congress is empowered to authorize federal jurisdiction on the basis of diversity as long as at least one plaintiff and one defendant are diverse. *See id.* With respect to aliens, the Supreme Court early construed Article III as authorizing diversity suits only between a citizen of a state and an alien, *see Mossman v. Higginson,* 4 US. (4

Dall.) 12, 14 (1800) (citing Judiciary Act of 1789, ch. 20, sec. 11, 1 Stat. 73, 78); *Montalet v. Murray,* 8 U.S. (4 Cranch) 46, 47 (1807); *Hodgson v. Bowerbank,* 9 U.S. (5 Cranch) 303, 304 (1809), and the statute now does not expressly provide that one alien may sue another in federal court. *See* 28 U.S.C. § 1332(a)(2) (granting jurisdiction in cases between "citizens of a State and citizens or subjects of a foreign state.")

More than a decade ago when confronted with a case where an alien was one of several plaintiffs suing an alien defendant, we held that the complete diversity required under *Strawbridge* was lacking. *See Field v. Volkswagenwerk AG,* 626 F.2d 293, 296 (3d Cir. 1980). Other circuits have also construed the diversity statute to apply the complete diversity requirement to aliens. . . .

In light of these precedents, plaintiff argues that because the decedent Ram Singh was an alien (a permanent resident alien) and defendant Daimler–Benz is an alien (a nonresident alien), complete diversity is lacking and there is no subject matter jurisdiction. However, the cases upon which Singh relies construed the diversity statute before Congress expanded the definition of "citizen" for purposes of diversity to provide that "an alien admitted to the United States for permanent residence shall be deemed a citizen of the State in which such alien is domiciled." 28 U.S.C. § 1332(a) (1988). The district court relied on the plain language of the new provision to find that the Singhs (including, significantly, the decedent) are deemed citizens of Virginia. The court concluded that as one defendant is an alien and the other is an American corporation with citizenship in Delaware and New Jersey, "there is complete diversity between the parties." The court reiterated this view on reconsideration.

Plaintiff contends that the district court's reading of the statute is erroneous. He claims that it will lead to a dramatic increase in the number of diversity suits maintained in federal court, and that Congress could not have intended, nor did it have the power, to overrule the longstanding prohibition of suits between aliens. Under plaintiff's view, the new provision was intended only to bar suits where a permanent resident alien sues a citizen of the same state, and did not establish a new definition of citizenship for permanent resident aliens in all cases.

A. Statutory Language

In resolving a question of statutory interpretation we turn first to the language of the provision. *See Comm. v. Engle,* 464 U.S. 206, 214 (1984). We find no support there for plaintiff's position. The amended diversity jurisdiction statute reads:

(a) The district courts shall have original jurisdiction of all civil actions where the matter in controversy exceeds the sum or value of $50,000 . . . and is between—

(1) citizens of different States;

(2) citizens of a State and citizens or subjects of a foreign state;

(3) citizens of different States and in which citizens or subjects of a foreign state are additional parties; and

(4) a foreign state . . . as plaintiff and citizens of a State or of different States.

For the purposes of this section, section 1335, and section 1441, an alien admitted to the United States for permanent residence shall be deemed a citizen of the State in which such alien is domiciled.

28 U.S.C. § 1332(a) (1988) (emphasis added).

There is no ambiguity in the emphasized language. With this new provision, which became effective on May 18, 1989, *see* David D. Siegel, *Commentary on 1988 Revision,* 28 U.S.C.A. § 1332, at 5 (West.Supp.1993), Congress directed that permanent resident aliens, who heretofore were considered "citizens or subjects of a foreign state" for purposes of diversity jurisdiction, are now considered "citizen[s] of the State in which [they are] domiciled." The provision represents a straightforward congressional direction.

Plaintiff concedes, at least implicitly, that this is the plain reading of the statute. He argues, however, that such a construction is contrary to the legislative intent, and that, if adhered to, it would lead to an unconstitutional result. Because the statutory language is plain, our inquiry should be complete. *See Garcia v. United States,* 469 U.S. 70, 75 (1984). Nonetheless, we will proceed to consider the legislative history, as it may provide some helpful insight in our statutory construction. *See Darby v. Cisneros,* 509 U.S. 137 (1993) ("Recourse to the legislative history . . . is unnecessary in light of the plain meaning of the statutory text. Nevertheless, we consider that history briefly because both sides have spent much of their time arguing about its implications.").

B. Legislative History

The provision deeming a permanent resident alien a state citizen for the purpose of diversity was included in the Judicial Improvements and Access to Justice Act (1988 Act), Pub.L. No. 100–702, 102 Stat. 4642 (1988). The 1988 Act follows verbatim the language of S. 1482, 100th Cong., 2d Sess. (1988), *reprinted in* 134 Cong.Rec. 31,040 (1988), described as an "omnibus court reform bill," 134 Cong.Rec. 31,049 (1988) (statement of Sen. Heflin), which was considered by the Senate on October 14, 1988, *id.* at 31,039, and which had a somewhat tangled legislative history.[1]

Although Singh directs us to language in the legislative history of the 1988 Act expressing concern about the "delay caused by rising caseloads," H.R.Rep. No. 889, 100th Cong., 2d Sess. 23 (1988), *reprinted in* 1988 U.S.C.C.A.N. 5982, 5984, we note that these remarks were taken from the House Report and were therefore directed to the House version of the bill. The anti-diversity sentiment of some House members is reflected in a provision of one of the earlier versions of the bill which would have virtually eliminated diversity jurisdiction, *see id.* at 25, 1988 U.S.C.C.A.N. at 5985–86, a bill reported favorably by the Subcommittee on Courts, Civil Rights, and the Administration of Justice of the House Committee on the Judiciary, *see id.* at 45, *reprinted in* 1988 U.S.C.C.A.N. at 6005. The full Committee deleted that provision, adopting instead an increase in the amount in controversy. *See id.* at 25, *reprinted in* 1988 U.S.C.C.A.N. at 5985–86. We cannot glean much assistance about the purpose for the permanent resident alien provision from the House Report, because that provision was not in the House proposal.

As Senator Heflin explained, S. 1482 was the "culmination of many months of negotiation with members of the Subcommittee on Courts and Administrative Practice, the Senate Judiciary Committee, and the House of Representatives." 134 Cong.Rec. 31,050 (1988). The claims for the bill in the Senate with respect to diversity were considerably more modest than Singh suggests. Senator Heflin, the floor sponsor of S. 1482, introduced the bill by stating "[t]his bill provides a procedure for the promulgation of rules issued by the courts, establishes a Committee of the Judicial Conference to study the problems and needs of the Federal judiciary, *makes modest adjustments to the scope of diversity jurisdiction,* provides for the early resolution of district court jurisdictional issues under the Tucker Act, reauthorizes the State justice institute, amends both the Court Interpreter and Jury Selection and Service Acts, and makes other improvements proposed by the Judicial Conference." *Id.* (emphasis added).

The most far reaching feature of Title II, the title of the ten title bill that deals with diversity jurisdiction, was that raising the amount in controversy for diversity purposes from $10,000 to $50,000. The House Report gives two reasons for the increase. One

1. *See* Cong. Index (CCH) 35,062, 35,102 (1988) (chronology of the history of H.R. 3152 and H.R. 4807); 134 Cong. Rec. 31,050 (1988) (statement of Sen. Heflin) (describing House and Senate treatment of H.R. 3152, H.R. 4807 and S. 1482); John B. Oakley, *Recent Statutory Changes in the Law of Federal Jurisdiction and Venue: The Judicial Improvements Acts of 1988 and 1990,* 24 U.C. Davis L. Rev. 735, 736 n.1 (1991).

was to reduce the "basis for Federal court jurisdiction based solely on diversity of citizenship." H.R.Rep. No. 889, *supra,* at 44, *reprinted in* 1988 U.S.C.C.A.N. at 6005. The other was to adjust for the effect of inflation since 1958 when the $10,000 threshold was enacted. Although Senator Heflin noted in reviewing the various titles of the bill that the increase in amount in controversy was estimated by some to reduce the diversity caseload by up to 40 percent (an estimate included in the House report), he described the provisions of Title II of the bill relating to diversity jurisdiction as making "*modest amendments* to reduce the basis for federal court jurisdiction based solely on diversity of citizenship." 134 Cong.Rec. 31,051 (1988) (emphasis added). A similar approach was taken by Senator Thurmond who, when speaking on the floor of the Senate on the increase in the amount in controversy, stated "[t]his provision simply reflects the present diversity amount adjusted for inflation." *Id.* at 31,066.

Nothing in the remarks of Senator Heflin or any of the other three members of the Senate Judiciary Committee who spoke briefly in favor of the bill on the floor supports Singh's argument that the overall goal of the bill was "to reduce diversity jurisdiction to relieve caseload pressures." Appellant's Brief at 27. The overall bill was clearly designed to improve federal court administration and efficiency, including, for example, a provision permitting a controlled experiment in court-annexed arbitration which Senator Grassley lauded. *See* 134 Cong.Rec. 31,067 (1988) (discussing § 901, 102 Stat. at 4659–64 (codified at 28 U.S.C. §§ 651–58)).

There were two other provisions in Title II of S. 1482 relevant to diversity jurisdiction. One altered the citizenship rules for cases involving multistate corporations (who will hereafter be deemed citizens of any state in which they have been incorporated as well as of their principal place of business), insurers (in direct actions the citizenship of the insured will also be attributed to the insurer), and representative parties—estates, infants, and incompetents (whose citizenship will be determined by reference to the citizenship of the "represented" party). *See* 134 Cong.Rec. 31,051 (1988) (Statement of Sen. Heflin) (discussing § 202, 102 Stat. at 4646 (codified at 28 U.S.C. § 1332(a))). The latter measure, one of those added by the Senate, was designed to eliminate the artificial manufacture of diversity by naming representatives from other states, *see id.* at 31,055, but its impact on caseload was not discussed.

The third change in existing law effected by Title II of S. 1482 was the provision dealing with the citizenship of permanent resident aliens, the provision at issue here. Because the permanent resident alien provision was not part of the bill at the time the House Report was written, and there was no Senate Report, there is only scant legislative history. This provision appears to have been added by Senator Heflin very late in the process of congressional consideration of the version of S. 1482 as enacted, and the only references to the provision in the Congressional Record are on the day it was adopted unanimously by the Senate.

The section-by-section analysis that Senator Heflin introduced into the Congressional Record first noted that "large numbers of persons" are permanent resident aliens, and then continued, "[t]here is no apparent reason why actions between persons who are permanent residents of the same State should be heard by Federal courts merely because one of them remains a citizen or subject of a foreign state." 134 Cong.Rec. 31,055 (1988). No senator spoke to this provision.

The introduction of the Senate bill containing the permanent resident alien provision followed shortly after the September 1988 meeting of the Judicial Conference of the United States at which the Conference agreed to recommend "that Congress amend 28 U.S.C. § 1332(a) to treat a permanent resident alien as a citizen of the state of his or her domicile." Judicial Conference of the United States, *Reports of the Proceedings of the Judicial Conference of the United States Held in Washington, D.C. March 15, 1988 and September 14, 1988, at 77* (1988) (*Proceedings of the Judicial Conference*). The Conference action in turn followed the report and recommendation of its Committee on Federal–State Jurisdiction.

Because the Committee's consideration of this issue was the genesis of the statutory provision, we include the relevant portion of its Report:

> 28 U.S.C. § 1332(a)(2) currently gives the district courts diversity jurisdiction over actions between citizens of a State and citizens or subjects of a foreign state. Section 1332(a)(3) covers actions between citizens of different States in which citizens or subjects of a foreign State are parties. Diversity jurisdiction exists under these provisions even though the alien may have been admitted to the United States as a permanent resident. Review of immigration statistics indicates that a large number of persons falls within this category.
>
> There seems to be no reason why actions involving persons who are permanent residents of the United States should be heard by Federal courts merely because one of them remains a citizen or subject of a foreign state or has not yet become a citizen of the United States.

Report of the Judicial Conference Committee on Federal–State Jurisdiction 6–7 (Sept.1988) (Federal–State Committee), *summarized in Proceedings of the Judicial Conference, supra,* at 76–77. The above language of the Judicial Conference's Committee Report was substantially adopted in the Senate's section-by-section analysis of S. 1482. *See* 134 Cong.Rec. 31,055 (1988).

There is ample basis in the report of the Federal–State Committee to support Singh's view that the reduction of the diversity caseload was a factor in the proposed change as to the treatment of permanent resident aliens. *See* Federal–State Committee, *supra,* at 7 ("The Committee believes that a proposal to eliminate diversity of citizenship jurisdiction under these circumstances is consistent with recent Judicial Conference positions to encourage justifiable piecemeal reductions in diversity jurisdiction in the face of the substantial opposition to total abolition.").

It is far less clear that the Judicial Conference Committee's perspective represented the view of the Senate. Senator Heflin did not espouse it, and in fact his comments on Title II of the bill dealing with diversity jurisdiction noted that "[w]hile the Judicial Conference of the United States has long supported total abolition of diversity jurisdiction, such measures are very controversial." 134 Cong.Rec. 31,051 (1988).

The Senate's consideration of the resident alien provision focused on the incongruity of permitting a permanent resident alien living next door to a citizen to invoke federal jurisdiction for a dispute between them while denying a citizen living across the street the same privilege. *See* 134 Cong.Rec. 31,055 (1988). This does not mean that the reduction in diversity caseload may not have been a factor in the acceptance of the provision. However, we have no basis to jump from the "modest" adjustment to the scope of diversity jurisdiction, which the provision undeniably accomplished, to Singh's claim that construing the alien permanent resident provision according to its plain language would contravene the legislative intent.

The 1988 Act also contained several provisions relating to procedure in removal of cases from state to federal court, but even those will not necessarily reduce diversity cases in a significant measure. The Act imposed an absolute one year time limit to remove a case from state to federal court on the basis of diversity of citizenship, *see* § 1016(b)(2)(B), 102 Stat. at 4669 (codified at 28 U.S.C. § 1446(b)), thereby changing the prior procedure permitting a case to be removed after the claims against defendants whose presence destroyed complete diversity were dismissed or dropped. While acknowledging that this provision would produce "a modest curtailment in access to diversity jurisdiction," the House Report emphasized instead that the change would prevent "removal after substantial progress has been made in state court." H.R.Rep. No. 889, *supra* at 72, *reprinted in* 1988 U.S.C.C.A.N. at 6032.

A related change was the inclusion of a provision requiring that the citizenship of defendants sued under fictitious names be disregarded, abrogating the Ninth Circuit's practice of permitting claims in California against a Doe defendant automatically to destroy diversity. *See* § 1016(a), 102 Stat. at 4669, (codified at 28 U.S.C. § 1441(a)); *see Oakley, supra,* at 753–56. It would not be surprising if this amendment requiring courts to ignore the citizenship of fictitious defendants increased, rather than decreased, the number of diversity cases. There is even some question if the impact on the federal courts' caseload of the increase in the amount in controversy requirement to $50,000, the one provision clearly designed to affect the number of diversity cases, will approach the predicted reduction.[3]

In short, while we agree with Singh that there is nothing in the legislative history of the 1988 Act that suggests that Congress intended the permanent resident alien provision to expand diversity jurisdiction, there is also nothing to support Singh's view that the entire 1988 Act was characterized by a "clarity of purpose" to reduce diversity jurisdiction. Appellant's Reply Brief at 3 n. 1. Instead the Act is more accurately viewed as Senator Heflin described it, "a noncontroversial judicial improvements bill with many authors." 134 Cong.Rec. 31,050 (1988).

We recognize that Congress may not have intended to enlarge diversity jurisdiction even in the limited situation presented by this case, but the possible unintended effect of permitting a permanent resident alien to invoke diversity jurisdiction when that party could not have done so before the amendment is not sufficient reason for us to torture or limit the statutory language. *See Pittston Coal Group v. Sebben,* 488 U.S. 105, 115 (1988) ("It is not the law that a statute can have no effects which are not explicitly mentioned in its legislative history. . . ."). Although Congress has from time to time recognized the need to restrict the availability of diversity jurisdiction, we are not free to go farther than it has chosen to go. *See Schwartz v. Electronic Data Systems, Inc.,* 913 F.2d 279, 284 (6th Cir. 1990). Had Congress intended to limit the language of the deeming provision to cases in which a permanent resident alien of a state is suing a citizen or another permanent resident of the same state, it could easily have so provided by limiting the deeming provision to be applicable only to section 1332(a)(2). Instead, Congress's language is broad, and without limitation provides that "for purposes of this section," i.e., all of section 1332(a), a permanent resident alien "shall be deemed a citizen of the State in which such

---

3. At least one commentator believes that even the fivefold increase in the amount in controversy, which one would expect to have a substantial effect on the federal court dockets, has not had and will not have a great effect. *See* 1 James Wm. Moore et al., *Moore's Federal Practice* ¶ 0.71[4.–7] (2d ed. 1993).

alien is domiciled." 28 U.S.C. § 1332(a) (1988). Thus this includes as well section 1332(a)(3) which, when the deeming provision is applied, fits precisely this case ("citizens of different states [Singh (Virginia) v. Mercedes (Delaware and New Jersey)] and in which citizens or subjects of a foreign state [Daimler] are additional parties"). We must construe this as written, particularly because the legislative history does not provide an overriding reason not to do so.

C. Congressional Power to Define Citizenship

Singh does not argue explicitly that as a general matter Congress does not have the power to define who or what is a citizen for purposes of diversity jurisdiction. The history of Congress's various modifications of citizenship belies any such notion. There was no statutory elaboration on the word "citizen" used in the first Judiciary Act of 1789 in the grant of jurisdiction to the federal courts of controversies "between a citizen of the State where the suit is brought, and a citizen of another State." Act of Sept. 24, 1789, ch. 20, Sec. 11, 1 Stat. 73, 78. Since then, there have been a series of amendments by Congress which elaborate on the concept of citizenship. One example is the 1940 amendment which defined "States" to include the Territories, the District of Columbia, and the Commonwealth of Puerto Rico, and consequently extended citizenship for diversity purposes to their previously excluded citizens. *See* Act of Apr. 20, 1940, ch. 117, 54 Stat. 143 (codified at 28 U.S.C. § 1332(d)); *see also National Mut. Ins. Co. v. Tidewater Transfer Co.,* 337 U.S. 582 (1949) (provision upheld by fractured Supreme Court on inconsistent rationales).

Congress's periodic revisions in the treatment of corporations for purposes of their citizenship consistently has been accepted by the courts. Thus, Congress's power to enact the 1958 amendment to section 1332(c) deeming a corporation to be a citizen not only of the state of its incorporation but also of the state of its principal place of business is unquestioned. *See, e.g. Kelly v. United States Steel Corp.,* 284 F.2d 850 (3rd Cir. 1960).

We know of no appellate court decision to consider the new statute but there are numerous district court decisions which have agreed (some in dicta) that the permanent resident alien provision must be interpreted according to its literal language. *See Iscar, Ltd. v. Katz,* 743 F.Supp. 339, 345 (D.N.J. 1990) (resident alien party who was not a permanent resident when the action was filed but became one by the time the court considered the motion to dismiss is "a citizen of New Jersey ... [and t]hus the parties are completely diverse"); *D'Arbois v. Sommelier's Cellars,* 741 F. Supp. 489, 490 (S.D.N.Y. 1990) (dictum) (although amended diversity statute could not be applied retroactively, it might have cured jurisdictional defect in case brought by alien plaintiff against permanent resident alien among others by deeming latter a citizen of a particular state); *see also Syed v. Syed,* 1991 WL 70851 at *1 (dictum) (dismissing complaint on ground, *inter alia* that if both plaintiff and defendant were resident aliens, "the last sentence of Section 1332(a) ... [would] requir[e] that they be domiciled in different states"); *Nakanishi v. Kanko Bus Lines, Inc.,* 1989 WL 1183124, at *2 (S.D.N.Y. 1989) (dictum) ("recent amendment may remove the jurisdictional bar" to action by plaintiff resident alien of New Jersey against United States citizen defendants and defendant permanent resident alien of New York).

Two other courts have applied the plain meaning of the statute in cases turning on related issues, such as whether a person qualifies as a "permanent resident." For example, in a case with an alien plaintiff and as defendants a United States citizen and an alien with a work permit, the court in *Kristensen v. de Dampierre,* 1990 WL 103957, at *1 (S.D.N.Y. 1990), found that there was no subject matter jurisdiction, but indicated that had the defendant alien been a permanent resident, the result would have been different under the amended statute. *See also Miller v. Thermarite Pty. Ltd.,* 793 F. Supp. 306, 307–08 (S.D. Ala. 1992) (same, for nonimmigrant temporary worker).

Singh does not challenge Congress's *power* to deem a permanent resident alien to be a citizen of the state of his or her domicile. In fact, Singh acknowledges that Congress could redefine permanent resident aliens to be citizens of the states of their domiciles, but seeks to limit that definition to situations where the effect will be to defeat diversity jurisdiction between a citizen of a state and an alien permanently domiciled in the same state. Singh urges this court not to apply the same deeming provision in any other context, and to follow the holding of the district court in *Arai v. Tachibana,* 778 F. Supp. 1535 (D. Haw. 1991). In that case the court dismissed the complaint brought by Japanese aliens against both a Hawaii corporation and Japanese citizens who were permanent residents of Hawaii, although it acknowledged that the statutory language of the permanent resident alien provision was clear.

The *Arai* court gave two reasons for its failure to follow that language, both of which Singh presses here. We have already rejected the first such reason, the inconsistency with the asserted purpose of the 1988 Act. The other reason given in *Arai* and repeated by Singh here is that any other reading would "countenance diversity jurisdiction in the situation where an alien permanently residing in one state sues an alien permanently residing in another state, a plainly unconstitutional result." Appellant's Brief at 28.

Singh warns that we are ignoring the Supreme Court's direction to avoid a construction of a statute which will lead to unconstitutional applications. Singh suggests that because this Court in *Field v. Volkswagenwerk AG,* 626 F.2d 293, 296 (3d Cir. 1980), enunciated the principle that the complete diversity requirement denied jurisdiction "in an action by an alien against citizens of a state and another alien," we cannot apply the plain language of the statute.

The holding in *Field* is not at issue here, because the issue on appeal there was the district court's refusal to permit the resident alien plaintiff to withdraw and thereby remove the impediment to diversity jurisdiction. Nothing in *Field* suggests there is any constitutional infirmity in applying diversity jurisdiction in the instant situation, where a permanent resident alien deemed by the amended statute to be a citizen of Virginia sues a nonresident alien and a citizen of states other than Virginia. At a minimum, Congress's deeming provision falls within its power to invest the federal courts with jurisdiction when there is minimal diversity.

Thus the potential unconstitutional application of the deeming provision as to the citizenship of permanent residents is limited to situations in which a permanent resident alien sues as the sole defendant either a permanent resident alien domiciled in another state or a nonresident alien. Some commentators have suggested that the plain reading of the provision in those situations will lead to constitutional problems. *See* 1 *Moore's, supra,* ¶ 0.71[4.–7], 0.75[1.–2–2] ("unless the courts can ignore the plain language of the clause and hold that it does not apply in [the two scenarios described above], the legislation is unconstitutional"); Richard Bisio, *Changes in Diversity Jurisdiction and Removal,* 69 Mich. Bar. J. 1026, 1028 (1990) ("The amendment probably oversteps the Article III constitutional grant of judicial power if it is applied to allow suits solely between aliens."); Oakley, *supra,* at 741 (provision "invites courts to adjudicate cases that may be beyond the constitutional power of the federal courts").

The alleged constitutional issue that might arise when one alien sues another is not presented in this case because there is a citizen party, thereby satisfying minimal diversity. Moreover, the resolution of the constitutional issue is not as clear as may appear from first glance. Even accepting the general view that the Supreme Court's decision in *Hodgson v. Bowerbank,* 9 U.S. (5 Cranch) 303 (1809) (diversity jurisdiction does not extend to actions between aliens) is a construction of the diversity clause of Article III, this would not necessarily preclude Congress from authorizing federal jurisdiction in suits between aliens grounded on other Constitutional bases. *See, e.g., Verlinden B.V. v. Central Bank of Nigeria,* 461 U.S. 480 (1983) (relying on "Arising Under" clause of

Article III); *Tidewater,* 337 U.S. at 583 (opinion of Jackson, J.) (relying on Article I power to legislate re District of Columbia). We leave this intriguing issue for another day because we are bound to follow the injunction applicable to all federal courts not to reach to decide a constitutional issue unless it is squarely presented. It is sufficient for us to hold today that we see nothing in the Constitution which would turn us from applying the plain statutory language in the case before us.

III.   Conclusion

Because in this case there is a deemed citizen of Virginia suing an alien and a citizen of Delaware and New Jersey, the district court properly found that there is the requisite diversity of citizenship. Accordingly, we will affirm the judgment of the district court.

Notes

8–1.   Several years after *Singh*, the D.C. Circuit addressed similar facts, but reached a result opposite to the Third Circuit.

Respectfully, we conclude that the Third Circuit gave insufficient attention to the statements in the legislative history on the purpose of the 1988 amendment. Despite the reference in the legislative history indicating that Congress intended to eliminate complete diversity in lawsuits between a citizen and an alien admitted for permanent residence in the same state, that is not the whole history. The diversity provisions of the Judicial Improvements Act were enacted after more than a decade of congressional debate on the continuing need for diversity jurisdiction in light of the heavy caseload of the federal courts. *See* 134 Cong. Rec. at 31,050. The Judicial Conference's recommendation was premised on the need for a reduction in diversity jurisdiction, and the House bill, which provided for the same increase of the amount-in-controversy requirement as the Senate bill, was evidently a compromise between those who wished to abolish diversity jurisdiction almost entirely, and those who wished to retain it. *Id.*; H. Rep. at 44, 1988 U.S.C.C.A.N. at 6005. In adding the alienage provision, the Senate, and ultimately the Congress, evidenced a purpose consistent with the policies of the other diversity reforms. There is no evidence to the contrary. Although its overall goal, as the Third Circuit noted, was to improve the administration and efficiency of the federal courts, with regard to diversity the Judicial Improvements Act was designed to contract the scope of jurisdiction.

Saadeh v. Farouki, 107 F.3d 52 (D.C. Cir. 1997). A majority of district courts have followed the reasoning of *Saadeh* rather than *Singh*. Why hasn't Congress resolved this "ambiguity"?

8–2.   Crowded federal dockets and respect for federalism have led many prominent judges, legislators and commentators—including Judge Sloviter—to advocate the abolition or significant curtailment of diversity jurisdiction. *See, e.g.,* Dolores K. Sloviter, *A Federal Judge Views Diversity Jurisdiction Through the Lens of Federalism,* 78 Va. L. Rev. 1671, 1672–74 (1992). Which cases involving aliens belong in federal as opposed to state courts? (Revisit each of the Hypotheticals presented at the beginning of this chapter.) Which party in *Singh* was trying to invoke federal court jurisdiction? What might this anecdotal evidence suggest about the need for a federal forum for foreign plaintiffs? For foreign defendants?

Chapter 9

CHOICE OF LAW

Materials in this chapter address the question what law applies when the administration of justice requires a choice between two or more systems of law. American lawyers often refer to this branch of study as "Conflicts of Law"; European lawyers tend to use the term "Private International Law." The different terminology is revealing. In the United States, there are three categories of "conflicts": (1) intra-state vertical conflicts that present a choice between federal and state law; (2) inter-state horizontal conflicts where the court must choose between the laws of two states; and (3) international horizontal conflicts that involve the application vel non of foreign law. European and other countries that do not have overlapping layers of federal and state governments are most familiar with conflicts associated with the third category—international conflicts.

In the United States, intra-state vertical conflicts, which present a choice between federal and state law, are resolved pursuant to the *Erie* doctrine. *See Erie R.R. Co. v. Tompkins,* 304 U.S. 64 (1938). That doctrine provides that, in diversity cases, federal courts should apply their own procedural law but must apply the substantive law of the state in which the court sits. The *Erie* doctrine is a central component of the American civil procedure course and is not addressed here. It is worth emphasizing, however, that *Erie* and other side-effects of federalism are not universal phenomena. Countries with a single layer of courts would not encounter the same issues.

Inter-state and inter-national conflicts arise because law-making bodies of various jurisdictions see the world differently. If the law were uniform in all jurisdictions there would be no conflicts. But of course we must expect if not also appreciate that the laws of states and countries will differ in their protections of rights, prohibitions of conduct, promotions of norms and the like. But when a dispute crosses a jurisdictional boundary, there must be some principle to mediate the policy determinations of the different jurisdictions—to determine what law applies.

If one Californian negligently injures another Californian in an automobile accident while the two are in Nevada, should California or Nevada negligence law determine the standard of care? If a Texan and an Austrian enter into a contract that does not include a choice-of-law clause, what law governs the availability of punitive damages for a willful breach of contract? Resolution of such issues are significant not only as to the individual case presenting the conflict, but also for establishing a pattern or network of relations between and among the competing jurisdictions. Justice Story invoked the latter concern in his explanation of why one jurisdiction would ever apply another's law:

> The true foundation on which the administration of international law must rest is that the rules which are to govern are those which arise from mutual interest and utility, from a sense of the inconveniences which would result from a contrary doctrine, and from a spirit of moral necessity to do justice, in order that justice may done to us in return.*

Of course an understanding of *why* a court would apply the law of another jurisdiction does not explain exactly *when* a court would or should do so. And we have centuries of experience searching for a satisfactory resolution to this enduring if basic problem. The many dimensions of this subject can hardly be addressed in full in a Conflict of Laws elective; the brief introduction provided here only scratches the surface.

Theoretical approaches to resolving conflicts among competing laws can be grouped into three categories. In the discussion of each of these categories, the word "state" is used as a generic reference to include not only one of the United States, but also a foreign state.

Lex fori. One approach to the question what jurisdiction's law applies is simply not to pose the question at all. The court in which the transaction is litigated could simply always apply its own law. Judges are most familiar with the law of the forum. Its application is therefore easier, less time-consuming, and (there being no need for a foreign law expert) more efficient than resort to the rules of decision of some alien legal system. This approach recognizes that judges cannot apply the law of another state with fidelity and accuracy, and thus relieves judges of that responsibility. After all, is

---

* J. Story, Commentaries on the Conflict of Laws, Foreign and Domestic § 35, at p. 34 (1834) *quoted in* Eugene F. Scoles, Peter Hay, et al., Conflict of Laws 19 (West 4th ed. 2004).

it realistic to expect a Texas judge meaningfully to apply Austrian law?

The primary disadvantage of a lex fori approach, however, is that it can reward plaintiffs who file in whatever state offers them the most favorable law. Forum shopping can be unfair to defendants and lead to absurd applications. If either of the plaintiffs in the previous hypotheticals files suit in Iowa, should the substantive law of Iowa apply? Defenders of the lex fori approach argue that there are other motions (e.g., personal jurisdiction, venue, forum non conveniens, etc.) that prevent a suit from being prosecuted in a jurisdiction that has no connection to the parties or the lawsuit. But a lex fori approach would raise the already-high stakes on those other motions ever higher. Moreover, a strict lex fori approach would mean that a court could not provide a forum without also applying the forum state's law. Imagine, for example, that the Texas and Austria litigants in the earlier example both have corporate operations in Chicago and would prefer to litigate there even though the transaction has no connection to Illinois. Must the decision to litigate in Illinois be tied to the determination that Illinois law apply?

Lex fori is at least a part of almost every jurisdiction's conflicts doctrine. No matter the jurisdiction's conflict of laws methodology for determining what *substantive* law to apply, the forum will almost always apply the *procedural* law of the forum. Importantly, that procedural law of the forum will include the conflict of laws methodology itself. In other words, if a Texas plaintiff files suit in Illinois against an Austrian defendant, the Illinois court will apply Illinois conflict of laws principles to determine what substantive law to apply; and even if the Illinois court determines that the substantive law of some state other that Illinois should be applied, the litigation would proceed pursuant to the procedural law of the Illinois forum.

Multilateralism. A second theoretical approach is to reach multilateral consensus on a set of jurisdiction-selection rules. Such rules identify a determinative contact for every controversy, and use that single contact to select the law that will govern the conflict. For example, the determinative contact for a tort could be the place of injury. If the states of California and Nevada have agreed on that jurisdiction-selection rule, the same substantive law would be applied irrespective of whether the litigation takes place in California or Nevada. Such a system ensures more predictable and uniform results and discourages forum shopping: if the plaintiff was injured in an accident in Nevada, both states would apply the substantive law of Nevada.

Jurisdiction-selection rules tend to be rather absolute. Although a jurisdiction-selection rule could be written to permit a court to apply some other law under certain circumstances, these escape hatches would undermine the expectation of decisional harmony that justifies the multilateral compact. Absolute rules deliver certainty and predictability. Yet absolute rules cannot account for the unique considerations that might be presented in a particular application. In a tort case, for example, the place of injury might be some remote location where the plaintiff just happened to be located when the defendant's defective product caused the injury. Can the standard of care fairly turn on something so unpredictable and beyond the control of the defendant? A different absolute rule can be drafted to anticipate that problem case, but will create other problems. For example, states might agree instead to require the application of the law of the place of the wrongful act. But if the wrongful act is the allegedly defective design of a product in New York, should New York law dictate the standard of care if a Massachusetts plaintiff purchased the product in Massachusetts from a Massachusetts defendant, was injured by that product in Massachusetts, and sues in Massachusetts?

Unilateralism. While multilateral approaches allocate transactions to a particular legal system, unilateralists approach choice-of-law problems in a rather different manner. Instead of focusing on a shared framework of rules, unilateral approaches favor a process of more discretionary decision-making that can be tailored to the unique needs of each particular case. This approach presumes that justice, fairness, and the best practical result require consideration, in each case, of the totality of the circumstances presented.

Discretion to invoke whatever law best resonates with the circumstances then presented is an expensive luxury. The high cost of "rough" justice is predictability and certainty. That the law should be uniform and impartial is among the most basic principles of American jurisprudence. But without meaningful constraints, the judicial decision-making process may be perceived as arbitrary or unfair. The ad hoc approach of a given judge may also fail to appreciate what Justice Story described as the true foundation on which the administration of international law must rest.

———

Most sovereigns have experimented at some time or other with variations and combinations of all three of these approaches, and the evolution continues. There is no single contemporary approach even among the various states of the United States, much less among the nation states of the rest of the world. The dominant approach to international or interstate conflicts issues in the United States is reflected in the Restatement (Second) of Conflict of Laws (the "Restatement"). The Restatement is an ambitious framework that tries to combine the virtues of both discretion *and* predictable rules. Many state courts have adopted some or all of the Restatement's methodology;* some foreign countries have a similar analytical structure.

The Restatement's approach is defined by the superseding principle that the law governing a particular issue should be the law of the state that has "the most significant relationship" to the occurrence and the parties. The factors relevant to that appraisal, are enumerated generally to include

(a) the needs of the interstate and international systems,

(b) the relevant policies of the forum,

(c) the relevant policies of the other interested states and the relative interests of those states in the determination of the particular issue,

(d) the protection of justified expectations,

(e) the basic policies underlying the particular field of law,

(f) certainty, predictability and uniformity of result, and

(g) ease in the determination and application of the law to be applied

Restatement (Second) of Conflict of Laws § 6(2).

Further, the Restatement enumerates an additional set of factors for each substantive category of law that should inform that inquiry as to which jurisdiction has "the most significant relationship." For example, in tort cases, the following contacts should be taken into account:

(a) the place where the injury occurred,

(b) the place where the conduct causing the injury occurred,

(c) the domicile, residence, nationality, place of incorporation and place of business of the parties, and

(d) the place where the relationship, if any, between the parties is centered.

Restatement (Second) of Conflict of Laws § 145(2).** Obviously, the combination of the Section 6 and Section 145 factors give courts

---

* Although the Full Faith and Credit Clause of the United States Constitution provides the power to federalize the law of interstate conflicts, that authority has been exercised in rather limited con-texts. Generally speaking, then, conflicts is a matter of state law.

** In contracts cases, the factors a court should consider include (a) the place of contracting; (b) the place of the

considerable flexibility in determining which jurisdiction has the "most significant relationship."

After enumerating those "general principles," the Second Restatement then offers a "secondary statement ... setting forth the choice-of-law the courts will *usually* make in given situations".*** The purpose of these sections is to infuse the methodology with some elements of certainty and predictability. In the torts section, for example, the Restatement creates rebuttable presumptions about the applicable law depending upon the nature of the tort. In most of these instances, there is a rebuttable presumption that the law of the place of injury should be applied**** The presumptions can be rebutted with evidence that some other state has the "most significant relationship." And that inquiry, already described above, is premised on the factors outlined in Sections 6 and 145.

The rules of the Second Restatement apply both to interstate and to international conflicts. This does not mean, however, that the source of the foreign law is irrelevant. Indeed, a court has considerable flexibility under the most significant relationship test, and may be more prone to choose forum law in international than in interstate cases. Note subparagraph (g) in Section 6(2), *supra*. But of course the opposite may also be true. Perhaps because of the importance of comity in international relations, a court may be more willing to apply a foreign law in an international case than in an interstate case involving similar facts.

Notes

9–1. The drafters of the Second Restatement recognized, in the Introduction to their work, that "the jettisoning of ... rigid rules in favor of standards of greater flexibility ... reduces certitude" and "leaves the answer to specific problems very much at large." pp. vii–viii. That comment reflects the shift from the fairly rigid jurisdiction-selecting rules that characterized the First Restatement of Conflict of Laws to the more discretionary framework of the Second Restatement.

9–2. Note the return of *Erie*'s torment regarding the hazy line between substance and procedure. Even in cases where a jurisdiction applies another state's substantive law, in most cases a court will apply

---

negotiation of the contract; (c) the place of performance; (d) the location of the subject matter of the contract; and (e) the domicil, residence, nationality, place of incorporation and place of business of the parties. Restatement (Second) of Conflict of Laws § 188(2).

*** Restatement (Second) of Conflict of Laws viii.

**** In contracts cases, the presumptions are more varied: for contracts involving the sale of land, the location of the property; for contracts involving the sale of chattel, the place of delivery; for most insurance contracts, the location of the risk; for most service contracts, the place where the services will be rendered. Restatement (Second) of Conflict of Laws §§ 189–197.

its own procedural law. Whether an issue is characterized as a matter of substance or of procedure, then, could be consequential. Similar characterization issues arise when the methodology provides different rules for different types of cases or different rules for different issues within cases. The pigeon-hole characterization of the action as one of contract or tort, for example, could, in turn, be dispositive of the case.

9–3. Most substantive laws are premised on the assumption that they will be litigated in that jurisdiction's courts and pursuant to that jurisdiction's procedural rules. Can such a law be removed from that fabric and "applied" in isolation by some other court in another jurisdiction—pursuant to different discovery rules, rules of evidence, and trial procedures?

9–4. Contracting parties can resolve conflicts questions definitively by negotiating a choice of law clause. Most conflict methodologies respect party autonomy and, subject to certain limitations, the parties are free to select the law governing their contract. *See, e.g.,* Restatement (Second) of Conflict of Laws § 187.

9–5. Statutory mandates may also preempt the most significant relationship test. Restatement (Second) of Conflict of Laws § 6(1). A state's commercial code, for example, may require the application of a particular law.

9–6. Dépeçage is an important term in conflicts doctrine. It is defined as "applying the rules of different states to determine different issues" in the same case. *See* Willis L.M. Reese, *Dépeçage: A Common Phenomenon in Choice-of-Law*, 73 Colum. L. Rev. 58, 58 (1973). For example, there may be situations where a court applies one state's law to determine the standard of care, yet apply another state's law to determine the standard for the measure of damages.

9–7. Another important term in conflicts doctrine is renvoi. This term refers to situations where a court, having concluded that another state's law should apply, recognizes that the conflicts methodology of that other state would have directed that court to apply some law other than its own. For example, a Texas court, having determined that Austrian law should apply because Austria had the most significant relationship, might recognize that, had the case proceeded in Austria, the Austrian courts would not have applied Austrian law. The dilemma, then, is whether the Texas court should apply Austrian law when the Austrian courts themselves would not have applied Austrian law. This is referred to as the problem of *renvoi*. Continuing with our example, consideration of Austrian conflicts principles might reveal that Austrian courts would have applied Texas law; or perhaps the Austrian courts would have applied, say, Belgian law. The hypothesized invocation of Texas law presents what is often referred to as a *remission*; the invocation of a third sovereign presents a *transmission*. To avoid the renvoi problem, American conflicts law generally presumes that the application of another state's law refers exclusively to that state's "internal law," and not the "whole law" which would include consideration of that state's conflicts principles.

9–8. A principal difference between conflicts doctrines in Europe and the United States is that conflicts doctrines are more likely to be codified in Europe. Germany codified additional components of its conflicts law in 1999, and translated excerpts from the tort rules follow:

Article 40: Tort

(1) Claims arising from tort are governed by the law of the state in which the person liable to provide compensation acted. The injured person may demand, however, that the law of the state where the result took effect be applied instead. The right to make this election may be exercised only in the court of first instance and then only until the end of the first oral proceeding or the end of the written trial proceeding.

(2) If the person liable to provide compensation and the injured person had their habitual residence in the same state at the time the act took place, the law of that state shall be applied. In the case of enterprises, associations, or legal persons the place of their principal administration, or, in the case of a branch, its location, shall be the equivalent of a habitual residence.

(3) Claims that are governed by the law of another state may not be entertained to the extent that they

1. go substantially beyond that which is required for appropriate compensation for the injured person,

2. obviously serve purposes other than provision of appropriate compensation for the injured person, or

3. conflict with provisions concerning liability contained in a treaty that is in force with respect to the Federal Republic of Germany. . . .

Article 41: Substantially Closer Connection

(1) If there is a substantially closer connection to the law of a state other than the law that would be applicable under [Article 40 paragraphs 1 and 2] the law of that state shall be applied.

(2) In particular, a substantially closer connection may be the result of

1. a special legal or factual relationship between the parties in connection with an obligation. . .

Article 42: Party Autonomy

After the event giving rise to a non-contractual obligation has occurred, the parties may choose the law that shall apply to the obligation; rights of third parties remain unaffected.

Act on the Revision of the Private International Law (1999). Compare and contrast this methodology to the approach of the Second Restatement.

9–9.   Multilateral efforts among the Member States have made substantial progress toward ensuring that certain types of claims are adjudicated under the same law no matter where, in the European Union, that claim is litigated. Since the 1980 Rome Convention (Rome I), the Member States of Europe have enjoyed principles applicable to contracts between parties that are domiciliaries to an EU country. The central feature of the framework is the principle of freedom of choice, whereby the parties are free to choose the law applicable to their contract. Where the parties have not determined what law is to be applicable to their contract, it will be governed by the law of the country with which it has the closest connection. Like the Brussels I Regulation, the Rome Convention contains special rules to protect the weaker parties, meaning consumers and employed persons. A Rome II Convention is being drafted to consider conflict of laws rules for torts and other non-contractual relations.

Chapter 10

RECOGNITION AND ENFORCEMENT OF FOREIGN JUDGMENTS

This chapter considers the significance of the fact that a controversy has already been litigated in some foreign court. A civil judgment has no formal effect beyond the national boundary of the court that rendered the judgment. Foreign judgments have local effect only if the state acquiesces or is bound by treaty to give the foreign judgment effect. Materials in this chapter explore the role of such treaties and also the elastic rationale for according preclusive effect to foreign judgments.

The basic tension that underlies the study of recognition and enforcement practice is rather straightforward. A state may be inclined to recognize and enforce foreign judgments because it may be inefficient or unfair to allow parties to relitigate what has already been adjudicated elsewhere. Recognition and enforcement of foreign judgments also fosters stability and collaboration among participants in a global community where an increasing number of social and economic activities have multi-national contacts. By recognizing and enforcing judgments entered in other countries, a country anticipates that others will return the courtesy. But enforcing a judgment may involve more than a mere expression of courtesy. Any civil judgment is a product of the rendering jurisdiction's procedural and substantive laws; and judgments carry the baggage of political, social and cultural norms that may conflict with the norms of the country that is being asked to recognize or enforce that judgment. Respecting or ratifying a foreign judgment that flouts domestic values thus can create serious political problems or run afoul of local values.

Treaties offer one solution for contracting states united in their desire to harmonize and stabilize their domestic laws on the enforcement of judgments. The Brussels I Regulation, for example, provides rules for the recognition and enforcement of the judgments of Member States. The Rules are brief and rather straightforward. Provided that the Member State's court proceedings from which the judgment emanated fall within the definition of civil and commercial matters, there are few exceptions to the general proposition that the judgment of another contracting state must be recognized or enforced. According to Article 34 of the Regulation, a judgment shall not be recognized:

1. if such recognition is manifestly contrary to public policy in the Member State in which recognition is sought;

2. where it was given in default of appearance, if the defendant was not served with the document which instituted the proceedings or with an equivalent document in sufficient time and in such a way as to enable him to arrange for his defence, unless the defendant failed to commence proceedings to challenge the judgment when it was possible for him to do so;

3. if it is irreconcilable with a judgment given in a dispute between the same parties in the Member State in which recognition is sought;

4. if it is irreconcilable with an earlier judgment given in another Member State or in a third State involving the same cause of action and between the same parties, provided that the earlier judgment fulfils the conditions necessary for its recognition in the Member State addressed.

The Regulation (and its predecessors) were designed to harmonize and stabilize the domestic law on the enforcement of judgments within the European Community. Uniform principles allow the free circulation of judgments, promoting trade and inspiring confidence. On an initial application for recognition, the court must sua sponte examine whether any of these grounds for refusal exist. And "[u]nder no circumstances may a foreign judgment be reviewed as to its substance."*

But such treaties require a certain "mutual trust in the administration of justice" that is not always present.** The United States is a party to some very specialized tax and "friendship, commerce, and navigation" treaties that require the recognition of judgments under certain limited circumstances. The United States has also ratified and implemented the United Nations Convention on the Recognition and Enforcement of Foreign Arbitral Awards. *See* 9

---

* Brussels I Regulation, Art. 36.   ** *Id.*, Preamble, Para. 16.

U.S.C. §§ 201–208 (Federal Arbitration Act). The Convention, often referred to as the New York Convention,

> is the primary legal basis for enforcing international commercial arbitration awards. If a consumer dispute is commercial in nature and is between parties in different countries or parties in the same country seeking to enforce the aware in a third country, then the arbitration may result in a "foreign" arbitration award for the purposes of the New York Convention. For example, under the New York Convention, an award rendered in Ohio, United States, and enforced in Paris, France, is subject to the New York convention. Should the parties seek to enforce the award in Massachusetts or California, then the New York Convention no longer applies, and the party seeking to enforce the award must rely on the municipal law of the United States or of the individual state. The New York Convention does not require that the parties come from different countries or even that at least one of the parties be a citizen of a state that is a signatory to the New York Convention. It merely requires that the award be issued in a member country or if issued in a non-member country, enforced in a member country that does not require reciprocity.

> In international commercial arbitration, there is the strong presumption that arbitrations are valid and the award should be enforced. The New York Convention's "pro-enforcement bias" prevents any count from reviewing the merits of the underlying dispute when the prevailing party seeks to convert the arbitral award into a court judgment. Therefore, one must exclude the dispute or the resulting arbitral award from one governed under the New York Convention in order for a shifting standard of review proposal to work....

Llewellyn Joseph Gibbons, *Creating a Market for Justice; A Market Incentive Solution to Regulating the Playing Field: Judicial Deference, Judicial Review, Due Process, and Fair Play in Online Consumer Arbitration*, 23 Nw. J. Int'l L. & Bus. 1 (2002). Adhered to by nearly half of the world's states, including almost all of the major trading states and all of the principal centers of international arbitration, the New York Convention gives arbitral awards greater currency even than formal judgments of courts. Although the Convention identifies a few specific and limited grounds upon which an arbitral award may be denied recognition, the pro-enforcement bias is as renowned as Professor Gibbons suggests.

Further, at the suggestion of the United States delegation, in 1992 the Hague Conference on Private International Law began work on a multilateral convention that would govern jurisdiction and recognition and enforcement of foreign judgments in civil and commercial matters. The effort produced several drafts and had been the subject of considerable discussion, but its broad ambitions were not realized. Fundamental differences about the appropriate scope of personal jurisdiction stalled the development of a convention, even though provisions dealing with the recognition and enforcement of foreign judgments had been relatively uncontroversial.

Salvaged from those efforts was the Convention on Choice of Court Agreements, which was signed on behalf of the Members States of the Hague Conference on June 30, 2005. The new treaty has been described as the litigation counterpart to the New York Convention. Like the New York Convention, it will establish rules for enforcing private party agreements regarding the forum for the resolution of disputes, and rules for recognizing and enforcing the decisions issued by the chosen forum. Designed to "promote international trade and investment though enhanced judicial co-operation," the new Convention applies to international business-to-business agreements with exclusive choice of court clauses. Judgments resulting from jurisdiction exercised in accordance with an exclusive choice of court agreement must be recognized and enforced in the courts of other Contracting States. Professor Ron Brand, a member of the United States delegation explained:

> The Convention includes safeguards acknowledging governmental interests that might otherwise be frustrated by the parties' choice of court. Thus, in addition to the exclusion of consumer transactions, it excludes application to employment relationships, family law matters, insolvency proceedings, nuclear damage, and personal injury claims, among others. It also allows courts not chosen to ignore choice of court agreements and courts asked to recognize judgments to refuse recognition and enforcement under limited circumstances that are consistent with traditional rules found in national and regional law. Thus, for example, recognition or enforcement of a judgment may be refused if it "would be manifestly incompatible with the public policy of the requested State." ... An additional safeguard ... allows refusal of recognition and enforcement of a judgment "if, and only to the extent that, the judgment awards damages, including exemplary or punitive damages, that do not compensate a party for actual loss or harm suffered." This provision recognizes existing practice in the use of public policy defenses to refuse recognition and enforcement of punitive damage awards....

Ronald A. Brand, *The New Hague Convention on Choice of Court Agreements*, The American Society of International Law, July 26, 2005.

Even if not obliged by a treaty, a country might recognize and enforce the judgments of other countries. Indeed, the United States has long been among the countries in the world most receptive to the recognition and enforcement of foreign judgments notwithstanding the fact that the United States has not been a party to any comprehensive bilateral or multilateral treaty concerning such matters. Even more impressive, this receptiveness is the product not of Congressional legislation, but rather a coordinated effort among the states to adopt a common analytical framework.

To that end, a majority of states have adopted some version of the Uniform Foreign Money Judgments Recognition Act. However, because not all states have adopted the Uniform Act, and because the Uniform Act is limited to money judgments, a second and similar analytical framework also serves an important function in the recognition and enforcement practice in the United States. The Restatement (Third) of Foreign Relations Law, summarizes the prevailing common and statutory law of the States of the United States.

RESTATEMENT (THIRD) OF FOREIGN RELATIONS LAW

(1987)

§ 481. Recognition and Enforcement of Foreign Judgment. Except as provided in § 482, a final judgment of a court of a foreign state granting or denying recovery of a sum of money, establishing or confirming the status of a person, or determining interests in property, is conclusive between the parties, and is entitled to recognition in courts in the United States. . . .

Comment:

. . . c. Effect of foreign judgment. A foreign judgment is generally entitled to recognition by courts in the United States to the same extent as a judgment of a court of one State in the courts of another State. As in the case of a sister-State judgment, a judgment of a foreign country ordinarily has no greater effect in the United States than in the country where the judgment was rendered. . . .

d. Reciprocity in enforcement of foreign judgments. A judgment otherwise entitled to recognition will not be denied recognition or enforcement because courts in the rendering state might not enforce a judgment of a court in the United States if the circumstances were reversed. *Hilton v. Guyot*, 159 U.S. 113 (1895), declared a limited reciprocity requirement applicable when the judgment creditor is a national of the state in which the judgment creditor is a national of the state in which the judgment was rendered and the judgment debtor is a national of the United

States. Though that holding has not been formally overruled, it is no longer followed in the great majority of State and federal courts in the United States. . . .

g. Proceedings to enforce foreign judgments in the United States. In many States, including those that have adopted the Uniform Foreign Money Judgments Recognition Act, . . . an action to enforce a foreign money judgment may be initiated through expedited procedures, such as a motion for summary judgment in lieu of a complaint. Enforcement of a foreign judgment may also be pursued by counterclaim, cross-claim, or affirmative defense.

§ 482   Grounds for Nonrecognition of Foreign Judgments.

(1) A court in the United States may not recognize a judgment of the court of a foreign state if:

(a) the judgment was rendered under a judicial system that does not provide impartial tribunals or procedures compatible with due process of law; or

(b) the court that rendered the judgment did not have [personal] jurisdiction over the defendant. . .

(2) A court in the United States need not recognize a judgment of the court of a foreign state if:

(a) the court that rendered the judgment did not have jurisdiction of the subject matter of the action;

(b) the defendant did not receive notice of the proceedings in sufficient time to enable him to defend;

(c) the judgment was obtained by fraud;

(d) the cause of action on which the judgment was based, or the judgment itself, is repugnant to the public policy of the United States or of the State where recognition is sought;

(e) the judgment conflicts with another final judgment that is entitled to recognition;

(f) the proceeding in the foreign court was contrary to an agreement between the parties to submit the controversy on which the judgment is based to another forum.

Notes

10–1.   Note that if one of the defenses listed in Paragraph (1) of Section 482 is established, the court where recognition is sought is required to deny recognition. If one of the defenses listed in Paragraph (2) is established, the court has the discretion to deny recognition

10–2.   By equating foreign judgments to sister state judgments, the statement in § 481 cmt. c establishes a strong policy in favor of recognizing and enforcing foreign judgments. Article IV Section 1 of the United States Constitution requires that "Full Faith and Credit shall be given in each State to the public Acts, Records, and judicial Proceedings of every other State."

10–3. The reference to *Hilton v. Guyot* in § 481 cmt. D deserves special attention. That case, decided in 1895, is the United States Supreme Court's only guidance about standards for the recognition and enforcement of foreign judgments. In that case, Justice Gray, writing for a Court divided 5–4, embraced principles of comity and expressed respect for the diversity of approaches in foreign systems, but ultimately adopted reciprocity as a touchstone for resolving questions about the recognition and enforcement of foreign judgments. The Court refused to enforce the French judgment obtained by French plaintiffs against an American defendant because, were the roles reversed, the French court would not have enforced the American judgment. The legacy of that opinion rests not in its holding (common law that bound only *federal* courts sitting in diversity until 1938, when general federal common was extinguished), but rather in its articulation of the need for comity and deference to foreign legal systems.

10–4. Reciprocity requirements still are a fundamental component of the recognition and enforcement practices of many countries. On one hand, adoption of a reciprocity requirement indicates that a country is open to enforcing the judgments from other countries that are willing to do the same in return. But on the other hand, it forces the "other" country to act first—to establish a record of enforcing the judgments of the country that has the reciprocity requirement. If both (or all) countries have a reciprocity requirement, who acts first? Does a policy that punishes non-cooperation ultimately encourage cooperation? Is there another more effective yet equally cautious method of demonstrating a receptiveness to enforcing foreign judgments provided the same courtesy is returned?

SOCIETY OF LLOYD'S v. ASHENDEN

233 F.3d 473 (7th Cir. 2000)

POSNER, CIRCUIT JUDGE:

These are diversity suits brought in the federal district court in Chicago by Lloyd's, a foreign corporation, against American members ("Names") of insurance syndicates that Lloyd's manages. Lloyd's wanted to use the Illinois Uniform Foreign Money–Judgments Recognition Act to collect money judgments, each for several hundred thousand dollars, that it had obtained against the defendants in an English court after the names' repeated efforts in earlier litigation to knock out the forum-selection clause in their contracts with Lloyd's had failed. Pursuant to this strategy, Lloyd's filed the judgments in the district court and then issued "citations" pursuant to the Illinois procedure for executing a judgment. The filing of the judgments inaugurated this federal-court proceeding to collect them; and state law, in this case the Illinois citations statute, 735 ILCS 5/2–1402, supplies the procedure for executing a federal-court judgment. Fed. R. Civ. P. 69(a). The statute allows the holder of a judgment to depose the judgment debtor respecting the existence, amount, and whereabouts of assets that can be seized to satisfy the judgment; to impose a lien on those assets; and to command the debtor to turn over to the judgment creditor as many of the seizable assets as may be necessary to satisfy the judgment.

The defendants ignored the citations and instead asked the district court not to recognize the English judgments as being enforceable in Illinois. They argued that those judgments had denied them due process of law and therefore were not enforceable under the foreign money-judgments recognition act, which makes a judgment rendered by a court outside the United States unenforceable in Illinois if

> the judgment was rendered under a *system* which does not provide impartial tribunals or procedures compatible with the requirements of due process of law.

735 ILCS 5/12–621 (emphasis added). The district court rejected the argument and granted summary judgment for Lloyd's, declaring the judgments enforceable and so the issuance of citations proper.

We have italicized the word that defeats the defendants' argument. The judgments about which they complain were rendered by the Queen's Bench Division of England's High Court, which corresponds to our federal district courts; they were affirmed by the Court of Appeal, which corresponds to the federal courts of appeals; and the Appellate Committee of the House of Lords, which corresponds to the United States Supreme Court, denied the defendants' petition for review. Any suggestion that this system of courts "does not provide impartial tribunals or procedures compatible with the requirements of due process of law" borders on the risible. The courts of England are fair and neutral forums. The origins of our concept of due process of law are English, and the English courts, especially the Supreme Court of Judicature (composed of the High Court and the Court of Appeal) and the Appellate Committee of the House of Lords, the tribunals involved in the judgments challenged here, are highly regarded for impartiality, professionalism, and scrupulous regard for procedural rights. The English judicial system ... is the very fount from which our system developed; a system which has procedures and goals which closely parallel our own. United States courts which have inherited major portions of their judicial traditions and procedure from the United Kingdom are hardly in a position to call the Queen's Bench a kangaroo court.

Not that the English concept of fair procedure is identical to ours; but we cannot believe that the Illinois statute is intended to bar the enforcement of all judgments of any foreign legal system that does not conform its procedural doctrines to the latest twist and turn of our courts regarding, for example, the circumstances under which due process requires an opportunity for a hearing in advance of the deprivation of a substantive right rather than afterwards. It is a fair guess that no foreign nation has decided to incorporate our due process doctrines into its own procedural law; and so we interpret "due process" in the Illinois statute (which, remember, is a uniform act, not one intended to reflect the idiosyncratic jurisprudence of a particular state) to refer to a concept of fair procedure simple and basic enough to describe the judicial processes of civilized nations, our peers. The statute requires only that the foreign procedure be "compatible with the requirements of due process of law," and we have interpreted this to mean that the foreign procedures are "fundamentally fair" and do not offend against "basic fairness." *Ingersoll Milling Machine Co. v. Granger*, 833 F.2d 680, 687–88 (7th Cir. 1987); *see also Hilton v. Guyot*, 159 U.S. 113, 202–03 (1895)....

It is true that no evidence was presented in the district court on whether England has a civilized legal system, but that is because the question is not open to doubt. We need not consider what kind of evidence would suffice to show that a foreign legal system "does not provide impartial tribunals or procedures compatible with the requirements of due process of law" if the challenged judgment had been rendered by Cuba, North Korea, Iran, Iraq, Congo, or some other nation whose adherence to the rule of law and commitment to the norm of due process are open to serious question, *see, e.g., Bank Melli Iran v. Pahlavi*, 58 F.3d 1406, 1411–12 (9th Cir. 1995); *Choi v. Kim*, 50 F.3d 244, 249–250 (3rd Cir. 1995)..., as England's are not. It is anyway not a question of fact. It is not, strictly speaking, a question of law either, but it is a question about the law of a foreign nation, and in answering such questions a federal court is not limited to the consideration of evidence that would be admissible under the Federal Rules of Evidence; any relevant material or source may be consulted. Fed. R. Civ. P. 44.1.

Rather than trying to impugn the English legal system en gross, the defendants argue that the Illinois statute requires us to determine whether the particular judgments that they are challenging were issued in proceedings that conform to the requirements of due process of law as it has come to be understood in the case law of Illinois and other American jurisdictions. The statute, with its reference to "system," does not support such a retail approach, which would moreover be inconsistent with providing a streamlined, expeditious method for collecting money judgments rendered by courts in other jurisdictions—which would in effect give the judgment creditor a further appeal on the merits. The process of collecting a judgment is not meant to require a second lawsuit, thus converting every successful multinational suit for damages into two suits. . . . But that is the implication of the defendants' argument. They claim to be free to object in the collection phase of the case to the procedures employed at the merits phase, even though they were free to challenge those procedures at that phase and indeed did so.

Notes

10–5. Judge Posner suggests that procedural systems should be viewed as a whole, because weakness in one aspect of "due process" may well be offset by strength in another. But aren't some threshold concepts of our system of due process, in a sense, non-negotiable? Can another system adequately "offset" notice and the right to be heard? The right to a jury trial? The right to cross-examine witnesses? The right to counsel? And if there are some processes that cannot be compromised, how does a court identify and protect them if not by using a "retail approach"?

10–6. Assuming that Judge Posner is right, a system committed to the rule of law and to the norm of due process will have offset a diminished Procedure X with an enhanced Procedure Y. Therefore, even with a calibration of X and Y that differs from the United States', citizens or subjects of that country would enjoy a system whereby the ordinary administration of justice contains an overall quantum of process similar to the United States. But a one-shot litigator in a foreign system might encounter only Procedure X without enjoying the benefits of (as, over time, citizens or subjects of the foreign country would) the compensating Procedure Y. Is that fair?

10–7. What sources will determine whether a nation has a commitment to the rule of law and to the norm of due process? Should the State Department maintain a definitive list for such purposes?

10–8. The generally favorable attitude of American courts toward judgments of other countries should not be equated to a "rubber stamp" approach to enforcement, however. The following case illustrates that United States courts will also refuse to enforce foreign judgments under certain circumstances.

BRIDGEWAY CORPORATION v. CITIBANK

201 F.3d 134 (2nd Cir. 2000)

CALABRESI, CIRCUIT JUDGE:

Bridgeway Corp. ("Bridgeway"), a Liberian corporation seeking to enforce a final judgment rendered by the Supreme Court of

Liberia, appeals from the district court's decision denying Bridgeway's motion for summary judgment and granting, sua sponte, summary judgment in favor of the nonmoving party, Citibank. The district court held, first, that Citibank was not judicially estopped from challenging the fairness of the Liberian judicial system simply because it had participated voluntarily in litigation in Liberia and, second, that the evidence in the record established, as a matter of law, that the Liberian judicial system was not "a system that ... provide[s] impartial tribunals or procedures compatible with the requirements of due process." We affirm.

I. BACKGROUND

A. Overview of Liberian History

This appeal derives from an action by Bridgeway to enforce a money judgment against Citibank entered by the Supreme Court of Liberia on July 28, 1995. Because the merits of this case turn on the events surrounding the Liberian civil war during the first half of the 1990s, it is helpful to provide a brief overview of those circumstances before proceeding to discuss the case. The following facts are drawn from the district court's thoughtful opinion and are not traversed in the record before us.

Liberia was founded in 1817 to resettle freed American slaves, and in 1847 it became an independent republic. The original 1847 Constitution, amended in 1976 and again in 1986, established a government modeled on that of the United States. Under the 1986 Constitution, for example, the judicial powers of the Liberian government are vested in a Supreme Court and such subordinate courts as the Legislature may establish. The Supreme Court is composed of one chief justice and four associate justices. Justices and judges are nominated by the President and confirmed by the Senate and have life tenure unless impeached.

From 1980 to 1989, Samuel Kanyon Doe headed a Liberian government marked by corruption and human rights abuses, as well as by rampant inflation. In 1989, a group of dissidents seized power and, in 1990, executed Doe. Doe's death marked the beginning of a violent seven-year civil war. By 1991, Liberia was in effect ruled by two governments: one controlled Monrovia, the capital, while the other controlled the remainder of the country. Following several short-lived cease fires, a formal peace accord was signed in August 1995. After another outbreak of violence in 1996, elections were held in July 1997. In August 1997, Charles Taylor was inaugurated and the 1986 Constitution was reinstated.

Throughout the period of civil war, Liberia's judicial system was in a state of disarray and the provisions of the Constitution concerning the judiciary were no longer followed. Instead, under an agreement worked out among the warring parties in 1992, the Supreme Court was reorganized, with various factions each unilaterally appointing a specified number of justices. The United States State Department Country Reports for Liberia during this period paint a bleak picture of the Liberian judiciary. The 1994 Report observed that "corruption and incompetent handling of cases remained a recurrent problem." The 1996 Report stated that, "the judicial system, already hampered by inefficiency and corruption, collapsed for six months following the outbreak of fighting in April."

In 1997, before elections were held, the leaders of the various factions acknowledged that the integrity of the Supreme Court had been compromised by factional loyalties since 1992 and agreed that the Court would have to be reconstituted so that it might gain the legitimacy that would enable it to resolve successfully disputes that might arise concerning the elections. The members of the Court were therefore dismissed and new members were appointed based on the recommendations of the Liberian National Bar Association.

B. This Case

Plaintiff-appellant Bridgeway is a Liberian corporation with its principal place of business in Monrovia, Liberia. Defendant-appellee, Citibank, is a United States banking corporation with its principal place of business in New York. For many years Citibank maintained a branch in Monrovia, but it closed that branch in January 1992 and completely withdrew from Liberia by 1995. As required by Liberian law, Citibank, before withdrawing, formulated a plan of liquidation, which was approved by the National Bank of Liberia. According to this plan, funds were to be remitted by Citibank to Meridian Bank Liberia Ltd., in order to meet Citibank's obligations to depositors. Citibank alerted its customers to its plans so that they could withdraw their funds. On April 21, 1995, the National Bank of Liberia indicated by letter that Citibank had satisfactorily completed the liquidation plan and was no longer licensed to do business in Liberia.

Bridgeway had an account at Citibank's Liberian branch with a balance of $189,376.66. In November 1992, Bridgeway brought suit in Liberia against Citibank, seeking a declaration that Citibank was obligated to pay Bridgeway its balance in United States (rather than Liberian) dollars. In August 1993, the trial court ruled in favor of Citibank. The court found that, under Liberian law, a person may not refuse to accept Liberian dollars for the discharge of an obligation unless there is an express agreement to the contrary and that Liberian law gives the Liberian dollar a par value equal to the value of the United States dollar. The trial court also found that under Bridgeway's contract with Citibank, the latter had the right to decide the currency in which a withdrawal would be paid. Bridgeway appealed to the Liberian Supreme Court, which reversed the lower court's decision and entered judgment for Bridgeway.

Bridgeway filed suit in New York state court to enforce the Liberian Supreme Court judgment, and Citibank removed the case to the federal district court. When it became apparent that Citibank was going to defend itself by challenging the legitimacy of the Liberian judicial system, Bridgeway moved for summary judgment—arguing that Citibank was estopped from questioning the fairness of the Liberian judiciary. But the district court denied that motion and, sua sponte, granted summary judgment for Citibank. Specifically, the court found that, as a matter of law, Liberia's courts did not constitute "a system of jurisprudence likely to secure an impartial administration of justice" and that, as a result, the Liberian judgment was unenforceable in the United States. Bridgeway now appeals.

II. Discussion

... [A].   Judicial Estoppel

Bridgeway ... argues that because Citibank voluntarily participated in litigation in Liberian courts, it was judicially estopped from raising any question as to the impartiality of those courts in the instant case. Bridgeway observes that Citibank has taken part in at least a dozen civil cases in Liberia since 1992. And in several of those cases, Citibank appeared as a plaintiff. Having availed itself of Liberia's courts without there raising any objections to the fairness of Liberian justice, Citibank should now be estopped, Bridgeway argues, from calling into question the validity of Liberian judgments. Citibank responds by arguing that its participation in Liberian litigation did not amount to an admission of the fairness of Liberian courts. Moreover, it argues that it could not have raised its objections to Liberia's judicial system in Liberia, because Liberian courts routinely sanction lawyers who question the Liberian judicial system. The district court agreed with Citibank.

Judicial estoppel "prevents a party from asserting a factual position in a legal proceeding that is contrary to a position previously taken by [the party] in a prior legal proceeding." In this Circuit, "[a] party invoking judicial estoppel must show that (1) the party against whom the estoppel is asserted took an inconsistent position in a prior proceeding and (2) that position was adopted by the first tribunal in some manner." We have described the type of inconsistency required as a "clear inconsistency between [the party's] present and former positions."

In order for Bridgeway to prevail, we must conclude that voluntarily participating in litigation in a foreign tribunal is fundamentally inconsistent with the belief that the tribunal is unlikely to provide an impartial forum or one that comports with notions of due process. Such a position is without merit. Defending a suit where one has been haled into court, and suing where jurisdiction and venue readily exist do not constitute assertions that the relevant courts are fair and impartial. Accordingly, we do not view Citibank's voluntary participation in Liberian litigation, even as a plaintiff, as clearly contradictory to its present position.

[B].   Fairness of Liberian Courts[1]

i.   Burden

The parties strenuously dispute who bears the ultimate burden of proof with respect to the fairness of the Liberian judicial system. Although there are cases in which the question of the burden might be significant, it does not ultimately matter here. Accordingly, we express no opinion on it. Even if Citibank were to bear both the burden of production and that of persuasion, it has come forward with sufficiently powerful and uncontradicted documentary evidence describing the chaos within the Liberian judicial system during the period of interest to this case to have met those burdens and to be entitled to judgment as a matter of law. Thus, the United States State Department Country Reports presented by Citibank indicate that the Liberian judicial system was in a state of disarray, as do, more subtly, the affidavits by Citibank's Liberian counsel, H. Varney G. Sherman.

The only evidence Bridgeway has introduced in support of its position are three statements by Liberian attorneys: (1) an affidavit of James E. Pierre, Esq., a member of the Liberian Bar, stating that the procedural rules of Liberia are modeled on those of New York State courts; (2) an affidavit introduced by Citibank, in which H. Varney G. Sherman, Citibank's Liberian counsel, states that "the Liberian Government is patterned after the state governments of the United States of America;" and (3) an affidavit of N. Oswald Tweh, former Vice President of the Liberian National Bar Association, that "Liberia's judicial system was and is structured and administered to afford party-litigants therein impartial justice."

---

1. In granting summary judgment, the district court reflexively applied New York law. Citibank argues that federal law should apply. Because of the similarity of the New York and federal standards concerning the enforcement of for- eign judgments, however, the district court's application of New York law did not affect the outcome. . . . We therefore express no view on whether the district court was correct.

The first statement concerns the design of the Liberian judicial system, but says nothing about its practice during the period in question.[2] The second, in addition to suffering from the same defect as the first, does not even discuss the Liberian judicial system directly. And the third is purely conclusory.

ii. Evidence

Summary judgment cannot be granted on the basis of inadmissible evidence. See Fed. R. Civ. P. 56(e). And Bridgeway raises many objections to the evidence relied upon by the district court in determining that Liberia's courts were, as a matter of law, unlikely to render impartial justice. Although the parties argue over a variety of different pieces of evidence, in the absence of any proof supporting Bridgeway's position, we need only consider whether Citibank adduced admissible evidence in sufficient amount to make the district court's decision regarding the performance of the Liberian judiciary during the civil war be supportable as well as uncontroverted. In fact, all of the district court's conclusions concerning this issue can be derived from just two sources: the affidavits of H. Varney G. Sherman ("Sherman affidavits") and the U.S. State Department Country Reports for Liberia for the years 1994–1997 ("Country Reports" or "Reports").

Bridgeway does not object to the admissibility of the Sherman affidavits (except on the ground that they support an argument that Bridgeway alleges Citibank is estopped from making). Indeed, in its brief, Bridgeway cites statements derived from these very affidavits in support of its own position. We will therefore assume that the Sherman material was properly relied upon by the district court.[3]

The district court also relied quite heavily on the Country Reports. Bridgeway argues that these Reports constitute excludable

---

2. Evidence concerning the design of a judicial system might be sufficient, in the absence of countervailing evidence. But where a party presents evidence concerning the actual practice of a judicial system, evidence about design is not likely to create a genuine issue of material fact.

3. Sherman's affidavits contain much of the information on the basis of which the district court made its decision and wrote its opinion: the history of the Liberian governmental system, the history of the civil war, and some of the effects of the civil war on the Liberian judicial system. Although Sherman was somewhat restrained in his description, he did indicate that during the civil war the constitutional provisions governing the appointment of Supreme Court justices were not followed, members of the Supreme Court served at the "will and pleasure of the appointing powers," and, when elections were finally called, the parties acknowledged that "membership on the Supreme Court had been based on factional appointment and with factional loyalties." Cf. Restatement (Third) of Foreign Relations § 482 cmt. b. (1987) ("Evidence that the judiciary was dominated by the political branches of government ... would support a conclusion that the legal system was one whose judgments are not entitled to recognition."). He concluded that "between July, 1990 and August, 1997, the Supreme Court was not organized in keeping with the 1986 Constitution."

hearsay. Citibank replies that the Reports are admissible under Fed. R. Evid. 803(8)(C), which allows the admission of "factual findings resulting from an investigation made pursuant to authority granted by law, unless the sources of information or other circumstances indicate lack of trustworthiness."

Rule 803(8) "is based upon the assumption that public officers will perform their duties, that they lack motive to falsify, and that public inspection to which many such records are subject will disclose inaccuracies." 31 Michael H. Graham, Federal Practice and Procedure § 6759, at 663–64 (Interim ed.1992). " 'Factual finding' includes not only what happened, but how it happened, why it happened, and who caused it to happen." Id. at 689. The rule therefore renders presumptively admissible "not merely . . . factual determinations in the narrow sense, but also . . . conclusions or opinions that are based upon a factual investigation." *Gentile v. County of Suffolk*, 926 F.2d 142, 148 (2d Cir. 1991).

In order to fit within the purview of Rule 803(8)(C), the evidence must (1) contain factual findings, and (2) be based upon an investigation made pursuant to legal authority. Once a party has shown that a set of factual findings satisfies the minimum requirements of Rule 803(8)(C), the admissibility of such factual findings is presumed. The burden to show "a lack of trustworthiness" then shifts to the party opposing admission. *See Ariza v. City of New York*, 139 F.3d 132, 134 (2d Cir. 1998).

In this case, there is little doubt that the Country Reports constitute "factual findings." Moreover, the Reports are certainly gathered pursuant to legal authority: federal law requires that the State Department submit the Reports annually to Congress, see 22 U.S.C. §§ 2151n(d), 2304(b) (1994 & Supp. 1999). They are therefore presumptively admissible.

Bridgeway attempts to rebut this presumption by arguing that the Reports are untrustworthy, and it points to language in the State Department's description of their preparation. The State Department says that "[w]e have given particular attention to attaining a high standard of consistency despite the multiplicity of sources and the obvious problems related to varying degrees of access to information, structural differences in political and social systems, and trends in world opinion regarding human rights practices in specific countries." Although this constitutes a frank recognition of the shortcomings intrinsic in any historical investigation, it does not amount (as Bridgeway argues) to an admission of the lack of trustworthiness required to reject the admissibility of these documents.

When evaluating the trustworthiness of a factual report, we look to (a) the timeliness of the investigation, (b) the special skills or experience of the official, (c) whether a hearing was held and the level at which it was conducted, and (d) possible motivation problems. See Fed. R. Evid. 803(8)(C) advisory committee's note. With the exception of (c), which is not determinative by itself, cf. id. ([T]he rule ... assumes admissibility in the first instance but with ample provision for escape if sufficient negative factors are present. (emphasis added)), nothing about the Reports calls into question their reliability with respect to these factors. The Reports are submitted annually, and are therefore investigated in a timely manner. They are prepared by area specialists at the State Department. And nothing in the record or in Bridgeway's briefs indicates any motive for misrepresenting the facts concerning Liberia's civil war or its effect on the judicial system there.[4] *See Bank Melli Iran v. Pahlavi*, 58 F.3d 1406, 1411 (9th Cir. 1995) (relying on Country Reports in granting summary judgment on the issue of the fairness of Iranian courts).

In addition to its reliance on the Sherman affidavits and the Country Reports, the district court took judicial notice of historical facts drawn from a variety of sources. Bridgeway objects to this. Even if we agreed with Bridgeway's objection, we would affirm the district court's decision because the facts of which the district court took judicial notice were merely background history and of no moment to the ultimate determination of the fairness of Liberia's courts during the period of the civil war. The information in the district court's opinion concerning the functioning of the Liberian courts during the war is drawn (or could easily be drawn) entirely from the Sherman affidavits and the Country Reports, both of which were clearly admissible.

Having found all of Bridgeway's contentions to be without merit, we affirm the judgment of the district court.

Notes

10–9. Why wasn't Citibank's prior voluntary participation (as a plaintiff) in the judicial system of Liberia sufficient to demonstrate that system's fundamental impartiality and fairness?

10–10. In Liberia, Citibank prevailed at the trial court but lost on appeal. Does this make it harder or easier for Citibank to argue that it was denied meaningful process?

4. One could certainly imagine situations in which motivational problems might plausibly be present (e.g., a country report on an avowed enemy or a significant ally of the United States), but Bridgeway has raised no such doubts here. Accordingly, we express no views on the admissibility of country reports in those circumstances.

10–11.   Upon consideration of whether to enforce the Liberian judgment, should the American court review the procedural protections of the Liberian appellate process, the trial process or both?

10–12.   After *Bridgeway*, are all Liberian judgments (during the relevant time period) unenforceable? In other words is Liberia now one of the countries that, like Cuba, North Korea, Iran, Iraq and Congo, Judge Posner described as lacking a commitment to the rule of law and to the norm of due process? Or might it vary on a case-by-case basis? (But vary based on what?)

Glossary and Index

References are to Pages

INTERNATIONAL CENTER FOR THE SETTLEMENT OF INVESTMENT DISPUTES (ICSID)

The ICSID provides facilities for the conciliation and arbitration of disputes between contracting states and investors who qualify as nationals of other contracting states. ICSID is an autonomous international organization; however, it has close ties with the World Bank. Recourse to ICSID dispute resolution is generally voluntary, but contracting states are required to recognize and enforce ICSID arbitral awards.

Generally, 13

INTERNATIONAL COURT OF JUSTICE (ICJ)

Located in The Hague in the Netherlands, the ICJ (sometimes referred to as the "World Court") is the judicial branch of the United Nations. Established in 1946, the ICJ issues rulings on disputes between states that have agreed to submit to its jurisdiction. The ICJ also issues advisory opinions, providing reasoned but non-binding rulings on certain questions of international law, usually at the request of the United Nations General Assembly. This court should not be confused with the International Criminal Court.

Generally, 11–12

INTERNATIONAL CRIMINAL COURT (ICC)

Countries ratifying the treaty that created the ICC grant it authority to try their citizens for genocide, crimes against humanity, and war crimes. Although a legally separate entity derived from a treaty, the impetus for the establishment of the ICC came from within the United Nations. The establishment of the ICC in 2002 followed the creation of several ad hoc tribunals to try war crimes in the former Yugoslavia and Rwanda. The contracting states desired to create a permanent tribunal so that an ad hoc tribunal would not have to be created after each occurrence of these crimes. More than 100 countries on six continents have ratified or acceded to the terms of the treaty, but not the US.

Generally, 12

INTERNATIONAL INSTITUTE FOR THE UNIFICATION OF PRIVATE LAW (UNIDROIT)

Based in Rome, UNIDROIT is an intergovernmental group that studies the need and methods for modernizing, harmonizing, and coordinating commercial law between states. The membership includes 59 member states, including the US, and draws from a variety of different legal, economic and political systems as well as different cultural backgrounds.

Generally, 14, 32

JURISDICTION

See Personal Jurisdiction; Subject Matter Jurisdiction

JURISDICTION-SELECTING RULES

See Choice of Law

JURY TRIALS,

Generally, 55–62
Avatar of democratic participation, 59
Collectivity, 59
Delorean, trial of John, 61
French Revolution, 58
Hamilton, Andrew, and, 60
Iconic status of, 60
Jefferson, Thomas, and, 60
Organ of government, 59
Popularity of, 58, 61–62
Right to vote, analogous to, 61
Tocqueville, Alexis de, and, 60–61
Transnational Rules of Civil Procedure, and, 62
Unanimity, 59–60
Zenger, trial of John Peter, 60

JUSTINIAN CODE

See Roman Law

LAISSEZ-FAIRE

American value, as, 55–62

LAW OF NATIONS

Alien Tort Claims Act, 148

LEGAL AID

Generally, 8, 16–27

LEGAL EXPENSE INSURANCE

Generally, 21–22

LETTER OF REQUEST

See Hague Evidence Convention

TAKING EVIDENCE
See Discovery

TERRITORIAL AUTHORITY
See Personal Jurisdiction

TOCQUEVILLE, ALEXIS DE
Observations about America, 55, 60

TRANSNATIONAL RULES OF CIVIL PROCEDURE
Generally, 15, 32,
Discovery, 50–54
Jury trial, 62
Pleading, 32

TRANSPLANTS
Comparative law, inspired by, 5, 55

TRIBUNALS, INTERNATIONAL
Generally, 11–13
Nuremberg, 12
Rwanda, 12
Tokyo, 12
Yugoslavia, Former Territories of, 12

UMBRELLA PROVISIONS
See Personal Jurisdiction; Brussels I
Regulation

UNIDROIT
See International Institute for the Unification of Private Law

UNIFORM FOREIGN MONEY JUDGMENTS RECOGNITION ACT
The Uniform Act, adopted by the National Conference of Commissioners on Uniform State Laws in 1962, provides that final foreign money judgments within the scope of the Act and not subject to any of the defenses listed in the act are to be deemed conclusive between the parties, and recognized and enforced in the same manner as sister-state judgments. A majority of the states in the US have adopted the Uniform Act.
Generally, 179

UNILATERAL
Approaches to choice of law, see Choice of Law

UNITED NATIONS CONVENTION ON THE RECOGNITION AND ENFORCEMENT OF FOREIGN ARBITRAL AWARDS
See New York Convention

UNITED NATIONS COMMISSION FOR INTERNATIONAL TRADE LAW (UNCITRAL)
Established by the United Nations General Assembly in 1966, the mission of UNCITRAL is to promote the harmonization of disparities in national laws governing international trade. UNCITRAL, or "the Commission," has become the core legal body of the United Nations system in the field of international trade law.
Generally, 13

WORLD TRADE ORGANIZATION (WTO)
The WTO is an international organization with 148 members. The WTO is the successor to the General Agreement on Tariffs and Trade, and operates with the broad goal of reducing or abolishing international trade barriers. WTO members are required to grant one another most favored nation status, such that (with some exceptions) trade concessions granted by a WTO member to another country must be granted to all WTO members.
Generally, 12

†